- generations not stag[...]
- intersections of gene[...]
- hist. of comm. & of opposition to comm

post 1968: "living 'as if'" (315)
 - naked emperor

' 1989 - no plan, just reaction against
 regime

' post - comm. => gen. seperated by
 ability to have comparative
 perspective

" history of a collective oedipal revolt"
 (327)

Maria Shore article

THE CAPTIVE MIND

BY CZESLAW MILOSZ

TRANSLATED FROM THE POLISH BY
JANE ZIELONKO

VINTAGE INTERNATIONAL
VINTAGE BOOKS
A DIVISION OF RANDOM HOUSE, INC.
NEW YORK

Vintage International Edition, August 1990

Foreword Copyright © 1981 by Czeslaw Milosz
Copyright 1951, 1953 by Czeslaw Milosz
Copyright renewed 1981 by Csezlaw Milosz

Chapter I of this book, "The Pill of Murti Bing," originally
appeared in the *Partisan Review*, September-October 1951,
under the title "The Happiness Pill."

Library of Congress Cataloging in Publication Data
Milosz, Czeslaw.
The captive mind.
Translated from the Polish by Jane Zielonko.
New York Vintage Books, 1955 [c1953]
1. Poland—Intellectual life. 2. Communism—Poland. 1. Title.
DK411.M5 1955   914.38
ISBN 679-72856-2   89-40503
CIP

Manufactured in the United States of America
29 28 27 26 25 24 23 22 21 20

WHEN *someone is honestly 55% right, that's very good and there's no use wrangling. And if someone is 60% right, it's wonderful, it's great luck, and let him thank God. But what's to be said about 75% right? Wise people say this is suspicious. Well, and what about 100% right? Whoever says he's 100% right is a fanatic, a thug, and the worst kind of rascal.*

AN OLD JEW OF GALICIA

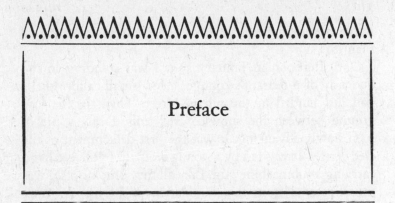

Preface

LIKE many of my generation, I could have wished that my life had been a more simple affair. But the time and place of his birth are matters in which a man has nothing to say. The part of Europe to which I belong has not, in our time, met with good fortune. Not many inhabitants of the Baltic States, of Poland or Czechoslovakia, of Hungary or Rumania, could summarize in a few words the story of their existence. Their lives have been complicated by the course of historic events.

It was in my country that the Second World War began. At that time, I was living in Warsaw. I had been through the rather strict education of a Catholic school, had read✓ law in one of the Polish universities, and had continued my studies in Paris. Literature was the real interest of my life. I had published two volumes of avant-garde verse, and some translations from French poetry.

I lived through five years of Nazi occupation. Today, looking back, I do not regret those years in Warsaw, which was, I believe, the most agonizing spot in the whole of terrorized Europe. Had I then chosen emigration, my life would certainly have followed a very different course. But my knowledge of the crimes which Europe has witnessed

pov has neg. def.

in the twentieth century would be less direct, less concrete than it is.

One afternoon in January 1945 I was standing in the doorway of a peasant's cottage; a few small-caliber shells had just landed in the village street. Then, in the low ground between the snow-covered hills, I saw a file of men slowly advancing. It was the first detachment of the Red Army. It was led by a young woman, felt-booted and carrying a submachine gun. Like all my compatriots, I was thus liberated from the domination of Berlin—in other words, brought under the domination of Moscow.

Hitherto, I had had no strong political affinities, and was only too ready to shut myself off from the realities of life. But reality would never let me remain aloof for long. The state of things in Poland inclined me towards left-wing ideas. My point of view can be defined negatively rather than positively: I disliked the right-wing groups, whose platform consisted chiefly of anti-Semitism. During the Nazi occupation I, like my colleagues, wrote for the clandestine publications, which were especially numerous in Poland. My experiences in those years led me to the conclusion that, after the defeat of Hitler, only men true to a socialist program would be capable of abolishing the injustices of the past, and rebuilding the economy of the countries of Central and Eastern Europe. My feelings for Russia were none too friendly. Pole and Russian have never loved one another, so I was no exception to the general rule. The exceptions were those—and some of my friends were among them—who before or during the war had become disciples of Stalin.

Such, then, was my state of mind as I watched the Russian girl with her submachine gun advance in my direction. To her, I was one of the millions of Europeans who had to be "liberated and educated." Perhaps I was even

change by degrees
writers = privileged

a member of the bourgeoisie . . . but that could not have seemed likely, since the shabby worker's overall which I was wearing was all I possessed in the world.

A few years later, a cultural attaché at the Embassy of the Warsaw government in Washington, D.C., was busy organizing concerts and exhibitions of Polish art; it was said he was not a communist. From 1945 to 1951, I was first a free-lance writer in Poland, and then cultural attaché, first in Washington and later in Paris. In the end I broke with the Warsaw government.

"But how," a reader may ask, "could you become a diplomatic official of that government, if you were not a member of the Party?" The answer lies, first, in the fact that in each of the people's democracies the political change developed by degrees (Jan Masaryk in Czechoslovakia could be, not a mere attaché, but the Minister of Foreign Affairs); and secondly, in the fact that writers in the people's democracies belong to the new privileged caste. It was thought that the appointment of a writer to a diplomatic post would produce a good impression abroad. "Yes," my reader may continue, "I can see that. But you— why did you agree to serve? For money?" No. I am no saint, but those who know me are aware that my needs are modest, and that I have no extravagant tastes except a love for books. I agreed to serve, not for material reasons, but through conviction.

We enter here upon the problems which form the subject of this book. The world of today is torn asunder by a great dispute; and not only a dispute, but a ruthless battle for world domination. Many people still refuse to believe that there are only two sides, that the only choice lies between absolute conformity to the one system or absolute conformity to the other. Call such people impractical, if you will; but it would be wrong to treat their hopes as

tongue and country

— loss of order in E. Euro post-Nazi

matter for contempt. Those who thought that they might succeed, while remaining within the Eastern bloc, in keeping clear of total orthodoxy and maintaining some degree of freedom of thought, have been defeated. The peasants' leaders were defeated, Masaryk was defeated, the socialists who tried to collaborate were defeated, Rajk was defeated in Hungary, Gomulka in Poland.

My mother tongue, work in my mother tongue, is for me the most important thing in life. And my country, where what I wrote could be printed and could reach the public, lay within the Eastern Empire. My aim and purpose was to keep alive freedom of thought in my own special field; I sought in full knowledge and conscience to subordinate my conduct to the fulfillment of that aim. I served abroad because I was thus relieved from direct pressure and, in the material which I sent to my publishers, could be bolder than my colleagues at home. I did not want to become an émigré and so give up all chance of taking a hand in what was going on in my own country. The time was to come when I should be forced to admit myself defeated.

To understand the course of events in Eastern and Central Europe during the first post-war years, it must be realized that pre-war social conditions called for extensive reforms. It must further be understood that the Nazi rule had occasioned a profound disintegration of the existing order of things. In these circumstances, the only hope was to set up a social order which would be new, but would not be a copy of the Russian regime. So what was planned in Moscow as a stage on the road to servitude, was willingly accepted in the countries concerned as though it were true progress. Men will clutch at illusions when they have nothing else to hold to.

The Method, the Diamat—that is, dialectical materialism

dialectical materialism
"New Faith"

as interpreted by Lenin and Stalin—possesses a strong magnetic influence on the men of the present day. In the people's democracies, the communists speak of the "New Faith," and compare its growth to that of Christianity in the Roman Empire. There has been instituted in France a group of worker-priests, who do regular work in the factories and bring the Gospel to the laboring masses while sharing fully in their living conditions. A large proportion of these men have abandoned Catholicism and been converted to communism. This example illustrates the intensity of the ideological struggle which is going on today. And let it be remembered that in the people's democracies indoctrination is enforced by the whole power of the State.

For several years I carried on a debate with those of my friends who were yielding, little by little, to the magic influence of the New Faith. The debate went on in my own mind also—more than a debate indeed, since that word gives no sense of the emotional stress which I experienced. As the nerve-centers of the country were mastered, one after the other, by the adherents of Moscow, I was forced to abandon my philosophic beliefs one after another, if I was to keep from throwing myself into the abyss. The abyss for me was exile, the worst of all misfortunes, for it meant sterility and inaction.

In the end, I found myself driven to the point where a final choice had to be made. This was when "socialist realism" was introduced into Poland. This is not, as some think, merely an esthetic theory to which the writer, the musician, the painter or the theatrical producer is obliged to adhere. On the contrary, it involves by implication the whole Leninist-Stalinist doctrine. If writers and painters are not forced to become members of the Party, that is because such a step is unnecessary. So long as they act in ac-

Abyss = exile

exile experiences

cordance with "socialist realism," they are automatically and inescapably enrolled among the followers of Stalin. "Socialist realism" is much more than a matter of taste, of preference for one style of painting or music rather than another. It is concerned with the beliefs which lie at the foundation of human existence. In the field of literature it forbids what has in every age been the writer's essential task—to look at the world from his own independent viewpoint, to tell the truth as he sees it, and so to keep watch and ward in the interest of society as a whole. It preaches a proper attitude of doubt in regard to a merely formal system of ethics but itself makes all judgment of values dependent upon the interest of the dictatorship. Human sufferings are drowned in the trumpet-blare: the orchestra in the concentration camp; and I, as a poet, had my place already marked out for me among the first violins.

Look, then, dispassionately at my problem. At home in Poland, my friends, my relatives, theaters where my translations of Shakespeare were being produced, publishers ready to print what I wrote. Above all, my own country and my own language—what is a poet who has no longer a language of his own? All these things were mine, if I would pay the price: obedience.

The actual moment of my decision to break with the Eastern bloc could be understood, from the psychological point of view, in more ways than one. From outside, it is easy to think of such a decision as an elementary consequence of one's hatred of tyranny. But in fact, it may spring from a number of motives, not all of them equally high-minded. My own decision proceeded, not from the functioning of the reasoning mind, but from a revolt of the stomach. A man may persuade himself, by the most logical reasoning, that he will greatly benefit his health by

refusing complicity in tyranny
(what does this imply about
those who stayed?)
W = also conformity

swallowing live frogs; and, thus rationally convinced, he may swallow a first frog, then the second; but at the third his stomach will revolt. In the same way, the growing influence of the doctrine on my way of thinking came up against the resistance of my whole nature.

The decision to refuse all complicity with the tyranny of the East—is this enough to satisfy one's conscience? I do not think so. I have won my freedom; but let me not forget that I stand in daily risk of losing it once more. For in the West also one experiences the pressure to conform —to conform, that is, with a system which is the opposite of the one I have escaped from. The difference is that in the West one may resist such pressure without being held guilty of a mortal sin.

My book takes the reader into the world inhabited by the intellectuals of Warsaw, Prague, Bucharest, and Budapest. It is a world familiar to me, but it may well seem to him foreign and even exotic. I try to explain how the human mind functions in the people's democracies. If I have been able to write this book, it is because the system invented by Moscow has seemed, and still seems to me infinitely strange. Any civilization, if one looks at it with an assumption of naive simplicity (as Swift looked at the England of his day), will present a number of bizarre features which men accept as perfectly natural because they are familiar. But nowhere is this so marked as in the new civilization of the East, which moulds the lives of eight hundred millions of human beings. We are, I think, only beginning to understand it, and in years to come thousands of books will be devoted to the study of this stupefying and loathsome phenomenon.

This book is at the same time a battlefield, in which I have given shape to my combats with the doctrine I have rejected. This, then, explains my method of writing; I give

How mind is led to conform
(democracy gives way to orthodoxy)

? the enemy his arms, I follow his arguments, at times I even copy his way of reasoning. In other words, I seek to create afresh the stages by which the mind gives way to compulsion from without, and to trace the road along which men in people's democracies are led on to orthodoxy.

CONTENTS

THE CAPTIVE MIND

CHAPTER I

The Pill of Murti-Bing

IT was only toward the middle of the twentieth century that the inhabitants of many European countries came, in general unpleasantly, to the realization that their fate could be influenced directly by intricate and abstruse books of philosophy. Their bread, their work, their private lives began to depend on this or that decision in disputes on principles to which, until then, they had never paid any attention. In their eyes, the philosopher had always been a sort of dreamer whose divagations had no effect on reality. The average human being, even if he had once been exposed to it, wrote philosophy off as utterly impractical and useless. Therefore the great intellectual work of the Marxists could easily pass as just one more variation on a sterile pastime. Only a few individuals understood the causes and probable consequences of this general ✓ indifference.

A curious book appeared in Warsaw in 1932. It was a novel, in two volumes, entitled *Insatiability*. Its author was Stanislaw Ignacy Witkiewicz, a painter, writer, and philosopher, who had constructed a philosophical system akin to the monadology of Leibnitz. As in his earlier novel, *Farewell to Autumn*, his language was difficult, full of neologisms. Brutal descriptions of erotic scenes al-

ternated with whole pages of discussions on Husserl, Car-
nap, and other contemporary philosophers. Besides, one
could not always tell whether the author was serious or
joking; and the subject matter seemed to be pure fantasy.

The action of the book took place in Europe, more precisely in Poland, at some time in the near future or even
in the present, that is, in the thirties, forties, or fifties. The
social group it portrayed was that of musicians, painters,
philosophers, aristocrats, and higher-ranking military officers. The whole book was nothing but a study of decay:
mad, dissonant music; erotic perversion; widespread use
of narcotics; dispossessed thinking; false conversions to
Catholicism; and complex psychopathic personalities. This
decadence reigned at a time when western civilization
was said to be threatened by an army from the East, a
Sino-Mongolian army that dominated all the territory
stretching from the Pacific to the Baltic.

Witkiewicz's heroes are unhappy in that they have no
faith and no sense of meaning in their work. This atmosphere of decay and senselessness extends throughout the
entire country. And at that moment, a great number of
hawkers appear in the cities peddling Murti-Bing pills.
Murti-Bing was a Mongolian philosopher who had succeeded in producing an organic means of transporting
a "philosophy of life." This Murti-Bing "philosophy of
life," which constituted the strength of the Sino-Mongolian
army, was contained in pills in an extremely condensed
form. A man who used these pills changed completely.
He became serene and happy. The problems he had struggled with until then suddenly appeared to be superficial
and unimportant. He smiled indulgently at those who
continued to worry about them. Most affected were all
questions pertaining to unsolvable ontological difficulties.
A man who swallowed Murti-Bing pills became imper-

vious to any metaphysical concerns. The excesses into which art falls when people vainly seek in form the wherewithal to appease their spiritual hunger were but outmoded stupidities for him. He no longer considered the approach of the Sino-Mongolian army as a tragedy for his own civilization. He lived in the midst of his compatriots like a healthy individual surrounded by madmen. More and more people took the Murti-Bing cure, and their resultant calm contrasted sharply with the nervousness of their environment.

The epilogue, in a few words: the outbreak of the war led to a meeting of the armies of the West with those of the East. In the decisive moment, just before the great battle, the leader of the Western army surrendered to the enemy; and in exchange, though with the greatest honors, he was beheaded. The Eastern army occupied the country and the new life, that of Murti-Bingism, began. The heroes of the novel, once tormented by philosophical "insatiety," now entered the service of the new society. Instead of writing the dissonant music of former days, they composed marches and odes. Instead of painting abstractions as before, they turned out socially useful pictures. But since they could not rid themselves completely of their former personalities, they became schizophrenics.

So much for the novel. Its author often expressed his belief that religion, philosophy, and art are living out their last days. Yet he found life without them worthless. On September 17, 1939, learning that the Red Army had crossed the eastern border of Poland, he committed suicide by taking veronal and cutting his wrists.

Today, Witkiewicz's vision is being fulfilled in the minutest detail throughout a large part of the European continent. Perhaps sunlight, the smell of the earth, little everyday pleasures, and the forgetfulness that work brings

can ease somewhat the tensions created by this process of
fulfillment. But beneath the activity and bustle of daily
life is the constant awareness of an irrevocable choice to
be made. One must either die (physically or spiritually),
or else one must be reborn according to a prescribed
method, namely, the taking of Murti-Bing pills. People
in the West are often inclined to consider the lot of converted countries in terms of might and coercion. That is
wrong. There is an internal longing for harmony and
happiness that lies deeper than ordinary fear or the desire
to escape misery or physical destruction. The fate of completely consistent, non-dialectical people like Witkiewicz
is a warning for many an intellectual. All about him, in
the city streets, he sees the frightening shadows of internal exiles, irreconcilable, non-participating, eroded by
hatred.

In order to understand the situation of a writer in a
people's democracy, one must seek the reasons for his
activity and ask how he maintains his equilibrium. Whatever one may say, the New Faith affords great possibilities
for an active and positive life. And Murti-Bing is more
tempting to an intellectual than to a peasant or laborer.
For the intellectual, the New Faith is a candle that he
circles like a moth. In the end, he throws himself into the
flame for the glory of mankind. We must not treat this
desire for self-immolation lightly. Blood flowed freely in
Europe during the religious wars, and he who joins the
New Faith today is paying off a debt to that European
tradition. We are concerned here with questions more
significant than mere force.

I shall try to grasp those profound human longings and
to speak about them as if one really could analyze what
is the warm blood and the flesh, itself, of man. If I should
try to describe the reasons why a man becomes a revolu-

tionary I would be neither eloquent nor restrained enough. I admit that I have too much admiration for those who fight evil, whether their choice of ends and means be right or wrong. I draw the line, however, at those intellectuals who *adapt* themselves, although the fact that they are adapted and not genuine revolutionaries in no way diminishes their newly acquired zeal and enthusiasm.

There are, I believe, a few key concepts which may lead us to understand why they accept Murti-Bing.

THE VOID — *lack of religion*

The society portrayed by Witkiewicz is distinguished by the fact that in it religion has ceased to exist as a force. And it is true that religion long ago lost its hold on men's minds not only in the people's democracies, but elsewhere as well. As long as a society's best minds were occupied by theological questions, it was possible to speak of a given religion as the way of thinking of the whole social organism. All the matters which most actively concerned the people were referred to it and discussed in its terms. But that belongs to a dying era. We have come by easy stages to a lack of a common system of thought that could unite the peasant cutting his hay, the student poring over formal logic, and the mechanic working in an automobile factory. Out of this lack arises the painful sense of detachment or abstraction that oppresses the "creators of culture." Religion has been replaced by philosophy which, however, has strayed into spheres increasingly less accessible to the layman. The discussions of Husserl by Witkiewicz's heroes can scarcely interest a reader of even better-than-average education; whereas the peasants remained bound to the Church, be it only emotionally and traditionally. Music, painting, and poetry became something completely foreign to the great majority of people. A theory developed that art should become a substitute for religion: "metaphysical feelings" were to be expressed in the "compression of pure form"; and so form soon came to dominate content.

To belong to the masses is the great longing of the "alienated" intellectual. It is such a powerful longing that, in trying to appease it, a great many of them who once looked to Germany or Italy for inspiration have now become converted to the New Faith. Actually, the rightist totalitarian program was exceptionally poor. The only gratification it offered came from collective *warmth*: crowds, red faces, mouths open in a shout, marches, arms brandishing sticks; but little rational satisfaction. Neither racist doctrines, nor hatred of foreigners, nor the glorification of one's own national traditions could efface the feeling that the entire program was improvised to deal with problems of the moment. But Murti-Bing is different. It lays scientific foundations. At the same time, it scraps all vestiges of the past. Post-Kantian philosophy, fallen into disrepute because of its remoteness from the life of men; art designed for those who, having no religion, dare not admit that to seek the "absolute" through a juxtaposition of colors and sounds is cowardly and inconclusive thinking; and the semi-magic, semi-religious mentality of the peasants—these are replaced by a *single* system, a single language of ideas. The truck driver and elevator operator employed by a publishing firm now read the same Marxist classics as its director or staff writers. A day laborer and a historian can reach an understanding on this basis of common reading. Obviously, the difference that may exist between them in mental level is no smaller than that which separated a theologian from a village blacksmith in the middle ages.

[handwritten: bringing masses + intellectuals together by obliterating religion & replacing w/ ideology]

But the fundamental principles are universal; the great spiritual schism has been obliterated. Dialectical materialism has united everyone, and philosophy (i.e., dialectics) once more determines the patterns of life. It is beginning to be regarded with a respect one reserves only for a force on which important things depend: bread and milk for one's children, one's own happiness and safety. The intellectual has once more become *useful*. He who may once have done his thinking and writing in his free moments away from a paying job in a bank or post office, has now found his rightful place on earth. He has been restored to society, whereas the businessmen, aristocrats, and tradespeople who once considered him a harmless blunderer have now been dispossessed. They are indeed delighted to find work as cloakroom attendants and to hold the coat of a former employee of whom they said, in pre-war days, "It seems he writes." We must not oversimplify, however, the gratifications of personal ambition; they are merely the outward and visible signs of social usefulness, symbols of a recognition that strengthens the intellectual's feeling of *belonging*.

THE ABSURD

Even though one seldom speaks about metaphysical motives that can lead to a complete change of people's political opinions, such motives do exist and can be observed in some of the most sensitive and intelligent men. Let us imagine a spring day in a city situated in some country similar to that described in Witkiewicz's novel. One of his heroes is taking a walk. He is tormented by what we may call the *suction* of the absurd. What is the significance of the lives of the people he passes, of the senseless bustle, the laughter, the pursuit of money, the stupid

animal diversions? By using a little intelligence he can
easily classify the passers-by according to type; he can
guess their social status, their habits and their preoccupa-
tions. A fleeting moment reveals their childhood, man-
hood, and old age, and then they vanish. A purely physiological study of one particular passer-by in preference to
another is meaningless. If one penetrates into the minds of
these people, one discovers utter nonsense. They are totally
unaware of the fact that nothing is their own, that everything is part of their historical formation—their occupations, their clothes, their gestures and expressions, their
beliefs and ideas. They are the force of inertia personified,
victims of the delusion that each individual exists as a
self. If at least these were souls, as the Church taught, or
the monads of Leibnitz! But these beliefs have perished.
What remains is an aversion to an atomized vision of life,
to the mentality that *isolates* every phenomenon, such as
eating, drinking, dressing, earning money, fornicating.
And what is there beyond these things? Should such a
state of affairs continue? Why should it continue? Such
questions are almost synonymous with what is known as
hatred of the bourgeoisie.

Let a new man arise, one who, instead of submitting to
the world, will transform it. Let him create a historical
formation, instead of yielding to its bondage. Only thus
can he redeem the absurdity of his physiological existence.
Man must be made to understand this, by force and by
suffering. Why shouldn't he suffer? He ought to suffer.
Why can't he be used as manure, as long as he remains
evil and stupid? If the intellectual must know the agony
of thought, why should he spare others this pain? Why
should he shield those who until now drank, guffawed,
gorged themselves, cracked inane jokes, and found life
beautiful?

The intellectual's eyes twinkle with delight at the persecution of the bourgeoisie, and of the bourgeois mentality. It is a rich reward for the degradation he felt when he had to be part of the middle class, and when there seemed to be no way out of the cycle of birth and death. Now he has moments of sheer intoxication when he sees the intelligentsia, unaccustomed to rigorously tough thinking, caught in the snare of the revolution. The peasants, burying hoarded gold and listening to foreign broadcasts in the hope that a war will save them from collectivization, certainly have no ally in him. Yet he is warm-hearted and good; he is a friend of mankind. Not mankind as it is, but as it *should* be. He is not unlike the inquisitor of the middle ages; but whereas the latter tortured the flesh in the belief that he was saving the individual soul, the intellectual of the New Faith is working for the salvation of the human species in general. ✓

NECESSITY

His chief characteristic is his fear of thinking for himself. It is not merely that he is afraid to arrive at dangerous conclusions. His is a fear of sterility, of what Marx called the misery of philosophy. Let us admit that a man is no more than an instrument in an orchestra directed by the muse of History. It is only in this context that the notes he produces have any significance. Otherwise even his most brilliant solos become simply a highbrow's diversions.

We are not concerned with the question of how one finds the courage to oppose the majority. Instead we are concerned with a much more poignant question: can one write well outside that one real stream whose vitality springs from its harmony with historical laws and the dynamics of reality? Rilke's poems may be very good, but if they are, that means there must have been some reason for them in his day. Contemplative poems, such as his, could never appear in a people's democracy, not only because it would be difficult to publish them, but because the writer's impulse to write them would be destroyed at its very root. The objective conditions for such poetry have disappeared, and the intellectual of whom I speak is not one who believes in writing for the bureau drawer. He curses and despairs over the censorship and demands of the publishing trusts. Yet at the same time, he is profoundly suspicious of unlicensed literature. The publishing license he himself receives does not mean that the editor appreciates the artistic merits of his book, nor that he expects it to be popular with the public. That license is simply a sign that its author reflects the transformation of reality with scientific exactness. Dialectical materialism in the Stalinist version both reflects and directs this transformation. It creates social and political conditions in which a man ceases to think and write otherwise than as necessary. He accepts this "must" because nothing worth while can exist outside its limits. Herein lie the claws of dialectics. The writer does not surrender to this "must" merely because he fears for his own skin. He fears for something much more precious—the significance of his work. He believes that the by-ways of "philosophizing" lead to a greater or lesser degree of graphomania. Anyone gripped in the claws of dialectics is forced to admit that the thinking of private philosophers, unsupported by citations from authorities, is sheer nonsense. If this is so, then one's total effort must be directed toward following the line, and there is no point at which one can stop.

The pressure of the state machine is nothing compared with the pressure of a convincing argument. I attended the artists' congresses in Poland in which the theories of socialist realism were first discussed. The attitude of the audience toward the speakers delivering the required reports was decidedly hostile. Everyone considered socialist realism an officially imposed theory that would have, as Russian art demonstrates, deplorable results. Attempts to provoke discussion failed. The listeners remained silent. Usually, however, one daring artist would launch an attack, full of restrained sarcasm, with the silent but obvious support of the entire audience. He would invariably be crushed by superior reasoning plus practicable threats against the future career of an undisciplined individual. Given the conditions of convincing argument plus such threats, the necessary conversion will take place. That is mathematically certain.

The faces of the listeners at these congresses were not completely legible, for the art of masking one's feelings had already been perfected to a considerable degree. Still one was aware of successive waves of emotion: anger, fear, amazement, distrust, and finally thoughtfulness. I had the impression that I was participating in a demonstration of mass hypnosis. These people could laugh and joke afterwards in the corridors. But the harpoon had hit its mark, and henceforth wherever they may go, they will always carry it with them. Do I believe that the dialectic of the speakers was unanswerable? Yes, as long as there was no fundamental discussion of methodology. No one among those present was prepared for such a discussion. It would probably have been a debate on Hegel, whose reading public was not made up of painters and writers. Moreover, even if someone had wanted to start it, he would have been silenced, for such discussions are permitted—and even then, fearfully—only in the upper circles of the Party.

These artists' congresses reveal the inequality between

the weapons of the dialectician and those of his adversary. A match between the two is like a duel between a foot soldier and a tank. Not that every dialectician is so very intelligent or so very well educated, but all his statements are enriched by the cumulated thought of the masters and their commentators. If every sentence he speaks is compact and effective, that is not due to his own merits, but to those of the classics he has studied. His listeners are defenseless. They could, it is true, resort to arguments derived from their observations of life, but such arguments are just as badly countenanced as any questioning of fundamental methodology. The dialectician rubs up against his public at innumerable meetings of professional organizations and youth groups in clubs, factories, office buildings, and village huts throughout the entire converted area of Europe. And there is no doubt that he emerges the victor in these encounters.

It is no wonder that a writer or painter doubts the wisdom of resistance. If he were sure that art opposed to the official line could have a lasting value, he probably would not hesitate. He would earn his living through some more menial job within his profession, write or paint in his spare time, and never worry about publishing or exhibiting his work. He believes, however, that in most cases such work would be artistically poor, and he is not far wrong. As we have already said, the objective conditions he once knew have disappeared. The objective conditions necessary to the realization of a work of art are, as we know, a highly complex phenomenon, involving one's public, the possibility of contact with it, the general atmosphere, and above all freedom from involuntary subjective control. "I can't write as I would like to," a young Polish poet admitted to me. "My own stream of thought has so many tributaries, that I barely succeed in damming

art no longer possible

off one, when a second, third, or fourth overflows. I get halfway through a phrase, and already I submit it to Marxist criticism. I imagine what X or Y will say about it, and I change the ending."

Paradoxical as it may seem, it is this subjective impotence that convinces the intellectual that the one Method is right. Everything proves it is right. Dialectics: I predict the house will burn; then I pour gasoline over the stove. The house burns; my prediction is fulfilled. Dialectics: I predict that a work of art incompatible with socialist realism will be worthless. Then I place the artist in conditions in which such a work *is* worthless. My prediction is fulfilled.

Let us take poetry as an example. Obviously, there is poetry of political significance. Lyric poetry is permitted to exist on certain conditions. It must be: 1) serene; 2) free of any elements of thought that might trespass against the universally accepted principles (in practice, this comes down to descriptions of nature and of one's feelings for friends and family); 3) understandable. Since a poet who is not allowed to *think* in his verse automatically tends to perfect his form, he is accused of formalism.

It is not only the literature and painting of the people's democracies that prove to the intellectual that *things cannot be different*. He is strengthened in this belief by the news that seeps through from the West. The Western world is the world of Witkiewicz's novel. The number of its aesthetic and philosophical aberrations is myriad. Disciples imitate disciples; the past imitates the past. This world lives as if there had never been a Second World War. Intellectual clans in Eastern Europe know this life, but know it as a stage of the past that isn't worth looking back on. Even if the new problems are so oppressive that they can break a great many people, at least they are con-

philosophers = dialecticians

temporary. And mental discipline and the obligation to be clear are undoubtedly precious. The work of really fine Western scholars and artists escapes notice. The only new names that are known are those of "democrats"—a delicate circumlocution for a non-pagan. In short, the recompense for all pain is the certainty that one belongs to the new and conquering world, even though it is not nearly so comfortable and joyous a world as its propaganda would have one think.

SUCCESS

Mystery shrouds the political moves determined on high in the distant Center, Moscow. People speak about prominent figures in hushed voices. In the vast expanses of Euro-Asia, whole nations can vanish without leaving a trace. Armies number into the millions. Terror becomes socially useful and effective. Philosophers rule the state—obviously not philosophers in the traditional sense of the word, but dialecticians. The conviction grows that the whole world will be conquered. Great hordes of followers appear on all the continents. Lies are concocted from seeds of truth. The philosophically uneducated bourgeois enemy is despised for his inherited inability to think. (Classes condemned by the laws of history perish because their minds are paralyzed.) The boundaries of the Empire move steadily and systematically westward. Unparalleled sums of money are spent on scientific research. One prepares to rule all the people of the earth. Is all this too little? Surely this is enough to fascinate the intellectual. As he beholds these things, historical fatalism takes root in him. In a rare moment of sincerity he may confess cynically, "I bet on this horse. He's good. He'll carry me far."

A patient has a hard time, however, when the moment

guilt

comes for him to swallow Murti-Bing in its *entirety*. He
becomes such a nervous wreck that he may actually fall
ill. He knows it means a definitive parting with his
former self, his former ties and habits. If he is a writer, he
cannot hold a pencil in his hand. The whole world seems
dark and hopeless. Until now, he paid a minimal tribute:
in his articles and novels, he described the evils of capitalist
society. But after all, it isn't difficult to criticize capitalism,
and it can be done honestly. The charlatans of the stock
exchange, feudal barons, self-deluding artists, and the in-
stigators of nationalistic wars are figures who lend themselves readily to his pen. But now he must begin to *approve*. (In official terminology this is known as a transition
from the stage of critical realism to that of socialist realism.
It occurred in the newly-established people's democracies
about the year 1950.) The operation he must perform on
himself is one that some of his friends have already undergone, more or less painfully. They shake their heads sympathetically, knowing the process and its outcome. "I
have passed the crisis," they say serenely. "But how he is
suffering. He sits at home all day with his head in his
hands."

The hardest thing to conquer is his feeling of guilt. No
matter what his convictions, every man in the countries
of which I speak is a part of an ancient civilization. His
parents were attached to religion, or at least regarded it
with respect. In school, much attention was devoted to
his religious upbringing. Some emotional traces of this
early training necessarily remain. In any case, he believes
that injury to one's fellow-man, lies, murder, and the encouragement of hatred are evil, even if they serve to accomplish sublime ends. Obviously, too, he studied the
history of his country. He read its former poets and philosophers with pleasure and pride. He was proud of its

century-long battle to defend its frontiers and of its struggle for independence in the dark periods of foreign occupation. Consciously or unconsciously, he feels a certain
loyalty to his forefathers because of the history of toil and
sacrifice on their part. Moreover, from earliest childhood,
he has been taught that his country belongs to a civilization that has been derived from Rome rather than By-
zantium.

Now, knowing that he must enter a gate through which
he can never return, he feels he is doing *something wrong*.
He explains to himself that he must destroy this irrational
and childish feeling. He can become free only by weed-
ing out the roots of what is irretrievably past. Still the
battle continues. A cruel battle—a battle between an angel
and a demon. True, but which is the angel and which
the demon? One has a bright face he has known since
his childhood—this must be the angel. No, for this face
bears hideous scars. It is the face of the old order, of stupid
college fraternities, of the senile imbecility of politicians,
of the decrepitude of Western Europe. This is death and
decadence. The other face is strong and self-contained,
the face of a tomorrow that beckons. Angelic? That is
doubtful.

There is a great deal of talk about patriotism, about
fine, progressive, national traditions, about veneration of
the past. But no one is so naïve as to take such talk seriously. The reconstruction of a few historical monuments,
or a re-editing of the works of former writers cannot
change certain revealing and important facts. Each people's democracy becomes a province of the Empire, ruled
by edicts from the Center. It retains some autonomy, but
to an ever-diminishing degree. Perhaps the era of independent states is over, perhaps they are no more than
museum pieces. Yet it is saddening to say good-bye to

one's dreams of a federation of equal nations, of a United States of Europe in which differing languages and differing cultures would have equal status. It isn't pleasant to surrender to the hegemony of a nation which is still wild and primitive, and to concede the absolute superiority of its customs and institutions, science and technology, literature and art. Must one sacrifice so much in the name of the unity of mankind? The nations of Western Europe will pass through this phase of integration later, and perhaps more gently. It is possible that they will be more successful in preserving their native language and culture. By that time, however, all of Eastern Europe will be using the one universal tongue, Russian. And the principle of a "culture that is national in form, socialist in content" will be consummated in a culture of monolithic uniformity. Everything will be shaped by the Center, though individual countries will retain a few local ornaments in the way of folklore. The Universal City will be realized when a son of the Kirghiz steppes waters his horses in the Loire, and a Sicilian peasant plants cotton in Turkmen valleys. Small wonder the writer smiles at propaganda that cries for a freeing of colonies from the grasp of imperialistic powers. Oh, how cunning dialectics can be, and how artfully it can accomplish its ends, degree by degree!

All this is bitter. But what about the harbinger of the Springtime of Nations, and Karl Marx, and the visions of the brotherhood of mankind? After all, nothing can be accomplished without the iron rule of a single Master. And what about this Master? A great Polish poet, describing his journey to the East—where he went in 1824 as a political prisoner of the Tsar—compared the soul of the Russian nation to a chrysalis. He wondered anxiously what would emerge when the sun of freedom shone: "Then will a shining butterfly take flight, or a moth, a sombre creature of the night?" So far, nothing prophesies a joyous butterfly.

✓ The writer, in his fury and frustration, turns his thought to Western Communists. What fools they are. He can forgive their oratory if it is necessary as propaganda. But they believe most of what they proclaim about the sacred Center, and that is unforgivable. Nothing can compare to the contempt he feels for these sentimental fools.

Nevertheless, despite his resistance and despair, the crisis approaches. It can come in the middle of the night, at his breakfast table, or on the street. It comes with a metallic click as of engaged gears. *But there is no other way*. That much is clear. There is no other salvation on the face of the earth. This revelation lasts a second; but from that second on, the patient begins to recover. For the first time in a long while, he eats with relish, his movements take on vigor, his color returns. He sits down and writes a "positive" article, marveling at the ease with which he writes it. In the last analysis, there was no reason for raising such a fuss. Everything is in order. He is past the "crisis."

He does not emerge unscathed, however. The aftereffects manifest themselves in a particular kind of extinguishment that is often perceptible in the twist of his lips. His face expresses the peaceful sadness of one who has tasted the fruit from the Tree of the Knowledge of Good and Evil, of one who knows he lies and who feels compassion for those who have been spared full knowledge. He has already gone through what still awaits so many others.

In 1945, an eminent Soviet journalist came to Poland. He was an elderly gentleman, who looked like a middle-class lawyer. That he was an extremely clever and rather unscrupulous person was evidenced by the tenacity with which he had maintained his position—and by his advanced years. After his return to Warsaw from a tour of several provincial Polish towns, he laughingly recounted an incident that had occurred in Silesia. Someone had spread the report that a delegation of foreigners from the West had arrived. The journalist (whose round belly and honest expression were inducive to such effusive manifestations of confidence) was seized and embraced on the street by a man crying: "The English have come." "That's just how it was in the Ukraine in 1919," was the journalist's comment on the incident. This recurrence of sterile hopes amused him and he was flattered to be the representative of a country ruled according to infallible predictions; for nation after nation had indeed become part of its Empire, according to schedule. I am not sure that there wasn't in his smile something of the compassionate *superiority* that a housewife feels for a mouse caught in her trap.

The "post-crisis" writer may well expect one day to be sent on a similar journalistic mission to some newly acquired Western country. Such a prospect is not altogether distasteful. To observe people who know nothing, who still have everything to learn, must undoubtedly afford moments of unadulterated sweetness. The master knows that the trap in which the mouse has been caught is not an entirely agreeable place to live in. For the moment, however, the citizens of these newly converted countries will understand little of their new situation. They will be exhilarated at first by the flutter of national banners, the blare of marching bands, and the proclamations of long-awaited reforms. Only he, the observer, will see into the future like a god, and know it to be hard, necessarily hard, for such are the laws of History.

In the epilogue of Witkiewicz's novel, his heroes, who have gone over to the service of Murti-Bing, become schizo-

[margin note top: scizophrenics - old/new morality coexist]

[margin note: 22 new gen. ⇒old morality lingers in Churches]

phrenics. The events of today bear out his vision, even in this respect. One can survive the "crisis" and function perfectly, writing or painting as one must, but the old moral and aesthetic standards continue to exist on some deep inner plane. Out of this arises a split within the individual that makes for many difficulties in his daily life. It facilitates the task of ferreting out heretical thoughts and inclinations; for thanks to it, the Murti-Bingist can feel himself into his opponent with great acuteness. The new phase and the old phase exist simultaneously in him, and together they render him an experienced psychologist, a keeper of his brother's conscience.

One can expect that the new generation, raised from the start in the new society will be free of this split. But that cannot be brought about quickly. One would have to eradicate the Church completely, which is a difficult matter and one that demands patience and tact. And even if one could eliminate this reverenced mainstay of irrational impulses, national literatures would remain to exert their malignant influence. For example, the works of the greatest Polish poets are marked by a dislike of Russia, and the dose of Catholic philosophy one finds in them is alarming. Yet the state must publish certain of these poets and must teach them in its schools for they are the classics, the creators of the literary language, and are considered the forerunners of the Revolution. To place them on the index would be to think non-dialectically and to fall into the sin of "leftism." It is a difficult dilemma, more difficult in the converted countries than in the Center, where the identification of national culture with the interests of humanity has been achieved to a great degree. Probably, therefore, the schizophrenic as a type will not disappear in the near future.

Someone might contend that Murti-Bing is a medicine

[margin note bottom: conflict btw. nat'l (Polish) poets → catholic + anti Russ (can't get rid of)]

that is incompatible with human nature. That is not a very strong argument. The Aztecs' custom of offering human sacrifices to their gods, or the mortification of the flesh practiced by the early Christian hermits scarcely seem praiseworthy. The worship of gold has become a motive power second to none in its brutality. Seen from this perspective, Murti-Bing does not violate the nature of humankind.

Whether a man who has taken the Murti-Bing cure attains internal peace and harmony is another question. He attains a relative degree of harmony, just enough to render him active. It is preferable to the torment of pointless rebellion and groundless hope. The peasants, who are incorrigible in their petty bourgeois attachments, assert that "a change must come, because *this can't go on*." This is an amusing belief in the natural order of things. A tourist, as an anecdote tells us, wanted to go up into the mountains, but it had been raining for a week. He met a mountaineer walking by a stream, and asked him if it would continue to pour. The mountaineer looked at the rising waters and voiced the opinion that it would not. When asked on what basis he had made his prediction, he said, "Because the stream would overflow." Murti-Bing holds such magic judgments to be phantoms of a dying era. The "new" is striving to overcome the "old," but the "old" cannot be eliminated all at once.

The one thing that seems to deny the perfection of Murti-Bing is the apathy that is born in people, and that lives on in spite of their feverish activity. It is hard to define, and at times one might suppose it to be a mere optical illusion. After all, people bestir themselves, work, go to the theater, applaud speakers, take excursions, fall in love, and have children. Yet there is something impalpable and unpleasant in the human climate of such cities as Warsaw or Prague. The collective atmosphere, resulting from an exchange and a re-combination of individual fluids, is bad. It is an aura of strength and unhappiness, of internal paralysis and external mobility. Whatever we may call it, this much is certain: if Hell should guarantee its lodgers magnificent quarters, beautiful clothes, the tastiest food, and all possible amusements, but condemn them to breathe in this aura forever, that would be punishment enough.

No propaganda, either pro or con, can capture so elusive and little-known a phenomenon. It escapes all calculations. It cannot exist on paper. Admitting, in whispered conversation, that something of the sort does exist, one must seek a rational explanation for it. Undoubtedly the "old," fearful and oppressed, is taking its vengeance by spilling forth its inky fluid like a wounded octopus. But surely the socialist organism, in its growth toward a future of guaranteed prosperity, is already strong enough to counteract this poison; or perhaps it is too early for that. When the younger generation, free from the malevolent influence of the "old," arises, everything will change. Only, whoever has observed the younger generation in the Center is reluctant to cast such a horoscope. Then we must postpone our hopes to the remote future, to a time when the Center and every dependent state will supply its citizens with refrigerators and automobiles, with white bread and a handsome ration of butter. Maybe then, at last, they will be satisfied.

Why won't the equation work out as it should, when every step is logical? Do we have to use non-Euclidian geometry on material as classic, as adaptable, and as plastic as a human being? Won't the ordinary variety satisfy him? What the devil does a man need?

how to eradicate old?

CHAPTER II

Looking to the West

"ARE Americans *really* stupid?" I was asked in Warsaw. In the voice of the man who posed the question, there was despair, as well as the hope that I would contradict him. This question reveals the attitude of the average person in the people's democracies toward the West: it is despair mixed with a residue of hope.

During the last few years, the West has given these people a number of reasons to despair politically. In the case of the intellectual, other, more complicated reasons come into play. Before the countries of Central and Eastern Europe entered the sphere of the Imperium, they lived through the Second World War. That war was much more devastating there than in the countries of Western Europe. It destroyed not only their economies, but also a great many values which had seemed till then unshakeable.

Man tends to regard the order he lives in as *natural*. The houses he passes on his way to work seem more like rocks rising out of the earth than like products of human hands. He considers the work he does in his office or factory as essential to the harmonious functioning of the world. The clothes he wears are exactly what they should be, and he laughs at the idea that he might equally well be wear-

ing a Roman toga or medieval armor. He respects and
envies a minister of state or a bank director, and regards
the possession of a considerable amount of money as the
main guarantee of peace and security. He cannot believe
that one day a rider may appear on a street he knows well,
where cats sleep and children play, and start catching
passers-by with his lasso. He is accustomed to satisfying
those of his physiological needs which are considered
private as discreetly as possible, without realizing that such
a pattern of behavior is not common to all human societies.
In a word, he behaves a little like Charlie Chaplin in *The
Gold Rush*, bustling about in a shack poised precariously
on the edge of a cliff.

His first stroll along a street littered with glass from
bomb-shattered windows shakes his faith in the "naturalness" of his world. The wind scatters papers from hastily
evacuated offices, papers labeled "Confidential" or "Top
Secret" that evoke visions of safes, keys, conferences,
couriers, and secretaries. Now the wind blows them
through the street for anyone to read; yet no one does, for
each man is more urgently concerned with finding a loaf
of bread. Strangely enough, the world goes on even though
the offices and secret files have lost all meaning. Farther
down the street, he stops before a house split in half by a
bomb, the privacy of people's homes—the family smells,
the warmth of the beehive life, the furniture preserving
the memory of loves and hatreds—cut open to public
view. The house itself, no longer a rock, but a scaffolding
of plaster, concrete, and brick; and on the third floor, a
solitary white bathtub, rain-rinsed of all recollection of
those who once bathed in it. Its formerly influential and
respected owners, now destitute, walk the fields in search
of stray potatoes. Thus overnight money loses its value and
becomes a meaningless mass of printed paper. His walk

becoming accustomed to "nat."
environment

takes him past a little boy poking a stick into a heap of smoking ruins and whistling a song about the great leader who will preserve the nation against all enemies. The song remains, but the leader of yesterday is already part of an extinct past.

He finds he acquires new habits quickly. Once, had he stumbled upon a corpse on the street, he would have called the police. A crowd would have gathered, and much talk and comment would have ensued. Now he knows he must avoid the dark body lying in the gutter, and refrain from asking unnecessary questions. The man who fired the gun must have had his reasons; he might well have been executing an Underground sentence.

Nor is the average European accustomed to thinking of his native city as divided into segregated living areas, but a single decree can force him to this new pattern of life and thought. Quarter A may suddenly be designated for one race; B, for a second; C, for a third. As the resettlement deadline approaches, the streets become filled with long lines of wagons, carts, wheelbarrows, and people carrying bundles, beds, chests, cauldrons, and bird cages. When all the moves are effected, 2,000 people may find themselves in a building that once housed 200, but each man is at last in the proper area. Then high walls are erected around quarter C, and daily a given lot of men, women, and children are loaded into wagons that take them off to specially constructed factories where they are scientifically slaughtered and their bodies burned.

And even the rider with the lasso appears, in the form of a military van waiting at the corner of a street. A man passing that corner meets a leveled rifle, raises his hands, is pushed into the van, and from that moment is lost to his family and friends. He may be sent to a concentration camp, or he may face a firing squad, his lips sealed with

adaptive

killing

plaster lest he cry out against the state; but, in any case, he serves as a warning to his fellow-men. Perhaps one might escape such a fate by remaining at home. But the father of a family must go out in order to provide bread and soup for his wife and children; and every night they worry about whether or not he will return. Since these conditions last for years, everyone gradually comes to look upon the city as a jungle, and upon the fate of twentieth-century man as identical with that of a cave man living in the midst of powerful monsters.

It was once thought obvious that a man bears the same name and surname throughout his entire life; now it proves wiser for many reasons to change them and to memorize a new and fabricated biography. As a result, the records of the civilian state become completely confused. Everyone ceases to care about formalities, so that marriage, for example, comes to mean little more than living together.

Respectable citizens used to regard banditry as a crime. Today, bank robbers are heroes because the money they steal is destined for the Underground. Usually they are young boys, mothers' boys, but their appearance is deceiving. The killing of a man presents no great moral problem to them.

The nearness of death destroys shame. Men and women change as soon as they know that the date of their execution has been fixed by a fat little man with shiny boots and a riding crop. They copulate in public, on the small bit of ground surrounded by barbed wire—their last home on earth. Boys and girls in their teens, about to go off to the barricades to fight against tanks with pistols and bottles of gasoline, want to enjoy their youth and lose their respect for standards of decency.

Which world is "natural"? That which existed before,

or the world of war? Both are natural, if both are within the realm of one's experience. All the concepts men live by are a product of the historic formation in which they find themselves. Fluidity and constant change are the characteristics of phenomena. And man is so plastic a being that one can even conceive of the day when a thoroughly self-respecting citizen will crawl about on all fours, sporting a tail of brightly colored feathers as a sign of conformity to the order he lives in.

The man of the East cannot take Americans seriously because they have never undergone the experiences that teach men how relative their judgments and thinking habits are. Their resultant lack of imagination is appalling. Because they were born and raised in a given social order and in a given system of values, they believe that any other order must be "unnatural," and that it cannot last because it is incompatible with human nature. But even they may one day know fire, hunger, and the sword. In all probability this is what will occur; for it is hard to believe that when one half of the world is living through terrible disasters, the other half can continue a nineteenth-century mode of life, learning about the distress of its distant fellowmen only from movies and newspapers. Recent examples teach us that this cannot be. An inhabitant of Warsaw or Budapest once looked at newsreels of bombed Spain or burning Shanghai, but in the end he learned how these and many other catastrophes appear in actuality. He read gloomy tales of the N.K.V.D., until one day he found he himself had to deal with it. *If something exists in one place, it will exist everywhere.* This is the conclusion he draws from his observations, and so he has no particular faith in the momentary prosperity of America. He suspects that the years 1933–45 in Europe pre-figure what will occur elsewhere. A hard school, where ignorance was punished

not by bad marks but by death, has taught him to think
sociologically and historically. But it has not freed him
from irrational feelings. He is apt to believe in theories
that foresee violent changes in the countries of the West,
for he finds it unjust that they should escape the hardships
he had to undergo.

The only system of thought that is accessible to him is
dialectical materialism, and it attracts him because it
speaks a language that is understandable in the light of
his experience. The illusory "natural" order of the Western countries is doomed, according to dialectical materialism (in the Stalinist version), to crash as a result of a
crisis. Wherever there is a crisis, the ruling classes take
refuge in fascism as a safeguard against the revolution of
the proletariat. Fascism means war, gas chambers, and
crematoria. True, the crisis in America predicted for the
moment of demobilization did not occur; true, England
introduced social security and socialized medicine to a
hitherto unknown degree; and it is true, as well, that anti-
Communist hysteria in the United States, whatever else
may have inspired it, was largely motivated by fear of an
armed and hostile power. Still these are merely modifica-
tions of a formula that is being proved in other respects.
If the world is divided between Fascism and Communism,
obviously Fascism must lose since it is the last, desperate
refuge of the bourgeoisie. The bourgeoisie rules through
demagoguery, which in practice means that prominent
positions are filled by irresponsible people who commit
follies in moments of decision. Just such follies were Hitler's ruthless policy toward the Eastern peoples, or Mussolini's involvement of Italy in the war.

A man need not be a Stalinist to reason thus. On the
contrary, knowing how doubtful are any benefits from
the system evolved in the Center, he would be overjoyed

to see a gigantic meteor wipe that cause of his misery off the face of the earth. He is, however, only a man. He weighs his chances and concludes it is unwise to align himself with the side that has been damned by the Being which has taken the place of God in this century, i.e. History. The propaganda to which he is subjected tries by every means to prove that Nazism and Americanism are identical in that they are products of the same economic conditions. He believes this propaganda only slightly less than the average American believes the journalists who assure him that Hitlerism and Stalinism are one and the same.

Even if he stands on a higher rung of the hierarchy and so has access to information about the West, he is still unable to weigh the relative strength and weakness of that half of the world. The optical instrument he sees through is so constructed that it encompasses only pre-determined fields of vision. Looking through it, he beholds only what he expected to see. For example, accustomed to living in a society in which law exists exclusively as a Party tool, and in which the sole criterion of human action is its effectiveness, he finds it hard to imagine a system in which every citizen feels himself bound by the sanctions of the law. These sanctions may have been introduced in order to protect the interests of privileged groups, but they remain even after the interests change; and it is not easy to supplant old laws with new. Every citizen is entangled in a network of statutes whose origin lies in some remote past. As a result, the mechanism of collective life is so unwieldy that anyone who tries to be truly active struggles helplessly to free himself of its restrictions.

The inhabitant of Central or Eastern Europe is incapable of understanding delays, absurd decisions, political campaigns, mutual recriminations, public opinion polls,

and demagoguery, which he considers to be characteristic
of the West. But at the same time, these encumbrances
assure the private citizen a certain security. To seize a man
on the street and deport him to a concentration camp is
obviously an excellent means of dealing with an individual who displeases the administration; but such means
are difficult to establish in countries where the only criminal is the man who has committed an act clearly defined
as punishable in a specific paragraph of the law. Nazi and
Communist criminal codes are alike in that they efface the
frontier between penal and non-penal deeds—the first, by
defining crime as any act directed against the interests of
the German nation; the second, as any act directed against
the interests of the dictatorship of the proletariat. What the
man of the East calls the "lifeless formalism of the bourgeoisie" does, on the other hand, afford some guarantee
that the father of a family will return home for supper
instead of taking a trip to a region where polar bears
thrive but human beings do not.

Nor is it easy in legally minded countries to adopt the
use of scientific torture under which every man confesses
with equal fervor whether he be innocent or guilty. Propaganda tries to convince the citizens of the people's democracies that law in the West is no more than a fiction
subservient to the interests of the ruling classes. Perhaps it
is a fiction, but it is not too subservient to the wishes of the
rulers. If they want to condemn a man, they must sweat to
prove him guilty in fact; his defense lawyers hide behind
all the technicalities of the law; the case drags on through
various appeals, etc. Obviously, crimes are committed
under its cover, but so far Western law serves to bind the
hands of the rulers as well as of the ruled which, depending on one's beliefs, may be a source of either strength or
weakness.

Americans, aware of the nature of their law, compare democracy to an awkward raft on which everyone paddles in a different direction. There is much hubbub and mutual abuse, and it is difficult to get everyone to pull together. In comparison with such a raft, the trireme of the totalitarian state, speeding ahead with outspread oars, appears indomitable. But on occasion, the totalitarian ship crashes on rocks an awkward raft can sail over.

New developments in the West are not easily ascertained in the people's democracies. In certain Western countries, above all in the United States, something has occurred which is without analogy in the preceding centuries: a new civilization has arisen which is popular, vulgar, perhaps in some respects distasteful to more "refined" people, but which assures its masses a share in the output of its machine production. It is true that what these masses rejoice in is frequently tawdry and superficial, and that they purchase it with hard labor. Yet a girl working in a factory, who buys cheap mass-production models of a dress worn by a movie star, rides in an old but nevertheless private automobile, looks at cowboy films, and has a refrigerator at home, lives on a certain level of civilization that she has in *common* with others. Whereas a woman on a collective farm near Leningrad cannot foresee the day when even her great-granddaughter will live on a level that approaches such an average.

What he refers to as the "stupidity" of the American masses, who are satisfied by the purely material advantages of this new civilization, is exceptionally irritating to the Eastern intellectual. Raised in a country where there was a definite distinction between the "intelligentsia" and the "people," he looks, above all, for ideas created by the "intelligentsia," the traditional fermenting element in revolutionary changes. When he meets with a society in which the "intelligentsia," as it was known in Central or Eastern Europe, does not exist, he has great difficulty in translating his observations into conceptual terms. The ideas he finds are clearly obsolete and far outdistanced by economic and technical developments. The purely pragmatic and empirical resolution of problems and the inability to swallow even a small dose of abstraction (whereas the German bourgeoisie, for example, had this ability in abundance) introduce unknowns into his calculations. If one regards these characteristics as signs of "backwardness" in comparison with Europe, then one must acknowledge that the "stupidity" which produced a technology immeasurably superior to that of Europe is not entirely a source of weakness.

In fact, if the impetus to perfect and use new discoveries has lost none of its drive, the credit lies with the West. The effort Japan made to overtake the West ended unsuccessfully; and Japan was beaten by the peace-minded and internally disunited United States of Roosevelt's day. Russia, copying Western models of automobiles, airplanes, jet engines, television sets, atom bombs and submarines, and such things as radar and penicillin, has now entered the race. The youngest generation in Eastern Europe, raised in the worship of Russia, is beginning to believe that she is taking the foremost place in the realm of science and technology. The older people consider such a belief absurd; but, given her untapped natural resources, a planned economy and the subsequent ability to allocate unlimited sums of money to scientific research and experimentation, they feel she may be well on the way toward supremacy.

This supposition seems to be refuted by the purely practical aims of contemporary Russian science for, as we know, the greatest discoveries are perfected in the course of long, disinterested work on the part of many scientists and often bear no immediate concrete results. It seems to be refuted, as well, by the insistence with which propaganda attributes most discoveries to the Russians even while they copy American construction, from bridges to motors, in the minutest detail. Such propaganda, pushed often to the point of the ridiculous, does not indicate a high degree of self-confidence. And such occurrences as the sale of Swedish machinery to the people's democracies under the stamp of Russian manufacture disproves its boastful claims. Nonetheless, this propaganda effort to destroy the Russian inferiority complex and to raise "technological morale" is proof of the importance the Center places upon this scientific race. Who knows to what results such a concentration of will may lead? Perhaps all that Russia needs is time.

Let us admit—and the Eastern or Central European will do so—that *at this moment* the superiority of the West in potential production, technology, and replacement of human hands by machines (which means the gradual effacing of the distinction between physical and mental work) is unquestionable. But, the Eastern intellectual asks, what goes on in the heads of the Western masses? Aren't their souls asleep, and when the awakening comes, won't it take the form of Stalinism? Isn't Christianity dying out in the West, and aren't its people bereft of all faith? Isn't there a void in their heads? Don't they fill that void with chauvinism, detective stories, and artistically worthless movies? Well then, what can the West offer us? Freedom *from something* is a great deal, yet not enough. It is much less than freedom *for something*.

While such questions are posed, actually they can be countered with others. American Communists (mostly the intellectually minded sons of middle-class or lower middle-classes families) complain about the spiritual poverty of the masses. They do not realize, however, that the Imperium they pine for is a combination of material poverty and lack of technology, plus Stalinism. Nor do they realize how fascinating it might be to try to imagine a combination of prosperity and technology, plus Stalinism. The new man of the Imperium is being remolded under the slogan of the struggle against poverty (which is simultaneously induced and conquered), and the advancement of technology (which is simultaneously demolished and rebuilt). If these two powerful motives were absent, what would happen? One suspects that the wheels of that gigantic machine would then turn in a vacuum. The stage of fully realized Communism is the "holy of holies." It is Heaven. One dare not direct one's eyes toward it. Yet if one dared to visualize that Paradise, he would find it not unlike the United States in periods of full employment. He would find (granting the alleviation of fear, which is improbable) the masses living physiologically, profiting from the material achievements of their civilization. But their spiritual development would meet an insuperable obstacle in a doctrine which considers its aim to be the liberation of man from material cares towards something which it, itself, defines as sheer nonsense.

These are utopian considerations which Western Communists may avoid, but their Eastern brothers do not. I remember one who said, "I do not want to live to see Communism realized, it will probably be so boring." When the great re-educational task is accomplished and the hated "metaphysical being" in man is utterly crushed, what will remain? It is doubtful whether Party imitations of Christian liturgy, and mass-like rites performed

before portraits of the leaders will give the people perfect
satisfaction.

More than the West imagines, the intellectuals of the
East look to the West for *something*. Nor do they seek
it in Western propaganda. The *something* they look for is
a great new writer, a new social philosophy, an artistic
movement, a scientific discovery, new principles of painting or music. They rarely find this *something*. The people of the East have already become accustomed to thinking of art and society on an organizational and mass scale.
The only forms of culture in the West which attain such
a scale are movies, best sellers, and illustrated magazines.
No thinking person in the West takes most of these means   *mass*
of mass recreation seriously; whereas, in the East, where   *culture*
everything has a mass character, they take on the dignity
of being the sole representatives of the "decadent culture
of the West." It is easy to sneer at most films, novels, or
articles (to say nothing of the fact that one is well-paid
for such criticism and that it releases one from the more
painful obligation of writing enthusiastically about the
Center). Hence it is the pet activity of most Eastern journalists, and the influence that this sort of criticism has on
its public is considerable.

The real cultural life of the West is very different. But
even there the Eastern intellectual stumbles upon treacherous appearances, for he finds both imitation and innova-
tion, decadence and vigor, advertised mediocrity and
imperfectly recognized greatness. The social and intellectual currents, which he knows from his pre-war trips
to the West, continue to exist and arouse his impatience
as products of a stage he has left behind. Still these are ✓
the aspects that attract his attention, and not the new creative forces sending up shoots amid a forest of dead trees.

The gravest reproach leveled against Western culture is

use of "Center"
— cult of ugliness
38   *The Captive Mind*

that it is <u>exclusive and inaccessible to the</u> masses. This reproach is largely valid. Poetry, painting, and even music,
shutting themselves up in ivory towers, become susceptible to numerous stylistic maladies. At the same time, however, their link with the everyday life of the people is
considerably stronger than it seems to be at first glance.
For example, avant-garde painting which is so "difficult"
and "obscure" reaches a tremendous number of people
through its influence on advertising, dress design, stage
sets, interior decoration, and most important of all, perhaps, on the shape of universally used machines. In comparison with this, the "Soviet Empire" style, which is
based on the painting on huge canvases of groups of
dignitaries standing about in various positions and poses,
is completely severed from everyday life. By destroying
all experimentation in art, the Center confined its applied
art (if one can speak of its existence at all) to a clumsy
imitation of Western applied art which, however, is constantly renewed under the influence of experimental easel
painting. When the cult of ugliness reigns in painting or
sculpture and any daring passes as formalism, then applied art, cut off from its roots, is bound to prove sterile.

The multi-colored setting of Western life is subject to
the law of osmosis. The average citizen of the West has
no idea that a painter in a garret, a little-known musician,
or a writer of "unintelligible" verse is a magician who
shapes all those things in life which he prizes. Government officials give little thought to such matters for they
consider them a waste of time. Since it is not a planned
economy, the Western state cannot come to the aid of
people working in the various arts. They go on, each
pursuing his own chimera, sometimes dying of hunger;
while nearby, wealthy men, not knowing what to do with

their money, spend it on the latest whims of their be-
nighted souls.

This order of things revolts a person from the East. In
his country, anyone who displays any talent is used. In
the West, the same man would have very little chance of
success. Western economy squanders talent to an incredible degree; and the few who do succeed owe their success
as often to pure luck as to native ability. In the countries
of the New Faith, the counterpart to this waste lies in the
fact that the capacity to follow the political line is a selec-
tive criterion by which the most mediocre often attain
the greatest renown. Nevertheless, the artist or scholar in the
East earns his living more easily than his colleague in the
West. Even though the pressure of the Method is burdensome, its material compensations are not to be scorned.
Many musicians, painters, and writers who had the opportunity to flee to the West did not do so because they felt
it was better to compose, paint, or write somehow or other,
rather than to teach or work in a factory, with no time or
energy left in which to perfect their true craft. Many of
those who were abroad returned to their own countries
chiefly for this reason.

Fear of the indifference with which the economic system
of the West treats its artists and scholars is widespread
among Eastern intellectuals. They say it is better to deal
with an intelligent devil than with a good-natured idiot.
An intelligent devil understands their mutual interests
and lets them live by a pen, a chisel, or a brush, caring for
his clients and making his demands. A good-hearted idiot
does not understand these interests, gives nothing and
asks nothing—which in practice amounts to polite cruelty.

To the people of the East it is axiomatic that the basic
means of production should belong to the State, that they

should be regulated according to a planned economy, and that their proceeds should be used for hygienic, cultural, scientific, and artistic ends. It is naïve to seek partisans of capitalism in their midst. The *something* these people look for in the West is certainly not warmed-over watchwords of the French Revolution or the American War of Independence. They laugh at the argument that factories and mines should belong to private individuals. Their search for *something* springs from a more or less clear understanding of the fact that the New Faith is incapable of satisfying the spiritual needs of mankind, for its efforts in that direction have with inexorable regularity turned into caricature. If they were forced to formulate what they seek, they would undoubtedly reply that they want a system with a socialist economy, but one in which man need not struggle desperately in the snake-like embrace of the Method. So they seek some sign indicating that real cultural values can arise outside the scope of the Method. But they must be lasting values, geared to the future, and therefore not products of obsolete concepts. Anything less would serve merely to confirm the Method. The people in the countries of the New Faith know that *only* in the West can there appear works that will bear the seeds of hope for the future. Perhaps discoveries no less important than those of Marx or Darwin have already been perfected in the workrooms of isolated philosophers. But how does one find them?

The Eastern intellectual is a severe critic of everything that penetrates to him from the West. He has been deceived so often that he does not want cheap consolation which will eventually prove all the more depressing. The War left him suspicious and highly skilled in unmasking sham and pretense. He has rejected a great many books that he liked before the War, as well as a great many trends in painting or music, because they have not stood the test of experience. The work of human thought *should* withstand the test of brutal, naked reality. If it cannot, it is worthless. Probably only those things are worth while which can preserve their validity in the eyes of a man threatened with instant death.

A man is lying under machine-gun fire on a street in an embattled city. He looks at the pavement and sees a very amusing sight: the cobblestones are standing upright like the quills of a porcupine. The bullets hitting against their edges displace and tilt them. Such moments in the consciousness of a man *judge* all poets and philosophers. Let us suppose, too, that a certain poet was the hero of the literary cafés, and wherever he went was regarded with curiosity and awe. Yet his poems, recalled in such a moment, suddenly seem diseased and highbrow. The vision of the cobblestones is unquestionably real, and poetry based on an equally *naked* experience could survive triumphantly that judgment day of man's illusions. In the intellectuals who lived through the atrocities of war in Eastern Europe there took place what one might call the *elimination of emotional luxuries.* Psychoanalytic novels incite them to laughter. They consider the literature of erotic complications, still popular in the West, as trash. Imitation abstract painting bores them. They are hungry—but they want bread, not hors d'oeuvres.

Dialectical materialism awakens a response in them because it is *earthy.* They would willingly espouse a literature and art born outside the sphere of the Method, but on condition that it be earthy, strong, and healthy. If only they could find it! It is significant that everything in the West that is strong enough for their taste turns on questions of social structure and mass belief. Such books are frequently Stalinist, but even more often anti-Stalinist.

W offers no alternative

A great many of them have read Koestler's *Darkness at Noon*. A few have become acquainted with Orwell's *1984*; because it is both difficult to obtain and dangerous to possess, it is known only to certain members of the Inner Party. Orwell fascinates them through his insight into details they know well, and through his use of Swiftian satire. Such a form of writing is forbidden by the New Faith because allegory, by nature manifold in meaning, would trespass beyond the prescriptions of socialist realism and the demands of the censor. Even those who know Orwell only by hearsay are amazed that a writer who never lived in Russia should have so keen a perception into its life. The fact that there are writers in the West who understand the functioning of the unusually constructed machine of which they themselves are a part astounds them and argues against the "stupidity" of the West.

Usually, what is strong in the West is purely negative. Its criticism of the New Faith is often accurate, but despite this, it points no way out, and introduces nothing to replace the Method. One can, it is true, say that it introduces a living man unashamed of his thoughts and capable of moving without the stilts supplied by citations from the authorities. To the Eastern intellectual, this is insufficient. One does not defeat a Messiah with common-sense arguments.

The Christian religion which is restricted or even exterminated in the countries of the New Faith always evokes a considerable (albeit unhealthy) amount of interest. Do Western Christians take the necessary advantage of their freedom? One is forced to the conclusion that they do not. Religion has become something in the nature of a vestigial custom, instances of which one finds in the folklore of various nations. Perhaps some pressure is needed if Christianity is to be reborn. The religious fervor of the Christians in the people's democracies would seem to indicate as much. One merely wonders if theirs isn't the piety of a mouse caught in a trap, and if it hasn't come just a bit too late.

The official order is to evince the greatest horror of the West. Everything is evil there: trains are late, stores are empty, no one has money, people are poorly dressed, the highly praised technology is worthless. If you hear the name of a Western writer, painter, or composer, you must scoff sarcastically, for to fight against "cosmopolitanism" is one of the basic duties of a citizen. Cosmopolitanism is defined as admiration for the (bourgeois) culture of the West. The term was invented in Moscow, and is not new in the history of Russia. Over a hundred years ago, Tsarist historians spoke with aversion of the "decadent West." It was in the decadent West of that time that Marx and Engels were writing, and it is from that West that it later proved necessary to import not only their work, but many other discoveries as well. In practice the fight against cosmopolitanism in the people's democracies takes the form of elaborate prescriptions indicating which Western writers of the past (those "progressive for their day") can be translated, what Western painting and music (usually created before 1870) is "healthy," etc.

No mattter how much trouble these detailed orders create for editors, publishers, and music directors, the "fight against cosmopolitanism" is not entirely without rational justification. Its motive in the Center is clear: too broad a scale of comparison is incompatible with the moral health of the citizens. In the people's democracies, which have been subjected to Western influence for centuries, it is a question of liquidating bad habits. You break a smoker of his habit by taking away his cigarettes.

In convincing himself that the Center is not completely wrong to combat "cosmopolitanism," the intellectual argues thus: the religion of Rome spread more or less over the area in which so-called European civilization arose. Those countries which today form the Western provinces of the Imperium were for centuries the eastern peripheries of that civilization. The growth of modern Europe, with its concurrent development of trade and industry, deepened the rift between "Europe" and its outlying "Eastern Marches." A citizen of Iowa asked to define what he means by "Europe" would probably name France, Holland, Italy, Germany. He would go no farther East, and he would imagine the inhabitants of that distant area to be a mixture of untrustworthy, backward tribes.

It is possible that our Iowan is an example of "historical lag," that his ideas are the products of concepts which no longer coincide with facts. Nevertheless, his opinions are characteristic, and in fact reflected in American political moves which did not see Russia's occupation of the "Eastern Marches" as a loss that could have serious consequences. After all, it was in Western Europe that money and power accumulated through the centuries and that culture patterns arose which later spread to the East. (For example, Polish churches and palaces were built by Italian architects; Polish popular art was shaped by Baroque; Polish poets admiringly followed the forms of French verse, etc.). The countries of Central and Eastern Europe were traditionally "poor relations," a semi-colonial terrain. The West's attitude toward them was in general patronizing, and still does not differ much from the somewhat oversimplified opinions of the citizen of Iowa.

The Pole, Czech, or Hungarian of average education knows a good bit about France, Belgium, or Holland. The Frenchman, Belgian, or Hollander of average education

*& spurned by w, solidarity
w/ Russia*

knows little about Poland, Czechoslovakia, or Hungary. The Eastern individual finds this state of affairs unreasonable, and feels a certain solidarity with the Russian who has old and unpleasant scores to settle with the West. Even though he is irritated by Russia's inferiority complex, which leads her to demand constant homage and assurances of her unquestionable superiority, the West's disdain of Central and Eastern Europe upsets him even more, for it seems to spring from a lack of recognition of the change in proportion which has occurred in the twentieth century. These countries have a large population which has displayed a definite ability to adapt itself to the exigencies of modern technology. They are rich in natural resources, and their mining and heavy industry are rapidly developing. Their worker no longer resembles the helpless emigrant who, setting out for the West in search of bread, was forced to accept the lowest type of manual labor. Their technicians and scholars can compete successfully with their Western colleagues. Their writers and musicians cannot complain of any lack of talent.

And what is more, from every point of view, these countries seem to be the most important part not only of Europe, but of the whole world: if we assume that the New Faith will spread throughout the earth, then these are the first and therefore most interesting areas of the experiment outside Russia itself. If we assume that the Center will lose, then the economic and culture patterns that will arise subsequently in these countries will certainly be new, for there is no such thing in history as a return to the status quo. Then is one not justified in checking this idolatry of Western models which was so prevalent among the cultivated circles of the "Eastern Marches"? Why should present-day French painting, born in a coun-

try living on remembered glories, be imitated in Prague or
Warsaw? Why should English plays, written for a completely different public, be played in these Eastern capitals?
One must break that habit of imitation which was inevitable as long as French, English, or Belgian capital, in-
vesting in the mines, railroads, and factories of the "Eastern Marches," pushed its books, films, and styles upon
them. Just as nationalized industry now stands on its own
✓ feet, so Eastern European cultures must learn to stand
by their own strength.

Unhappily, in freeing themselves from the spell of the
West, the literature, science, and art of these Marches became totally dependent on the new metropolis. Once
imitation was spontaneous and voluntary, but now it is
obligatory. Any attempt to find one's own way is de-
nounced as Titoism. Any attempt to reach into one's own
national past is possible only to the extent that that past
parallels the development of the Russian nation. One may
turn to folklore, obviously, and to the realistic plays of the
nineteenth century. But, for example, Poland has a tradition of romantic drama which does not lend itself to
realistic representation. It also possesses a tradition of stage
production which is known as "monumental theater." To
continue such traditions would smack of dangerous heresy.
The fight against "cosmopolitanism" is in reality nothing
more than the act of emptying a retort and refilling it
with a different fluid. In the past, a particular substance
was created in this retort through the interaction of native
and imported elements. Today the imported element appears in much purer form, for a sufficient number of
laboratory workers are eager to maintain the necessary
respect for the formula.

In the last century, the "decadent West" was condemned
by patriotic Russian historians because it was liberal, and

because the ideas that emanated from it threatened autocratic governments. Nor was it only these defenders of the throne who criticized it mercilessly. One has but to read Tolstoi's *What Is Art?* to get a picture of the scorn for Western sophistication that is so typical of the Russians. Tolstoi regarded Shakespeare's plays as collections of bloody crimes, and French painting (this was the period of the flowering of Impressionism) as the daubs of degenerates. After the Revolution, when once again the social system of Russia differed from that of the West, it was not difficult to enlarge on this precedent with a goodly number of arguments. Didn't Russia's strength lie in its suspicion of the West; and weren't even the Tsarist historians working for the Revolution by cultivating Russia's self-assurance and faith in the special calling of the nation? Conscious of their hitherto latent power, the "Scythians," as the great Russian poet Blok called his nation, at last began to march. Therefore, it would seem that the nations lying between the Baltic and Mediterranean seas would do well to imitate this Russian self-assurance and free themselves from the bad habit of parroting the West.

The intellectual understands, of course, that he himself is "cosmopolitan" since he looks to the West for *something*. This does not mean, however, that he complains about the orders that have banished Parisian boulevard art, or American detective stories from his country. A great many cultural phenomena which excite the "elite" in Western countries are distasteful to him. Asked whether T. S. Eliot's *The Cocktail Party* should be played in his native land, he would undoubtedly answer "No"; whereas, he finds *The Wasteland* by the same author an interesting piece of poetry. The new acquisition that the people of Central and Eastern Europe will never want to relinquish is the feeling of responsibility for what the public gets from editors or producers. If, for example, one considers a play bad, one should not present it even though it might be a considerable financial success. (Just imagine a Prague or Warsaw worker looking at *The Cocktail Party!*) On the other hand, the ban on Stravinsky's *Le Sacre du printemps* is obviously absurd. The "cosmopolitanism" of the intellectual I describe is very moderate. He makes distinctions between what is worthy of his respect in the West and what owes its success to cheap publicity appealing to the taste of a dubious "elite."

The superiority of Russian realist painting (*pieredwizniki*) over French Impressionism has been proved in Moscow. Unfortunately, the eye is used in the appreciation of a painting, and the most learned discourse cannot transform an ugly canvas into a great work of art—which is obviously to be deplored! At every step, be it in the realm of aesthetics or ethics, one encounters the opposition that the strangeness of man raises against the wisest of theories. It is reasonable that a responsibly raised child should inform on his father if he observes his behavior to be contrary to the good of the social order on whose well-being the happiness of all mankind depends. And yet the disgust such behavior awakens in many people is just as inexplicable as their preference for Manet over Russian nineteenth-century realists.

The recklessness with which the Russians are carrying out their mental operations in the people's democracies is reaching dangerous proportions. Consistent reasoning which orders one to by-pass a fact when a concept comes into conflict with reality must eventually lead to costly errors. Hitler's war on "degenerate art" sprang from the same seed as the new ethics of his party which ordered the slaughter of "inferior races"; and in these very ideas lay the causes of his defeat. Knowing the Center's demand that science and art conform to the Method instead of searching for objective truth and beauty, the intellectual comes to the conclusion that it is not the wisdom of the West that will cause the downfall of the Imperium, but rather the aberrations to which the Method leads.

Announcing Mendelian genetics to be wrong, the Center used roughly three groups of arguments: 1) It contradicts the dialectical interpretation of Darwin's theory of the natural selection of species because it stresses those elements of his theory which are the reflection of the social circumstances of Darwin's day, namely, the pitiless struggle for existence in a capitalist society. (In place of the struggle for existence within a given species, one must substitute cooperation within a given species.) 2) It does not yield satisfactory practical results in agriculture. 3) It can serve as the basis for racist theories, since an individual is "better" or "worse" according to his genes. All these arguments evidence the wish that reality were all one longs for it to be. Yet what will happen if Mendelian genetics proves to be consistent with scientific observation? No matter how loudly he applauds the speakers who annihilate Western genetics, the Eastern intellectual suspects he is the dupe of an enormous hoax similar to the hoaxes of German scholars who scientifically proved whatever was necessary to the Nazis at a particular moment.

This constitutes one step in the direction of doubt about the dialectical method itself. Is it not based at times on an interpretation of signs in nature and in history which the interpreter carefully placed there himself? Dialectics is the "logic of contradictions" applicable, according to the wise men, to those cases where formal logic is inadequate, namely to phenomena in motion. Because human concepts as well as the phenomena observed by men are in

In motion — contradictions
=> a beard example
50   The Captive Mind

motion, "contradictions contained in the concepts are but reflections, or translations into the language of thought, of those contradictions which are contained in the phenomena."

Very well; yet what about the example Plekhanov goes on to cite to prove the inadequacy of formal logic? Someone points to a young man whose beard is just beginning to grow and demands a reply to the question as to whether he does or does not have a beard. One cannot say he does not, for he has the beginnings of one. One cannot say he does, for it is not yet a beard. In a word, the beard is becoming; it is in motion; it is only a certain *quantity* of individual hairs which will one day become a *quality* called a beard. "Hell," mutters our intellectual, "these are nothing more than seventeenth-century rabbinical exercises." The hairs growing on the chin of a young man are absolutely indifferent as to what name one will give them. There is no "transition" here from "quantity to quality," as the faithful so piously proclaim. The problem "beard or no beard" arises from the language we use, from our system of classification. What boundless vanity it is to ascribe to phenomena the contradictions in which we are entangled because of our clumsy concepts.

But this is a very serious matter. The fate of the Imperium hangs on that unhappy chin. If all the historical analyses carried out according to the Method operate on the same sort of trickery—that is, if it first introduces the concepts, and then takes their contradictions to be the contradictions of the material observed—then the new Imperium may at any time trip itself in its own acrobatics.

And yet the Eastern intellectual is terrorized by the Method. How can one explain this? Without confessing to anyone, he admits to himself that falseness exists in the very core of the Method. But this does not prevent him

from ascribing to the Method any success he may have in
working with material by other techniques. The Method
exerts a magnetic influence on contemporary man because
it alone emphasizes, as has never before been done, the
fluidity and interdependence of phenomena. Since the
people of the twentieth century find themselves in social
circumstances where even the dullest mind can see that
"naturalness" is being replaced by fluidity and interdependence, thinking in categories of motion seems to be
the surest means of seizing reality in the act. The Method
is mysterious; no one understands it completely—but that
merely enhances its magic power. Its elasticity, as exploited by the Russians, who do not possess the virtue of
moderation, can result at times in the most painful edicts.
Nevertheless, history shows us that a healthy, reasoning
mind was rarely an effective guide through the labyrinth
of human affairs.

The Method profits from the discoveries of Marx and
Engels, from their moral indignation, and from the tactics
of their successors who have denied the rightness of moral
indignation. It is like a snake, which is undoubtedly a
dialectical creature: "Daddy, does a snake have a tail?"
asked the little boy. "Nothing but a tail," answered the
father. This leads to unlimited possibilities, for the tail
can begin at any point. Asking himself why he cannot
escape from its embrace (even if he should want to), the
intellectual replies that the measure of the Method's accuracy lies in the strength of those who rule in its name.
They know how to erect a building with mobile walls on
ground that is constantly shaken by earthquakes; while
the West, lacking equally perfected blueprints, clings to
a traditional architecture that threatens to crash. Certain
walls of the dialectical structure are so monstrous that
they make the inhabitants fear for the future of a build-

ing so constructed. But when they compare it with the static architecture of the West, they believe at times that all humanity will have to move into more mobile apartments.

The Eastern intellectual's attitude toward the West is therefore complicated, and not reducible to formulas of sympathy or antipathy. It is somewhat like disappointed love, and as we know, such deception often leaves a sediment of sarcasm. It took such a calamity to enable the new system, entirely contrary to the predictions of Marx, to have been born in backward Russia, and for the Revolution to have become an enterprise directed by the bureaucrats of the Center and extended by military conquest. It took such a calamity to bring matters to the point where Europeans seeking to change the obsolete order of their countries must agree, also contrary to the predictions of Marx, to submit to a nation which has never known how to rule itself, and which in all its history has never known prosperity or freedom. What a terrible fate to have been born in such an era! This is what our intellectual thinks even as he pronounces a speech about the "supreme honor" it is to live in the "great Stalinist epoch." His function is, as he defiantly calls it, to "inoculate" others with the "basic principles of enthusiasm." It does not seem entirely unlikely to him that the West may emerge triumphant in its dispute with the Method. Still the Method, that is the revision of Marx according to Russian patterns, though it has many weaknesses, is a stronger weapon in the hands of the rulers than tanks or guns alone. And it works effectively.

Experience has taught the Eastern intellectual to measure his moves carefully. He has seen too many who fell into the abyss of disfavor for a single thoughtless step, for a single impulsively written article. If the Imperium falls, it may prove possible in the ensuing chaos to seek new means of survival and action. Until that happens, one must work devotedly for the triumph of the Imperium, secretly nourishing the hope that the "stupidity" of the West is not so unbounded as one is led to suppose. If only the people in the West really understood the mechanism of the "great Stalinist epoch," and if only they would act accordingly! Everything would seem to indicate that they do not understand. But perhaps, perhaps they will?

ΛΛΛΛΛΛΛΛΛΛΛΛΛΛΛΛΛΛΛΛΛΛΛΛΛΛΛΛΛΛ

CHAPTER III

Ketman

OFFICIALLY, contradictions do not exist in the minds of the citizens in the people's democracies. Nobody dares to reveal them publicly. And yet the question of how to deal with them is posed in real life. More than others, the members of the intellectual elite are aware of this problem. They solve it by becoming actors.

It is hard to define the type of relationship that prevails between people in the East otherwise than as acting, with the exception that one does not perform on a theater stage but in the street, office, factory, meeting hall, or even the room one lives in. Such acting is a highly developed craft that places a premium upon mental alertness. Before it leaves the lips, every word must be evaluated as to its consequences. A smile that appears at the wrong moment, a glance that is not all it should be can occasion dangerous suspicions and accusations. Even one's gestures, tone of voice, or preference for certain kinds of neckties are interpreted as signs of one's political tendencies.

A visitor from the Imperium is shocked on coming to the West. In his contacts with others, beginning with porters or taxi drivers, he encounters no resistance. The people he meets are completely relaxed. They lack that internal concentration which betrays itself in a lowered head

acting convincingly

or in restlessly moving eyes. They say whatever words come to their tongues; they laugh aloud. Is it possible that human relations can be so direct?

Acting in daily life differs from acting in the theater in that everyone plays to everyone else, and everyone is fully aware that this is so. The fact that a man acts is not to his prejudice, is no proof of unorthodoxy. But he must act well, for his ability to enter into his role skillfully proves that he has built his characterization upon an adequate foundation. If he makes a passionate speech against the West, he demonstrates that he has at least 10 per cent of the hatred he so loudly proclaims. If he condemns Western culture lukewarmly, then he must be attached to it in reality. Of course, all human behavior contains a significant amount of acting. A man reacts to his environment and is molded by it even in his gestures. Nevertheless, what we find in the people's democracies is a conscious mass play rather than automatic imitation. Conscious acting, if one practices it long enough, develops those traits which one uses most in one's role, just as a man who became a runner because he had good legs develops his legs even more in training. After long acquaintance with his role, a man grows into it so closely that he can no longer differentiate his true self from the self he simulates, so that even the most intimate of individuals speak to each other in Party slogans. To identify one's self with the role one is obliged to play brings relief and permits a relaxation of one's vigilance. Proper reflexes at the proper moment become truly automatic. *ID self*

This happens in literature as well. A poet writing a piece of propaganda does not confine himself to a purely rationalistic approach. Imbued with the thought that poetry ideally should be suited to recitation in chorus at a meeting, he begins by tuning himself to an appropriate

pitch of collective emotion before he can release himself
in words. In the theater, the actor who plays the Cid, for
example, *is* the Cid on stage. Yet not every actor, even if
he is young and well-built, can play the Cid; he must have
an inborn capacity to release himself emotionally in that
role. Poetry as we have known it can be defined as the
individual temperament refracted through social convention. The poetry of the New Faith can, on the contrary, be
defined as social convention refracted through the individual temperament. That is why the poets who are
most adapted to the new situation are those endowed with
dramatic talent. The poet creates the character of an ideal
revolutionary and writes his verses as the monologue of
this character. He does not speak for himself but for the
ideal citizen. His results are reminiscent of songs written
to be sung on the march since the aim is the same—the
forging of the fetters of collectivity that bind together an
advancing column of soldiers. The best examples of such
song-slogans are certain verses of the German poet, Ber-
thold Brecht, which are superior to the works of other
Eastern poets because Brecht is fully conscious of the his-
trionic process involved.

Even though the identification of the play with private
thought-property is carried very far, a large residue of un-
assimilated matter remains which forces one to keep alert.
A constant and universal masquerade creates an aura that
is hard to bear, yet it grants the performers certain not in-
considerable satisfactions. To say something is white when
one thinks it black, to smile inwardly when one is out-
wardly solemn, to hate when one manifests love, to know
when one pretends not to know, and thus to play one's
adversary for a fool (even as he is playing you for one)—
these actions lead one to prize one's own cunning above all
else. Success in the game becomes a source of satisfaction.

inner sanctity - silence

Simultaneously, that which we protect from prying eyes
takes on a special value because it is never clearly formulated in words and hence has the irrational charm of things
purely emotional. Man takes refuge in an inner sanctuary
which is the more precious the greater the price he pays
in order to bar others from access to it.

Acting on a comparable scale has not occurred often in
the history of the human race. Yet in trying to describe
these new mores, we happen across a striking analogy in
the Islamic civilization of the Middle East. Not only was
the game played in defense of one's thoughts and feelings
well-known there, but indeed it was transformed into a
permanent institution and graced with the name of Ketman.

What is Ketman? I found its description in a book by
Gobineau entitled *Religions and Philosophies of Central
Asia*. Gobineau spent many years in Persia (from 1855 to
1858 he was a secretary in the French legation, from 1861
to 1863 he was French minister), and we cannot deny his
gift for keen observation, even though we need not necessarily agree with the conclusions of this rather dangerous
writer. The similarities between Ketman and the customs
cultivated in the countries of the New Faith are so striking
that I shall permit myself to quote at length.

The people of the Mussulman East believe that "He
who is in possession of truth must not expose his person,
his relatives or his reputation to the blindness, the folly,
the perversity of those whom it has pleased God to place
and maintain in error." One must, therefore, keep silent
about one's true convictions if possible.

"Nevertheless," says Gobineau, "there are occasions
when silence no longer suffices, when it may pass as an
avowal. Then one must not hesitate. Not only must one
deny one's true opinion, but one is commanded to resort

to all ruses in order to deceive one's adversary. One makes all the protestations of faith that can please him, one performs all the rites one recognizes to be the most vain, one falsifies one's own books, one exhausts all possible means of deceit. Thus one acquires the multiple satisfactions and merits of having placed oneself and one's relatives under cover, of not having exposed a venerable faith to the horrible contact of the infidel, and finally of having, in cheating the latter and confirming him in his error, imposed on him the shame and spiritual misery that he deserves.

"Ketman fills the man who practices it with pride. Thanks to it, a believer raises himself to a permanent state of superiority over the man he deceives, be he a minister of state or a powerful king; to him who uses Ketman, the other is a miserable blind man whom one shuts off from the true path whose existence he does not suspect; while you, tattered and dying of hunger, trembling externally at the feet of duped force, your eyes are filled with light, you walk in brightness before your enemies. It is an unintelligent being that you make sport of; it is a dangerous beast that you disarm. What a wealth of pleasures!"

How far Ketman can go is demonstrated by the founder of one sect, Hadzhi-Sheikh-Ahmed. "Although he left behind many works of theology, he never openly advanced in his books, as even his most passionate disciples avow, anything which could place the reader on the path of the ideas attributed to him today. But everyone affirms he practiced Ketman and that in private he was extremely daring and precise in establishing order in the doctrines which bear his name today." We cannot wonder, therefore, that, as a certain Persian admitted in conversation with Gobineau, "there is not a single true Moslem in Persia."

Not everyone was as careful as Hadzhi-Sheikh-Ahmed. To some, Ketman was useful in the preparatory period,

(margin note: Ketman practice of deception/silence)

but when they felt themselves sufficiently strong, they proclaimed their heresy openly. Here, for example, is the description of the itinerant preachings of Sadra, the disciple of Avicenna.

"He too was afraid of the mullahs. To incite their distrust was inevitable, but to provide a solid basis, furnish proof for their accusations, that would have been to expose himself to endless persecutions, and to compromise at the same time the future of the philosophical restoration he meditated. Therefore he conformed to the demands of his times and resorted to the great and splendid expedient of Ketman. When he arrived in a city he was careful to present himself humbly to all the moudjteheds or doctors of the region. He sat in a corner of their salons, their talars, remained silent usually, spoke modestly, approved each word that escaped their venerable lips. He was questioned about his knowledge; he expressed only ideas borrowed from the strictest Shiite theology and in no way indicated that he concerned himself with philosophy. After several days, seeing him so meek, the moudjteheds themselves engaged him to give public lessons. He set to work immediately, took as his text the doctrine of ablution or some similar point, and split hairs over the prescriptions and inner doubts of the subtlest theoreticians. This behavior delighted the mullahs. They lauded him to the skies; they forgot to keep an eye on him. They themselves wanted to see him lead their imaginations through less placid questions. He did not refuse. From the doctrine of ablution he passed to that of prayer; from the doctrine of prayer, to that of revelation; from revelation, to divine unity and there, with marvels of ingenuity, reticence, confidences to the most advanced pupils, self-contradiction, ambiguous propositions, fallacious syllogisms out of which only the initiated could see their way, the whole heavily

seasoned with unimpeachable professions of faith, he succeeded in spreading Avicennism throughout the entire
lettered class; and when at last he believed he could reveal himself completely, he drew aside the veils, repudiated
Islam, and showed himself the logician, the metaphysician
that he really was."

Islamic Ketman and the Ketman of the twentieth century in Europe seem to differ only in that the boldness
Sadra permitted himself would instantly have brought
him to a sad end in Europe. Nevertheless, Ketman in its
narrowest and severest forms is widely practiced in the
people's democracies. As in Islam, the feeling of superiority over those who are unworthy of attaining truth constitutes one of the chief joys of people whose lives do not
in general abound in pleasures. "Deviations," the tracing
of which creates so many troubles for the rulers, are not
an illusion. They are cases of accidental unmaskings of
Ketman; and those who are most helpful in detecting
deviations are those who themselves practice a similar
form of Ketman. Recognizing in other acrobats the tricks
they themselves employ, they take advantage of the first
occasion to down an opponent or friend. Thus they protect themselves; and the measure of dexterity is to antici-
pate by at least one day the similar accusation which could
be leveled against them by the man they denounce. Since
the number of varieties of Ketman is practically unlimited,
the naming of deviations cannot keep pace with the weed-
ing of a garden so full of unexpected specimens of heresy.
Every new commentary on the precepts of the New Faith
proclaimed by the Center multiplies the internal reservations of those who are externally the most faithful. It is
impossible to enumerate all the forms of Ketman that one
can discover in the people's democracies. I shall try, how-

ever, to proceed somewhat in the manner of a naturalist determining major groups and families.

National Ketman is broadly diffused throughout the masses, and even the upper brackets of the Party in the various dependent states are not free of it. Because Tito, like Sadra, announced his heresy to all the world, millions of human beings in the people's democracies must employ exceedingly ingenious means of masking themselves. Instructive displays of condemnation of those who wished to follow the national road to socialism in individual Eastern capitals taught the public what kind of phrases and reflexes can expose one to reproach for harboring this fatal tendency. The surest safeguard is to manifest loudly one's awe at Russia's achievements in every field of endeavor, to carry Russian books under one's arm, to hum Russian songs, to applaud Russian actors and musicians enthusiastically, etc. A writer who has not consecrated a single work to outstanding Russian figures or to Russian life, but has confined himself to national themes, cannot consider himself entirely safe. The chief characteristic of the people who practice this Ketman is an unbounded contempt for Russia as a barbaric country. Among the workers and peasants it is most often purely emotional, and based on observation of either the soldiers of the liberating army, or (since during the war a great many were in areas directly administered by the Russians) of Russians in their daily life.

Because until now the living standard of the masses in Russia was so much lower than that of the so-called people's democracies, national Ketman finds abundant nourishment. It cannot be defined simply as nationalism. For many centuries hatred existed between the Central European Slavs and the Germans, still it was colored

among the Slavs by a respect for Germany's material
achievements. On the other hand, perceiving by comparison the greater refinement of his own customs, his
greater organizational ability (be it only in respect to
transportation or the handling of machinery), the Central European would express his attitude toward Russia,
if he could, by a disdainful shrug of his shoulders—which,
however, doesn't prevent him from shuddering in fear before the countless hordes pouring out of the Euro-Asian
continent.

But this Ketman is not exclusively emotional in its appeal. Amid the young intelligentsia of working-class origin
the overwhelming opinion can be summed up shortly as
"Socialism—yes, Russia—no"; and this is where the sub-
tleties of doctrinal differences arise. The countries of Europe, this line of reasoning begins, are infinitely more prepared to realize socialism than Russia. Their population
is more intelligent; most of their land is under cultivation;
their systems of communication and their industry are
more highly developed. Measures based on absolute cruelty
are unnecessary and even pointless since there exists a
greater degree of social discipline. Nevertheless, "the national road to socialism" has been condemned and many
efforts made to prove that whoever is opposed to total
adaptation to Russian models and to surrendering to Russian dictatorship is a traitor who must share the fate of
Tito—that is, must come out against the Center and thus
weaken its war potential without which there can be no
revolution on a world scale. To pronounce oneself against
this thesis would be to deny the New Faith and to introduce in its place a different faith, for example one directly
linked to Marx and Engels. Many do so. Others, seeing
in the alliance between Tito and the West an example of
historical fatality, and rejecting the idea that this fatality

may be due simply to the Center's policy toward dependent nations, shut themselves up in a Ketman which does not hamper the Center in its external acts. A true Moslem, even though he be deeply attached to his Ketman, never seeks to injure Islam in those areas where it is fighting for its life against unbelievers. Such Ketman expresses itself only in practical moves which do no harm in the world struggle, but which on the other hand safeguard national interests whenever possible.

The Ketman of Revolutionary Purity is a rare variety, more common in the large cities of Russia than in the people's democracies. It is based on a belief in the "sacred fire of the revolutionary epoch of Lenin" which burns in such a poet as Mayakovski. Mayakovski's suicide in 1930 marked the end of an era distinguished by the flowering of literature, the theater, and music. The "sacred fire" was dampened, collectivization was introduced mercilessly, millions of Soviet citizens perished in slave labor camps, a ruthless policy toward non-Russian nations was established. Literature became flat and colorless under the influence of imposed theories; Russian painting was destroyed; Russian theater, then the foremost in the world, was deprived of freedom to experiment; science was subjected to directives from Party chiefs. A man who reasons thus hates Him with all his heart, holding Him responsible for the terrible lot of the Russian people and for the hatred they inspire in other nations.

Still, he is not altogether sure whether He is necessary or not. Perhaps in extraordinary periods such as the present the appearance of a tyrant must be considered desirable. Mass purges in which so many good communists died, the lowering of the living standard of the citizens, the reduction of artists and scholars to the status of yesmen, the extermination of entire national groups—what other man would dare undertake such measures? After all, Russia stood firm against Hitler; the Revolution weathered the attack of enemy armies. In this perspective, His acts seem effectiye and even justified, perhaps, by an exceptional historical stituation. If He had not instituted an exceptional terror in the year 1937, wouldn't there have been more people willing to help Hitler than there actually were? For example, doesn't the present-day line in scholarship and art, no matter how at odds it may be at times with common sense, effectually raise Russian morale in the face of the war that threatens? He is an infamous blot on the bright New Faith, but a blemish we must tolerate for the moment. And indeed we must even support Him. The "sacred fire" has not gone out. When victory is achieved, it will burst forth again with its old strength, the bonds He imposed will fall away, and relations between nations will operate on new and better principles. This variety of Ketman was widespread if not universal in Russia during the Second World War, and its present form is a rebirth of an already once-deceived hope.

Aesthetic Ketman is born of the disparity between man's longings and the sense-satisfactions the New Faith offers. A man of taste cannot approve the results of official pressure in the realm of culture no matter how much he applauds the latest verses, how many flattering reviews he writes of current art expositions, nor how studiously he pretends that the gloomy new buildings coincide with his personal preferences in architecture. He changes completely within the four walls of his home. There one finds (if he is a well-situated intellectual) reproductions of works of art officially condemned as bourgeois, records of modern music, and a rich collection of ancient authors in various languages. This luxury of splendid isolation is pardoned him so long as his creative work is effective prop-

aganda. To protect his position and his apartment (which
he has by the grace of the State), the intellectual is prepared to make any sacrifice or compromise; for the value
of privacy in a society that affords little if any isolation is
greater than the saying "my home is my castle" can lead
one to surmise. Two-way television screens installed in
private homes to observe the behavior of citizens in se-
clusion belong as yet to the future. Hence, by listening to
foreign radio stations and reading good books, he profits
from a moment of relaxation; that is, of course, if he is
alone, for as soon as guests arrive the play begins anew.

Never has there been a close study of how necessary to
a man are the experiences which we clumsily call aesthetic. Such experiences are associated with works of art
for only an insignificant number of individuals. The majority find pleasure of an aesthetic nature in the mere fact
of their existence within the stream of life. In the cities,
the eye meets colorful store displays, the diversity of
human types. Looking at passers-by, one can guess from
their faces the story of their lives. This movement of the
imagination when a man is walking through a crowd has
an erotic tinge; his emotions are very close to physiological
sensations. He rejoices in dresses, in the flash of lights;
while, for instance, Parisian markets with their heaps of
vegetables and flowers, fish of every shape and hue, fruits,
sides of meat dripping with every shade of red offer delights, he need not go seeking them in Dutch or Impres-
sionist painting. He hears snatches of arias, the throbbing
of motors mixed with the warble of birds, called greet-
ings, laughter. His nose is assailed by changing odors:
coffee, gasoline, oranges, ozone, roasting nuts, perfumes.

Those who have sung of the large cities have consecrated
many pages to the description of this joyous immersion in
the reservoir of universal life. The swimmer who trusts

himself to the wave, and senses the immensity of the element that surrounds him lives through a like emotion. I am thinking of such great singers of the city as Balzac, Baudelaire, and Whitman. It would seem that the exciting and invigorating power of this participation in mass life springs from the feeling of *potentiality*, of constant unexpectedness, of a mystery one ever pursues.

Even the life of the peasants, though it be dulled by brutalizing hand labor, allows for aesthetic expression in the rhythm of custom, the rites of the church, holy pictures, country fairs, native costumes, paper flower decorations, folk sculptures, music, and dances.

In the countries of the New Faith the cities lose their former aspect. The liquidation of small private enterprises gives the streets a stiff and institutional look. The chronic lack of consumer goods renders the crowds uniformly gray and uniformly indigent. When consumer products do appear, they are of a single second-rate quality. Fear paralyzes individuality and makes people adjust themselves as much as possible to the average type in their gestures, clothing, and facial expressions. Cities become filled with the racial type well-regarded by the rulers: short, square men and women, with short legs and wide hips. This is the proletarian type, cultivated to an extreme, thanks to binding aesthetic standards. (We know that these same dumpy women and stocky men could change completely under the influence of films, painting, and fashion, for America has proved that mass communication is at least as important as diet in determining physical appearance.) Streets, factories, and meeting places sport the inevitable red flags and painted slogans. The new buildings are monumental and oppressive, lightness and charm in architecture being condemned as formalistic. The number of aesthetic experiences accessible to a city-dweller in the countries of the New Faith is uncommonly limited. The only place of magic is the theater, for the spell of the theater exists even though confined by the commands of socialist realism which define both the contents of a play and stage décor. The tremendous popular success of authors like Shakespeare is due to the fact that their fantasy triumphs even within the bounds of naturalistic stage setting. The hunger for *strangeness* that is so great inside the Imperium should give the rulers pause; yet in all probability it does not, for they consider such longings derelicts from the past.

In the villages, where the entire former pattern of custom is to be abolished through the transformation of peasants into agricultural workers, there still remain survivals of the individual peasant cultures which slowly stratified over the centuries. Still, let us speak frankly, the main supports of this culture were usually the wealthier peasants. The battle against them, and their subsequent need to hide, must lead to the atrophy of peasant dress, decoration of huts, cultivation of private gardens, etc. There is a definite contradiction between the official protection of folklore (as a harmless form of national culture designed to satisfy patriotic tendencies) and the necessities of the new economic structure.

In these conditions aesthetic Ketman has every possibility of spreading. It is expressed not only in that unconscious longing for strangeness which is channeled toward controlled amusements like theater, film, and folk festivals, but also into various forms of escapism. Writers burrow into ancient texts, comment upon and re-edit ancient authors. They write children's books so that their fancy may have slightly freer play. Many choose university careers because research into literary history offers a safe pretext for plunging into the past and for converse with works of great aesthetic value. The number of translators of former prose and poetry multiplies. Painters seek an outlet for their interests in illustrations for children's books, where the choice of gaudy colors can be justified by an appeal to the "naïve" imagination of children. Stage managers, doing their duty by presenting bad contemporary works, endeavor to introduce into their repertoires the plays of Lope de Vega or Shakespeare—that is, those of their plays which are approved by the Center.

Some representatives of the plastic arts are so daring that they reveal their Ketman to no small degree by proclaiming the need of an aesthetic of everyday life, and by establishing special institutes to design fabrics, furniture, glass, and ceramics for industry. There is money for such enterprises, and they find support among the most intelligent dialecticians of the upper circles of the Party. Such efforts deserve respect when one considers that before the Second World War Poland and Czechoslovakia were, aside from Sweden and Finland, the leading countries in interior decoration. Nevertheless, there is no reason why that which passes as formalism in painting and architecture should be tolerated for any length of time in the applied arts.

The rationalization of aesthetic Ketman is obvious: since everything is planned in a socialist economy, why not proceed to a planned satisfaction of the aesthetic needs of human beings? Here, however, we trespass upon the treacherous territory of the demon, Psychology. To admit that a man's eye has need of exultant colors, harmonious forms, or light sunny architecture is to affirm that the taste of the Center is bad. However, even there one can see some progress. They are already erecting skyscrapers patterned after the buildings raised in Chicago about the year 1900. It is possible that in the year 2000 they will officially introduce art forms that today are considered modern in the West. But how can one still the thought that aesthetic experiences arise out of something organic, and that the union of color and harmony with fear is as difficult to imagine as brilliant plumage on birds living in the northern tundras?

Professional Ketman is reasoned thus: since I find myself in circumstances over which I have no control, and since I have but one life and that is fleeting, I should strive to do my best. I am like a crustacean attached to a crag on the bottom of the sea. Over me storms rage and huge ships sail; but my entire effort is concentrated upon clinging to the rock, for otherwise I will be carried off by the waters and perish, leaving no trace behind. If I am a scientist I attend congresses at which I deliver reports strictly adhering to the Party line. But in the laboratory I pursue my research according to scientific methods, and in that alone lies the aim of life. If my work is successful, it matters little how it will be presented and toward whose glory. Discoveries made in the name of a disinterested search for truth are lasting, whereas the shrieks of politicians pass. I must do all they demand, they may use my name as they wish, as long as I have access to a laboratory and money for the purchase of scientific instruments.

If I am a writer, I take pride in my literary achievements. Here, for example, is my treatise on Swift, a Marxist analysis. This type of analysis, which is not synonymous with the Method or the New Faith, makes possible a keen penetration into historical events. Marx had a genius for observation. In following him one is secure against attack, for he is, after all, the prophet; and one can proclaim one's belief in the Method and the New Faith in a preface fulfilling much the same function as dedications to kings or tsars in times past. Here is my translation of a sixteenth-century poem, or my novel whose scene is laid in the distant past. Aren't they of permanent value? Here are my translations from Russian. They are viewed with approbation and have brought me a large sum of money, but certainly Pushkin is a great poet, and his worth is not altered by the fact that today his poems serve Him as a means of propaganda. Obviously I must pay for the right to practice my profession with a certain number of articles and odes in the way of tribute. Still one's life on earth is not judged by transitory panegyrics written out of necessity.

These two examples of professional Ketman should demonstrate how little discomfort it creates for the rulers. It is the source of considerable dynamic force and one cause of the tremendous impetus toward education. The object is to establish some special field in which one can release one's energies, exploit one's knowledge and sensibility, and at the same time escape the fate of a functionary entirely at the mercy of political fluctuations. The son of a worker who becomes a chemist makes a *permanent* advance. The son of a worker who becomes a member of the security police rises to the surface, where large ships sail but where the sea is changeable and stormy. But most important of all, chemical experiments, bridges, translations of poetry, and medical care are exceptionally free of falsity. The State, in its turn, takes advantage of this Ketman because it needs chemists, engineers, and doctors. From time to time, it is true, there come from above muffled grumbles of hatred against those who practice Ketman in the realm of humanistic studies. Fadeyev, Moscow's literary overseer, attacked the University of Leningrad because one of its students had written a dissertation on the English poet, Walter Savage Landor. "Who needs Landor? Who ever heard of him?" cried Fadeyev. So it would seem that <u>moderation and watchfulness</u> are indicated for those who espouse this form of Ketman.

Sceptical Ketman is widely disseminated throughout intellectual circles. One argues that humanity does not know how to handle its knowledge or how to resolve the problems of production and division of goods. The first scientific attempts to solve social problems, made in the nineteenth century, are interesting but not precise enough. They happened, however, into the hands of the Russians who, unable to think otherwise than dogmatically, raised these first attempts to the dignity of dogma. What is happening in Russia and the countries dependent upon her bespeaks a kind of insanity, but it is not impossible that Russia will manage to impose her insanity upon the whole world and that the return to reason will occur only after two or three hundred years. Finding oneself in the very midst of an historical cyclone, one must behave as prudently as possible, yielding externally to forces capable of destroying all adversaries. This does not prevent one from taking pleasure in one's observations, since what one beholds is indeed unprecedented. Surely man has never before been subjected to such pressure, never has he had to writhe and wriggle so to adapt himself to forms constructed according to the books but obviously not to his size. All his intellectual and emotional capacities are put to the test.

Whoever contemplates this daily sight of repudiation and humiliation knows more about man than an inhabitant of the West who feels no pressure other than that of money. The accumulating of this store of observations is the activity of a miser who counts his treasure in secret. Since this Ketman is based on a total lack of belief in the Method, it helps one conform externally to the obligatory line by allowing for complete cynicism, and therefore for elasticity in adjusting oneself to changing tactics.

Metaphysical Ketman occurs generally in countries with a Catholic past. Most examples of it within the Imperium are found in Poland. This Ketman depends upon a *suspended* belief in a metaphysical principle of the world. A man attached to this Ketman regards the epoch in which he lives as anti-metaphysical, and hence as one in which no metaphysical faith can emerge. Humanity is learning to think in rationalistic and materialistic categories; it is burdened with immediate problems and entangled in a class war. Other-worldly religions are crumbling, living through a period of crisis and, what is worse, serving to defend the obsolete order. This does not mean that mankind will not return to a better and purified religion in the future. Perhaps the New Faith is an indispensable purgatory; perhaps God's purpose is being accomplished through the barbarians, i.e. the Center, who are forcing the masses to awaken out of their lethargy. The spiritual fare these masses receive from the New Faith is inferior and insufficient. Still one must commend the Center for breaking new ground and for demolishing externally splendid but internally rotten façades. One should cooperate in this task without betraying one's attachment to the Mystery. All the more so because the Mystery has no possibility of appearing in literature, for example, and because neither the language nor the ideas at the disposal of contemporary man are ripe enough to express it.

This metaphysical Ketman in its turn has a number of varieties. Certain practicing Catholics serve even in the security police, and *suspend* their Catholicism in executing their inhumane work. Others, trying to maintain a Christian community in the bosom of the New Faith, come out publicly as Catholics. They often succeed in preserving

Catholic institutions, because the dialecticians are ready to accept so-called "progressive" and "patriotic" Catholics who comply in political matters. The mutual game is rather ambiguous. The rulers tolerate such Catholics as a temporary and necessary evil, reasoning that the stage has not yet arrived at which one can utterly wipe out religion, and that it is better to deal with accommodating bigots than with refractory ones. "Progressive Catholics" are, however, conscious of being relegated to a not particularly honorable place, that of shamans or witch-doctors from savage tribes whom one humors until one can dress them in trousers and send them to school. They appear in various state spectacles and are even sent abroad as shining testimonials to the Center's tolerance toward uncivilized races. One can compare their function to that of "noble savages" imported to the metropolis by colonial powers for state occasions. Their defense against total degradation is metaphysical Ketman: they swindle the devil who thinks he is swindling them. But the devil knows what they think and is satisfied.

What holds for such Catholics can be applied to members of other religions, as well as to persons outside any denomination. One of the most ominous reproaches leveled against writers is the suspicion that their verses, plays, or novels contain a "metaphysical residue." Since a writer is a civilizer who dares not be a shaman or a sorcerer, the slightest signs of a metaphysical tendency in him are unforgivable. The literature of the countries which, until the Second World War, were free from Moscow's domination betrayed especially strong inclinations in that direction, so that metaphysical deviation is of constant and imperative concern to the rulers. For instance, a play that introduces "strangeness," revealing the author's interest in the tragedy of life, has no chance of being produced because the tragedy of human fate leads to thoughts about the mystery of human destiny. One forgives certain writers like Shakespeare these predispositions, but there is no question of permitting any contemporary author to harbor them. It is for this reason that Greek tragedies are not deemed suitable for theater repertoires. Marx loved the Greek tragedians, but let us not forget that the connection between the New Faith and Marx is rather superficial.

The New Faith is a Russian creation, and the Russian intelligentsia which shaped it had developed the deepest contempt for all art that does not serve social ends directly. Other social functions of art, probably the most important ones, consistently escaped its understanding. As for poetry, since its sources are hard to differentiate from the sources of all religion, it is singularly exposed to persecution. True, the poet is free to describe hills, trees, and flowers, but if he should feel that boundless exaltation in the face of nature that seized Wordsworth on his visit to Tintern Abbey, he is at once suspect. This is an excellent means of eliminating the legions of bad poets who like to confess their pantheistic flights publicly, but it is also a means of exterminating poetry as a whole and replacing it by jingles little better than the singing commercials broadcast over the radio in America. A painter, in turn, may be attacked quite as easily for using abbreviated and synthesized forms (formalism), as for an excessive love of the beauty of the world, i.e. a contemplative attitude which signifies that he is a metaphysicist by temperament. A musician should see to it that his compositions are easy to translate into the language of common activities (enthusiasm for work, folk festivities, etc.), and that no element remains which is difficult to grasp and hence dangerous. If metaphysical Ketman is tolerated in the "savages," i.e. those who profess the Christian religion, in the artists who are considered the educators of society, it is severely punished.

Ethical Ketman results from opposition to the ethics of the New Faith, which is based on the principle that good and evil are definable solely in terms of service or harm to the interests of the Revolution. Since exemplary behavior of citizens in their inter-relations aids the cause of socialism, great emphasis is placed upon individual morality.

"The development of a new man" is the key point in the New Faith's program. Demands made upon Party members are exceedingly harsh. One exacts of them no small degree of abstinence. As a result, admission to the Party is not unlike entrance into a religious order; and the literature of the New Faith treats this act with a gravity equal to that with which Catholic literature speaks of the vows of young nuns. The higher one stands in the Party hierarchy, the more attentively is one's private life supervised. Love of money, drunkenness, or a confused love-life disqualify a Party member from holding important offices. Hence the upper brackets of the Party are filled by ascetics devoted to the single cause of Revolution. As for certain human tools, deprived of real influence but useful because of their names, even if they belong to the Party one tolerates or sometimes encourages their weaknesses, for they constitute a guarantee of obedience. The general ethical ideal of the New Faith is puritanical. If it were feasible to lodge all the citizens in cells and release them only for work or for political meetings, that would undoubtedly be most desirable. But alas, one must make concessions to human nature. Procreation is possible only as a result of sexual relations between men and women, and one must take this inconvenience into account.

The "new man" is conditioned to acknowledge the

good of the whole as the sole norm of his behavior. He thinks and reacts like others; is modest, industrious, satisfied with what the state gives him; limits his private life to nights spent at home, and passes all the rest of his time amidst his companions at work or at play, observing them carefully and reporting their actions and opinions to the authorities. Informing was and is known in many civilizations, but the New Faith declares it a cardinal virtue of the good citizen (though the name itself is carefully avoided). It is the basis of each man's fear of his fellowmen. Work in an office or factory is hard not only because of the amount of labor required, but even more because of the need to be on guard against omnipresent and vigilant eyes and ears. After work one goes to political meetings or special lectures, thus lengthening a day that is without a moment of relaxation or spontaneity. The people one talks with may seem relaxed and careless, sympathetic and indignant, but if they appear so, it is only to arouse corresponding attitudes and to extract confidences which they can report to their superiors.

In effect this cult of the community produces something which poisons the community itself. The mentality of the Party's sages is, indeed, rather strange. They make concessions to physiological human weaknesses, but they refuse to admit that man has other foibles as well: that he feels fine when he can relax, and unhappy when he is afraid, that lying is bad for him because it creates internal tension. These weaknesses, together with others like the desire to better one's own lot at the expense of one's fellow-men, transform the ethic which was originally founded on cooperation and brotherhood into an ethic of a war pitting all men against all others, and granting the greatest chances of survival to the craftiest. Victory in this new struggle seems to belong to a breed different from that which was favored to win in the battle for money in the early days of industrial capitalism. If biting dogs can be divided into two main categories, noisy and brutal, or silent and slyly vicious, then the second variety would seem most privileged in the countries of the New Faith. Forty or fifty years of education in these new ethical maxims must create a new and irretrievable species of mankind. The "new man" is not merely a postulate. He is beginning to become a reality.

Ethical Ketman is not rare among highly placed figures in the Party. These persons, no matter how capable they are of murdering millions of people in the name of Communism, try to compensate for their professional severity and are often more honorable in their personal relations than people who affect individualistic ethics. Their capacity to sympathize and help is almost unlimited. Indeed this very feeling of compassion pushed them onto the road of revolution in their youth, and in this they reiterated the experience of Marx himself. One finds this Ketman chiefly among the old Communists. Conflicts between friendship and the interests of the Revolution are matters they weigh at length in their conscience; and they are pitiless only when completely convinced that, in shielding a friend or in refraining from denouncing him, they are injuring that cause which is most precious to them. Though they are usually esteemed as people of crystalline righteousness, they are not safe from frequent accusations of "intellectuality," a contemptuous epithet for those who are blameless as theoreticians, but hampered in action by an over-sensitivity to ethical considerations. A revolutionary should be without scruples. It is better to cut down human trees blindly than to wonder which among them are really rotten.

This variety of Ketman is one of the most prevalent in

the people's democracies because the new ethic is of recent inculcation, whereas the ethic vanquished by the New Faith was ensconced there for centuries. One can never foresee when and in whom this Ketman will appear, which makes for an element of surprise. Individuals who give one every reason to suppose that they do not denounce others turn out to be inveterate informers; individuals who are apparently most indifferent to "prejudices," show themselves inexplicably loyal toward their friends and even toward strangers. Since this Ketman augments the difficulties of controlling the citizens' thoughts, it is diligently sought out and penalized; yet the number of situations to which it can be applied is so great that it often eludes all manner of pressure.

The inhabitants of Western countries little realize that millions of their fellow-men, who seem superficially more or less similar to them, live in a world as fantastic as that of the men from Mars. They are unaware of the perspectives on human nature that Ketman opens. Life in constant internal tension develops talents which are latent in man. He does not even suspect to what heights of cleverness and psychological perspicacity he can rise when he is cornered and must either be skillful or perish. The survival of those best adapted to mental acrobatics creates a human type that has been rare until now. The necessities which drive men to Ketman sharpen the intellect.

Whoever would take the measure of intellectual life in the countries of Central or Eastern Europe from the monotonous articles appearing in the press or the stereotyped speeches pronounced there, would be making a grave error. Just as theologians in periods of strict orthodoxy expressed their views in the rigorous language of the Church, so the writers of the people's democracies make use of an accepted special style, terminology, and linguistic ritual. What is important is not what someone said but what he wanted to say, disguising his thought by removing a comma, inserting an "and," establishing this rather than another sequence in the problems discussed. Unless one has lived there one cannot know how many titanic battles are being fought, how the heroes of Ketman are falling, what this warfare is being waged over. Obviously, people caught up in this daily struggle are rather contemptuous of their compatriot political émigrés. A surgeon cannot consider a butcher his equal in dexterity; just so a Pole, Czech, or Hungarian practiced in the art of dissimulation smiles when he learns that someone in the emigration has called him a traitor (or a swine) at the very moment when this traitor (or swine) is engaged in a match of philosophical chess on whose outcome the fate of fifteen laboratories or twenty ateliers depends. They do not know how one pays—those abroad do not know. They do not know what one buys, and at what price.

Ketman as a social institution is not entirely devoid of advantages. In order to evaluate them, one need only look at life in the West. Westerners, and especially Western intellectuals, suffer from a special variety of *taedium vitae;* their emotional and intellectual life is too dispersed. Everything they think and feel evaporates like steam in an open expanse. Freedom is a burden to them. No conclusions they arrive at are binding: it may be so, then again it may not. The result is a constant uneasiness. The happiest of them seem to be those who become Communists. They live within a wall which they batter themselves against, but which provides them with a resistance that helps them define themselves. Steam that once evaporated into the air becomes a force under pressure. An even greater energy is generated in those who must hide their Communist convictions, that is, who must practice Ketman, a custom which is, after all, not unknown in the countries of the West.

In short, Ketman means self-realization *against* something. He who practices Ketman suffers because of the obstacles he meets; but if these obstacles were suddenly to be removed, he would find himself in a void which might perhaps prove much more painful. Internal revolt is sometimes essential to spiritual health, and can create a particular form of happiness. What can be said openly is often much less interesting than the emotional magic of defending one's private sanctuary. For most people the necessity of living in constant tension and watchfulness is a torture, but many intellectuals accept this necessity with masochistic pleasure.

He who practices Ketman lies. But would he be less dishonest if he could speak the truth? A painter who tries to smuggle illicit ("metaphysical") delight in the beauty of the world into his picture of life on a collective farm would be lost if he were given complete freedom, for the beauty of the world seems greater to him the less free he is to depict it. A poet muses over what he would write if he were not bound by his political responsibilities, but could he realize his visions if he were at liberty to do so? Ketman brings comfort, fostering dreams of what might be, and even the enclosing fence affords the solace of reverie.

Who knows whether it is not in man's lack of an internal *core* that the mysterious success of the New Faith and its charm for the intellectual lie? By subjecting man to pressure, the New Faith creates this core, or in any case the feeling that it exists. Fear of freedom is nothing more than fear of the void. "There is nothing in man," said a friend of mine, a dialectician. "He will never extract anything out of himself, because there is nothing there. You can't leave the people and write in a wilderness. Remember that man is a function of social forces. Whoever wants to be alone will perish." This is probably true, but I doubt if it can be called anything more than the law of our times. Feeling that there was *nothing* in him, Dante could not have written his *Divine Comedy* or Montaigne his *Essays*, nor could Chardin have painted a single still-life. Today man believes there is *nothing* in him, so he accepts *anything*, even if he knows it to be bad, in order to find himself at one with others, in order not to be alone. As long as he believes this, there is little one can reproach in his behavior. Perhaps it is better for him to breed a full-grown Ketman, to submit to pressure and thus feel that he *is*, than to take a chance on the wisdom of past ages which maintains that man is a creature of God.

But suppose one should try to live without Ketman, to challenge fate, to say: "If I lose, I shall not pity myself." Suppose one can live without outside pressure, suppose one can create one's own inner tension—then it is not true that there is nothing in man. To take this risk would be an act of faith.

CHAPTER IV

Alpha, the Moralist

THE HISTORY of the last decades in Central and Eastern Europe abounds in situations in regard to which all
epithets and theoretical considerations lose meaning. A
man's effort to match up to these situations decides his
fate. The solution each accepts differs according to those
impalpable factors which constitute his individuality.

Since the fate of millions is often most apparent in
those who by profession note changes in themselves and
in others, i.e. the writers, a few portraits of typical Eastern European writers may serve as concrete examples of
what is happening within the Imperium.

The man I call Alpha is one of the best-known prose
writers east of the Elbe. He was a close friend of mine, and
memories of many difficult moments that we went through
together tie us to each other. I find it hard to remain un-
moved when I recall him. I even ask myself if I should subject him to this analysis. But I shall do so because friendship would not prevent me from writing an article on
his books in which I would say more or less what I shall
say here.

Before the War, he was a tall, thin youth with horn-
rimmed glasses. He printed his stories in a certain right-
wing weekly that was held in low esteem by the literary

circles of Warsaw, which were made up chiefly of Jews or of people who looked with distaste on the racist and totalitarian yearnings of this publication. The editor of the weekly had to some degree discovered him, and had reason to congratulate himself upon his choice, for Alpha's talent was developing rapidly. Very shortly, his first novel began to appear serially in the weekly. It was later published by one of the leading houses, and created a great stir.

His main interest was directed toward tragic moral conflicts. At the time many young writers were under the spell of Joseph Conrad's prose. Alpha was particularly susceptible to Conrad's style because he had a tendency to create solemn and hieratic characters. Night fascinated him. Small people with their powerful passions in a night whose silence and mystery embraced their fate in its gigantic folds—this was the usual formula of his novels and stories. His youthful works resembled Conrad's in their majesty and silence, and in a sense of the immensity of the inhuman, indifferent world. Alpha's position was metaphysical and tragic. He was tormented by the enigma of purity—moral purity and purity of tone in what he wrote. He distilled his sentences. He wanted each to be not merely a statement but, like a phrase in a musical composition, irreplaceable and effective in its very sound.

This need for purity, I would say for other-worldly purity, was basic to his character; yet in his relations with people he was haughty and imperious. His pursuit of purity in his work was closely linked to his personal arrogance; the former was his sublimation, his other ego, the repository of all his hopes. The more he worried about his disordered private life, the more highly he prized his redeeming activity, which is what his writing was for him, and the more he accorded to it the nature of a solemn rite. The one rank that could have sated his ambition was that of a cardinal. Slow movements, the flow of scarlet silk, the proffering of a ring to kiss—this for him was purity of gesture, self-expression through the medium of a better self. There are certain comic actors who dream all their lives of playing a serious, dignified role; in him, much the same motives were at play. Alpha, who was gifted with an exceptional sense of humor in conversation, changed completely when he began to write; then he dwelt only in the highest registers of tragedy. His ambition reached further than fame as an author of well-written books. He wanted to be a moral authority.

The novel I mentioned, which was his first big success, was widely acclaimed as a Catholic novel, and he was hailed as the most gifted Catholic writer, which in a Catholic country like Poland was no small matter. It is hard to say whether or not he really was a Catholic writer. The number of twentieth-century Catholic authors is negligible. So-called conversions of intellectuals are usually of a dubious nature, not significantly different from transitory conversions to surrealism, expressionism, or existentialism.

Alpha was the kind of Catholic so many of us were. This was a period of interest in Thomism and of references to Jacques Maritain in literary discussion. It would be wrong to maintain that for all these "intellectual Catholics" literary fashion alone was at stake; one cannot reduce the clutching gestures of a drowning man to a question of fashion. But it would be equally incorrect to consider literary debates based on a skillful juggling of Thomist terminology as symptoms of Catholicism. Be that as it may, the "intellectual Catholics" colored certain literary circles. Theirs was a special political role; they were foes of racism and totalitarianism. In this they differed from the Catholics proper, whose political mentality was not entirely free of worship of "healthy organisms" (i.e. Italy and Germany) and approval of anti-Semitic brawls. The Communists despised Jacques Maritain's influence as degenerate, but they tolerated the "intellectual Catholics" because they opposed the ideas of the extreme right. Soon after he published his novel, Alpha began to frequent the circles of the "intellectual Catholics" and the left. Sensitive to the opinion people held of him, and taking the writer's role as a moral authority very seriously, he broke with the rightist weekly and signed an open letter against anti-Semitism.

Everyone looked for something different in Catholicism. Alpha, with his tragic sense of the world, looked for forms: words and concepts, in short, textures. This tragic sense in him was not unlike Wells's Invisible Man, who when he wanted to appear among people had to paste on a false nose, bandage his face and pull gloves over his invisible hands. Catholicism supplied Alpha's language. With concepts like sin and saintliness, damnation and grace he could grasp the experiences of the characters he described; and, even more important, the language of Catholicism automatically introduced the elevated tone that was so necessary to him and lulled his longing for a cardinal's scarlet. The hero of his book was a priest, a sure sign of the influence of French Catholic novelists, and above all Bernanos, but also an expression of Alpha's urge to create pure and powerful characters. The action took place in a village, and here his weaknesses revealed themselves. He was so preoccupied with building up moral conflicts that he was blind to concrete details and incapable of observing living people. Having been raised in the city, he knew little of peasants and their life. The village he described was a universal one; it could just as easily have been Breton or Flemish, and for this reason it was not a real village. The characters seemed to be wearing costumes alien to them (like young nobles dressed as shepherds in pastoral literature), and their speech was uniformly alike.

The story played itself out against a barely sketched-in background, but it was powerfully welded together and the critics received it enthusiastically. It ran into several editions quickly. He received a national award for it which brought him a large sum of money. It is possible that the prize jury took into account not only the artistic merits of the book, but also certain political advantages to themselves in choosing him. In those years, the government was clearly flirting with the extreme right and the choice of Alpha seemed a wise move. The right would certainly be satisfied; whereas the liberals would have no reason to attack the decision for after all everyone was then free to believe as he pleased and to write as he believed.

Despite fame and money, in his heart Alpha never considered his novel and his collection of short stories good books. Still, the position he had won permitted him to be as haughty as he loved to be. He was recognized as the author of profound and noble prose, whereas his colleagues could hardly hope to reach a wide public otherwise than by creating a cheap sensation. Their books were either glaringly naturalistic, especially in a physiological sense, or else they were psychological tracts disguised as novels. Men of letters lived in the intellectual ghetto of their literary cafés; and the more they suffered from their isolation from the life of the masses, the stranger and less comprehensible their styles became. The bitterness Alpha felt in spite of the success of his first books was something he found difficult to define, but the moment when he realized that there was something wrong with his writing was decisive for the rest of his life.

A great doubt assailed him. If his colleagues doubted the worth of their work, suspended as it was in a void, then his perplexity took on larger proportions. He wanted to attain a purity of moral tone, but purity in order to be genuine must be earthy, deeply rooted in experience and observation of life. He perceived that he had blundered into falseness by living in the midst of ideas about people, instead of among people themselves. What he knew about man was based on his own subjective experiences within the four walls of his room. His Catholicism was no more than a cover; he toyed with it as did many twentieth-century Catholics, trying to clothe his nudity in an esteemed, Old World cloak. He was seeking some means of awakening in his reader the emotional response he wanted, and obviously the reader on finding words like grace or sin, known to him since childhood, reacted strongly. But there is an element of dishonesty in such a use of words and concepts.

Alpha no longer knew whether the conflicts he created were real. Hailed as a Catholic writer, he knew that he was not; and his reaction was like that of a painter who having painted cubistically for a while is astonished to find that he is still called a cubist after he has changed his style. Critics, deceived by appearances, reckoned his books among those that were healthy and noble as opposed to the decadent works of his fellow-writers. But he realized that he was no healthier than his colleagues who at least did not attempt to hide their sorry nakedness.

The War broke out, and our city and country became a part of Hitler's Imperium. For five and a half years we lived in a dimension completely different from that which any literature or experience could have led us to know. What we beheld surpassed the most daring and the most macabre imagination. Descriptions of horrors known to us of old now made us smile at their naïveté. German rule in Europe was ruthless, but nowhere so ruthless as in the East, for the East was populated by races which, according to the doctrines of National Socialism, were either to be utterly eradicated or else used for heavy physical labor. The events we were forced to participate in resulted from the effort to put these doctrines into practice.

Still we lived; and since we were writers, we tried to write. True, from time to time one of us dropped out, shipped off to a concentration camp or shot. There was no help for this. We were like people marooned on a dissolving floe of ice; we dared not think of the moment when it would melt away. War communiqués supplied the latest data on our race with death. We had to write; it was our only defense against despair. Besides, the whole country was sown with the seeds of conspiracy and an "underground state" did exist in reality, so why shouldn't an underground literature exist as well. Except for two or three Nazi propaganda organs, no books or magazines were printed in the language of the defeated nation. Nonetheless, the cultural life of the country refused to be stifled. Underground publications were mimeographed on the run or illegally printed in a small format that was easy to circulate. Many underground lectures and authors' evenings were organized. There were even underground presentations of plays. All this raised the morale of the beaten but still fighting nation. National morale was good, too good, as events toward the end of the War proved.

In the course of these years, Alpha successfully realized his ambition to become a moral authority. His behavior was that of an exemplary writer-citizen. His judgments as to which actions were proper or improper passed in literary circles as those of an oracle, and he was often asked to decide whether someone had trespassed against the unwritten patriotic code. By unspoken accord, he became something of a leader of all the writers in our city. Underground funds went into his hands and he divided them among his needy colleagues; he befriended beginning writers; he founded and co-edited an underground literary review, typed copies of which were transmitted in rotation to "clubs" where they were read aloud in clandestine meetings. He ranked rather high among those initiated into the secrets of the underground network. His actions were characterized by real humanitarianism. Even before the War he had parted with his rightist patron who had voiced the opinion that the country needed to institute its own totalitarianism. (The patron was shot by the Gestapo in the first year of the War.) When the German authorities set out to murder systematically the three million Jews of Poland, the anti-Semites did not feel compelled to worry overmuch; they condemned this bestiality aloud, but many of them secretly thought it was not entirely unwarranted. Alpha belonged to those inhabitants of our town who reacted violently against this mass slaughter. He fought with his pen against the indifference of others, and personally helped Jews in hiding even though such aid was punishable by death.

He was a resolute opponent of nationalism, so nightmarishly incarnated in the Germans. This does not mean, however, that he had Communist leanings. The number of Communists in Poland had always been insignificant; and the cooperation between the Russians and the Germans after the Molotov-Ribbentrop pact created conditions particularly unfavorable to the activity of Moscow followers. The Communist Underground was weak. The hopes of the masses were turned toward the West, and the "underground state" was dependent on the Government-in-Exile in London. Alpha, with his barometer-like sensitivity to the moral opinions of his environment, felt no sympathy for a country that awakened friendly feelings in almost no one. But like the majority of his friends, he was anxious for far-reaching social reforms and for a people's government.

He and I used to meet often. It would hardly be an exaggeration to say that we spent the War years together. The sight of him was enough to raise one's spirits. He smiled in the face of all adversity; his manner was nonchalant; and to symbolize his contempt for hob-nailed boots, uniforms, and shouts of "Heil Hitler," he habitually carried a black umbrella. His tall, lean figure, the ironic flash of his eyes behind his glasses, and the anointed air with which he strode through the terror-plagued streets of the city added up to a silhouette that defied the laws of war.

Once, in the first year of the War, we were returning from a visit to a mutual friend who lived in the country. As I remember, we were arguing about the choice of a train. We decided against the advice of our host who had urged us to take a train leaving half an hour later. We arrived in Warsaw and walked along the streets feeling very satisfied with life. It was a beautiful summer morning. We did not know that this day was to be remembered as one of the blackest in the history of our city. Scarcely had I closed my door behind me when I heard shrieks in the street. Looking out the window, I saw that a general man-hunt was on. This was the first man-hunt for Auschwitz. Later millions of Europeans were to be killed there, but at the time this concentration camp was just starting to operate. From the first huge transport of people caught on the streets that day no one, it appears, escaped alive. Alpha and I had strolled those streets five minutes before the beginning of the hunt; perhaps his umbrella and his insouciance brought us luck.

These years were a test for every writer. The real tragedy of events pushed imaginary tragedies into the shade.
Whichever of us failed to find an expression for collective
despair or hope was ashamed. Only elementary feelings
remained: fear, pain at the loss of dear ones, hatred of the
oppressor, sympathy with the tormented. Alpha, whose
talent was in search of real and not imaginary tragedy,
sensed the material at hand and wrote a series of short
stories which were published as a book after the War and
widely translated. The theme of all these stories can be defined as loyalty. Not for nothing had Conrad been the favorite writer of his youth. This was a loyalty to something
in man, something nameless, but strong and pure. Before
the War, he tended to call this imperative sense of loyalty
moral, in the Catholic sense. Now, fearing falseness, he
affirmed merely that this imperative existed. When his
dying heroes turned their eyes toward a mute heaven, they
could find nothing there; they could only hope that their
loyalty was not completely meaningless and that, in spite
of everything, something in the universe responded to it.

The morality of his heroes was a lay morality, with a
question mark, with a pause, a pause that was not quite
faith. I think he was more honest in these stories than in
his pre-war writings. At the same time, he expressed accu-
rately and powerfully the state of mind of the countless
underground fighters dying in the battle against Nazism. Why did they throw their lives into the scale?
Why did they accept torture and death? They had no
point of support like the Führer for the Germans or the
New Faith for the Communists. It is doubtful whether
most of them believed in Christ. It could only have been
loyalty, loyalty to something called fatherland or honor,
but something stronger than any name. In one of his
stories, a young boy, tortured by the police and knowing

that he will be shot, gives the name of his friend because he is afraid to die alone. They meet before the firing squad, and the betrayed forgives his betrayor. This forgiveness cannot be justified by any utilitarian ethic; there is no reason to forgive traitors. Had this story been written by a Soviet author, the betrayed would have turned away with disdain from the man who had succumbed to base weakness. Forsaking Christianity, Alpha became a more religious writer than he had been before, if we grant that the ethic of loyalty is an extension of religious ethics and a contradiction of an ethic of collective goals.

In the second half of the War, a serious crisis in political consciousness took place in the "underground state." The underground struggle against the occupying power entailed great sacrifices; the number of persons executed or liquidated in concentration camps grew constantly. To explain the need of such sacrifice solely on the basis of loyalty left one a prey to doubt. Loyalty can be the basis of individual action, but when decisions affecting the fate of hundreds of thousands of people are to be made, loyalty is not enough. One seeks logical justification. But what kind of logical justification could there be? From the East the victorious Red Army was drawing near. The Western armies were far away. In the name of what future, in the name of what order were young people dying every day? More than one man whose task it was to sustain the morale of others posed this question to himself. No one was able to formulate an answer. Irrational dreams that something would happen to stop the advance of the Red Army and at the same time overthrow Hitler were linked with an appeal to the honor of the "country without a Quisling"; but this was not a very substantial prop for those of a more sober turn of mind. At this moment, Communist underground organizations began to be active, and were joined by some left-wing Socialists. The Communist program offered more realistic arguments than did the program of the London-directed "underground state": the country, it was fairly clear, was going to be liberated by the Red Army; with its aid one should start a people's revolution.

Gradually the intellectuals in the underground became impatient with the irrational attitudes that were spreading in the resistance movement. This irrationality began to reach the point of hysteria. Conspiracy became an end in itself; to die or to expose others to death, something of a sport. Alpha found himself surrounded by living caricatures of the ethic of loyalty he expounded in his stories. The patriotic code of his class prohibited him from approaching the small groups whose policy followed Moscow's dictates.

Like so many of his friends, Alpha felt himself in a trap. Then, for the first time in his writing he invoked his sense of humor, using it to point up the figures he knew so well, the figures of men mad for conspiracy. His satires bared the social background of underground hysteria. There is no doubt that the "underground state" was the handiwork of the intelligentsia above all, of a stratum never known in Western Europe, not to mention the Anglo-Saxon countries. Since the intelligentsia was, in its customs and ties, the legatee of the nobility (even if some members were of peasant origin), its characteristic traits were not especially attractive to the intellectuals. The intellectuals of Poland had made several attempts to revolt against the intelligentsia of which they themselves were a part, much as the intellectuals in America had rebelled against the middle class. When a member of the intelligentsia really began to think, he perceived that he was isolated from the broad masses of the population. Finding the social order at fault, he tended to become a radical in an effort to establish a tie with the masses. Alpha's satires on the intelligentsia of the Underground convinced him that this stratum, with its many aberrations, boded ill for the future of the country if the postwar rulers were to be recruited from its ranks—which seemed inevitable in the event of the London Government-in-Exile's arrival in Poland.

Just when he was passing through this process of bitter and impotent mockery, the uprising broke out. For two months, a kilometer-high column of smoke and flames stood over Warsaw. Two hundred thousand people died in the street fighting. Those neighborhoods which were not leveled by bombs or by the fire of heavy artillery were burned down by SS squads. After the uprising, the city which once numbered over a million inhabitants was a wilderness of ruins, its population deported, and its demolished streets literally cemeteries. Alpha, living in a distant suburb that bordered on fields, succeeded in escaping unharmed through the dangerous zone where people in flight were caught and sent to concentration camps.

In April of 1945, after the Germans had been expelled by the Red Army (the battles were then raging at the gates of Berlin), Alpha and I returned to Warsaw and wandered together over the mounds of rubble that had once been streets. We spent several hours in a once familiar part of the city. Now we could not recognize it. We scaled a slope of red bricks and entered upon a fantastic moon-world. There was total silence. As we worked our way downward, balancing to keep from falling, ever new scenes of waste and destruction loomed before us. In one of the gorges we stumbled upon a little plank fastened to a metal bar. The inscription, written in red paint or in blood, read: "Lieutenant Zbyszek's road of suffering." I know what Alpha's thoughts were at that time, and they were mine: we were thinking of what traces remain after the life of a man. These words rang like a cry to heaven from a shattered earth. It was a cry for justice. Who was Lieutenant Zbyszek? Who among the living would ever know what he had suffered? We imagined him crawling along this trail which some comrade, probably long-since killed, had marked with the inscription. We saw him as, with an effort of his will, he mustered his fleeting strength and, aware of being mortally wounded, thought only of carrying out his duty. Why? Who measured his wisdom or madness? Was this a monad of Leibnitz, fulfilling its destiny in the universe, or only the son of a postman, obeying a futile maxim of honor instilled in him by his father, who himself was living up to the virtues of a courtly tradition?

Further on, we came upon a worn footpath. It led into a deep mountain cleft. At the bottom stood a clumsy, huddled cross with a helmet on it. At the foot of the cross were freshly planted flowers. Somebody's son lay here. A mother had found her way to him and worn the path through her daily visits.

Theatrical thunder suddenly broke the silence. It was the wind rattling the metal sheets hanging from a cliff-like wall. We scrambled out of the heap of debris into a practically untouched courtyard. Rusting machines stood among the high weeds. And on the steps of the charred villa we found some account books listing profits and losses.

The Warsaw uprising begun at the order of the Government-in-Exile in London broke out, as we know, at the moment when the Red Army was approaching the capital and the retreating German armies were fighting in the outskirts of the city. Feeling in the Underground was

reaching a boiling point; the Underground Army wanted
to fight. The uprising was intended to oust the Germans
and to take possession of the city so that the Red Army
would be greeted by an already-functioning Polish government. Once the battle in the city began, and once it became obvious that the Red Army, standing on the other
side of the river, would not move to the aid of the insurgents, it was too late for prudence. The tragedy played itself out according to all the immutable rules. This was the
revolt of a fly against two giants. One giant waited beyond the river for the other to kill the fly. As a matter of
fact, the fly defended itself, but its soldiers were generally
armed only with pistols, grenades, and benzine bottles.
For two months the giant sent his bombers over the city
to drop their loads from a height of a few hundred feet;
he supported his troops with tanks and the heaviest artillery. In the end, he crushed the fly only to be crushed in
his turn by the second, patient giant.

There was no logical reason for Russia to have helped
Warsaw. The Russians were bringing the West not only liberation from Hitler, but liberation from the existing order,
which they wanted to replace with a good order, namely
their own. The " underground state " and the London
Government-in-Exile stood in the way of their overthrow
of capitalism in Poland; whereas, behind the Red Army
lines a different Polish government, appointed in Moscow,
was already in office. The destruction of Warsaw represented certain indisputable advantages. The people dying
in the street fights were precisely those who could create
most trouble for the new rulers, the young intelligentsia,
seasoned in its underground struggle with the Germans,
and wholly fanatic in its patriotism. The city itself in the
course of the years of occupation had been transformed
into an underground fortress filled with hidden printing

shops and arsenals. This traditional capital of revolts and insurrections was undoubtedly the most insubordinate city in the area that was to find itself under the Center's influence. All that could have argued for aid to Warsaw would have been pity for the one million inhabitants dying in the town. But pity is superfluous wherever sentence is pronounced by History.

Alpha, walking with me over the ruins of Warsaw, felt, as did all those who survived, one dominant emotion: anger. Many of his close friends lay in the shallow graves which abounded in the lunar landscape. The twenty-year-old poet Christopher, a thin asthmatic, physically no stronger than Marcel Proust, had died at his post sniping at SS tanks. With him the greatest hope of Polish poetry perished. His wife Barbara was wounded and died in a hospital, grasping a manuscript of her husband's verses in her hand. The poet Karol, son of the workers' quarter and author of a play about Homer, together with his inseparable comrade, the poet Marek, were blown up on a barricade the Germans dynamited. Alpha knew, also, that the person he loved most in his life had been deported to the concentration camp at Ravensbruck after the suppression of the uprising. He waited for her long after the end of the War until he finally had to accept the idea that she was no longer alive. His anger was directed against those who had brought on the disaster, that terrible example of what happens when blind loyalty encounters the necessities of History. Just as his Catholic words had once rung false to him, so now his ethic of loyalty seemed a pretty but hollow concept.

Actually, Alpha was one of those who were responsible for what had happened. Could he not see the eyes of the young people gazing at him as he read his stories in clandestine authors' evenings? These were the young people who had died in the uprising: Lieutenant Zbyszek, Christopher, Barbara, Karol, Marek, and thousands like them. They had known there was no hope of victory and that their death was no more than a gesture in the face of an indifferent world. They had died without even asking whether there was some scale in which their deeds would be weighed. The young philosopher Milbrand, a disciple of Heidegger, assigned to press work by his superiors, demanded to be sent to the line of battle because he believed that the greatest gift a man can have is the moment of free choice; three hours later he was dead. There were no limits to these frenzies of voluntary self-sacrifice.

Alpha did not blame the Russians. What was the use? They were the force of History. Communism was fighting Fascism; and the Poles, with their ethical code based on nothing but loyalty, had managed to thrust themselves beween these two forces. Joseph Conrad, that incorrigible Polish noble! Surely the example of Warsaw had demonstrated that there was no place in the twentieth century for imperatives of fatherland or honor unless they were supported by some definite end. A moralist of today, Alpha reasoned, should turn his attention to social goals and social results. The rebels were not even an enemy in the minds of the Germans; they were an inferior race that had to be destroyed. For the Russians, they were "Polish fascists." The Warsaw uprising was the swan-song of the intelligentsia and the order it defended; like the suicidal charges of the Confederates during the American Civil War, it could not stave off defeat. With its fall, the Revolution was, in effect, accomplished; in any case, the road was open. This was not, as the press of the new government proclaimed in its effort to lull the people, a "peaceful revolution." Its price was bloody, as the ruins of the largest city in the country testified.

But one had to live and be active instead of looking back at what had passed. The country was ravaged. The new government went energetically to work reconstructing, putting mines and factories into operation, and dividing estates among the peasants. New responsibilities faced the writer. His books were eagerly awaited by a human ant-hill, shaken out of its torpor and stirred up by the big stick of war and of social reforms. We should not wonder, then, that Alpha, like the majority of his colleagues, declared at once his desire to serve the new Poland that had risen out of the ashes of the old.

He was accepted with open arms by the handful of Polish Communists who had spent the war years in Russia and who had returned to organize the state according to the maxims of Leninism-Stalinism. Then, that is in 1945, everyone who could be useful was welcomed joyfully without any demand that he be a Red. Both the benevolent mask under which the Party appeared and the moderation of its slogans were due to the fact that there were so uncommonly few Stalinists in the country.

Unquestionably, it is only by patient and gradually increased doses of the doctrine that one can bring a pagan population to understand and accept the New Faith. Ever since his break with the rightist weekly, Alpha had enjoyed a good opinion in those circles which were now most influential. He was not reprimanded for having kept his distance from Marxist groups during the War; authors who had maintained such contacts could be counted on the fingers of one hand. Now the writers of Poland were a little like virgins—willing, but timid. Their first public statements were cautious and painstakingly measured. Still it was not what they said that mattered. Their names were needed as proof that the government was supported by the entire cultural elite. The program of behavior

toward various categories of people had been elaborated
by the Polish Communists while they were still in Moscow; and it was a wise program, based on an intimate understanding of conditions in the country. The tasks that
lay before them were unusually difficult. The country did
not want their government. The Party, which had barely
existed before the War, had to be reorganized and had to
reconcile itself to the knowledge that most of its new
members would be opportunists. Left-wing Socialists had
to be admitted into the government. It was still necessary
to carry on a complicated game with the Peasant Party,
for after Yalta the Western allies demanded at least the
semblance of a coalition. The most immediate job, therefore, was to bridge the gap between the small group of
Communists and the country as a whole; those who could
help most in building this bridge were famous writers
who were known as liberals or even as conservatives.
Alpha fulfilled every requirement. His article appeared on
the first page of a government literary weekly; it was an
article on humanism. As I recall it, he spoke in it of the
ethic of respect for man that revolution brings.

It was May, 1945, in the medieval city of Cracow. Alpha
and I, as well as many other writers and artists, had taken
refuge there after the destruction of Warsaw. The night
the news of the fall of Berlin came was lit with bursts of
rockets and shells, and the streets echoed with the fire of
small arms as the soldiers of the victorious Red Army
celebrated the prospect of a speedy return home. The
next morning, on a fine spring day, Alpha and I were sitting in the office of Polish Film, working on a scenario.
Tying up the loose ends of a film is a burdensome business; we were putting our feet up on tables and armchairs,
we were pacing the room, smoking too many cigarettes
and constantly being lured to the window through which

came the warble of sparrows. Outside the window was a courtyard with young trees, and beyond the courtyard a huge building lately transformed into a prison and the headquarters of the Security Police. We saw scores of young men behind the barred windows on the ground floor. Some had thrust their faces into the sun in an effort to get a tan. Others were fishing with wire hooks for the bits of paper which had been tossed out on the sand from neighboring cells. Standing in the window, we observed them in silence.

It was easy to guess that these were soldiers of the Underground Army. Had the London Government-in-Exile returned to Poland, these soldiers of the "underground state" would have been honored and feted as heroes. Instead, they were incarcerated as a politically uncertain element—another of History's ironic jokes. These young boys who had grown used to living with a gun in their hands and surrounded by perpetual danger were now supposed to forget their taste for conspiracy as quickly as possible. Many succeeded so well in forgetting that they pretended they had never been active in the Underground. Others stayed in the woods, and any of them that were caught were thrown behind bars. Although their foe had been Hitler, they were now termed agents of the class enemy. These were the brothers of the young people who had fought and died in the Warsaw uprising, people whose blind self-sacrifice lay on Alpha's conscience. I do not know what he was thinking as he looked at the windows of those prison cells. Perhaps even then he was sketching the plan of his first post-war novel.

As his whole biography demonstrates, his ambition was always boundless. He was never content to be just one among many; he had to be a leader so that he could justify his personal haughtiness. The novel he was writing should, he believed, raise him to first place among the writers active in the new situation. This was a time when writers were trying to change their style and subject matter, but they could not succeed without first effecting a corresponding change in their own personalities. Alpha was undergoing a moral crisis which was personal to him, but at the same time a reiteration of a conflict known to many of his countrymen. He sensed in himself a power that flowed from his individual but simultaneously universal drama. His feeling for the tragedy of life was seeking a new garment in which to appear in public.

Alpha did not betray his belief in himself. The novel he wrote was the product of a mature talent. It made a great impression on its readers. All his life he had circled around the figure of a strong and pure hero. In his pre-war novel, he had used a priest; now he drew a representative of the New Faith, a fearless old Communist who after spending many years in German concentration camps emerged unbroken in spirit. Returning to his devastated homeland, this hero found himself faced with a chaos which his clear mind and strong will were to convert into a new social order. The society he was to transform showed every sign of moral decay. The older generation of the intelligentsia, personally ambitious and addicted to drink, was still daydreaming of help from the Western allies. The youth of the country, educated to principles of blind loyalty and habituated to an adventurous life in the Underground, was now completely lost. Knowing no goals of human activity other than war against the enemy in the name of honor, it continued to conspire against a new enemy, namely the Party and the government imposed by Russia. But given post-war circumstances, the Party was the only power that could guarantee peace, reconstruct the country, enable the people to earn their daily bread, and start schools and universities, ships and railroads functioning. One did not have to be a Communist to reach this conclusion; it was obvious to everyone. To kill Party workers, to sabotage trains carrying food, to attack laborers who were trying to rebuild the factories was to prolong the period of chaos. Only madmen could commit such fruitless and illogical acts.

This was Alpha's picture of the country. One might have called it a piece of common-sense journalism had it not been for something that always distinguished him as a writer: pity, pity for the old Communist as well as for those who considered him their enemy. Because he felt compassion for both these forces, he succeeded in writing a tragic novel.

His shortcomings as a writer, so clearly evident in his pre-war works, now stood him in good stead. His talent was not realistic; his people moved in a world difficult to visualize. He built up moral conflicts by stressing contrasts in his characters; but his old Communist was as rare a specimen on the Polish scene as the priest he had made his hero before the war. Communists may, in general, be depicted as active, intelligent, fanatic, cunning but above all as men who take external acts as their domain. Alpha's hero was not a man of deeds; on the contrary, he was a silent, immovable rock whose stony exterior covered all that was most human—personal suffering and a longing for good. He was a monumental figure, an ascetic living for his ideas. He was ashamed of his personal cares, and his refusal to confess his private pain won the sympathy of the readers. In the concentration camp he had lost the wife he dearly loved; and now it was only by the greatest effort of his will that he could compel himself to live, for life had suddenly become devoid of meaning. He was a titan with a torn heart, full of love and forgiveness. In short, he emerged as a potential force capable of leading the world toward good. Just when his feelings and thoughts were purest he died, shot by a young man who saw in him only an agent of Moscow.

One can understand why Alpha, living in a country where the word "Communist" still had an abusive connotation, wanted to portray his hero as the model of a higher ethic; but that ethic can be evaluated properly only when we see it applied to concrete problems, only when its followers treat people as tools. As for the society the old Communist wanted to transform, an accurate observer would have seen in it positive signs and not merely symptoms of disintegration. The intelligentsia, that is every variety of specialist, were setting to work just as enthusiastically as the workers and peasants in mobilizing the factories, mines, railroads, schools, and theaters. They were governed by a feeling of responsibility toward the community and by professional pride, not by a vision of socialism along Russian lines. Nevertheless, their ethic of responsibility bore important results. Their political thinking was naïve, and their manners often characteristic of a by-gone era. Yet it was they, and not the Party, who reacted most energetically at first. The younger generation was lost and leaderless, but its terroristic deeds were at least as much a product of despair as of demoralization. The boys that Alpha and I had seen in the windows of the prison were not there because of any crimes they had committed, but only because of their war-time service in the "underground state." Alpha could not say all this because of the censorship, but his expressed pity for these boys permitted the reader to guess at what he left unsaid. However, his failure to present all the facets of the situation altered the motivation of his characters.

His book was entirely dominated by a feeling of anger

against the losers. This anger was essential to the existence of Alpha and many like him. The satiric attitude toward the underground intelligentsia which marked the stories he wrote toward the end of the War now manifested itself in the chapters of the novel that mocked absurd hopes for a sudden political change. In reality, these hopes, no matter how absurd the form they took in members of the white collar class, were far from alien to the peasants and workers. Alpha never knew the latter intimately, so he could, with much greater ease, attribute the belief in a magic removal of the Russians to a special characteristic of the intelligentsia which, unfortunately, was not distinguished for its political insight.

A novel that favorably compared the ethic of the New Faith with the vanquished code was very important to the Party. The book was so widely publicized that it quickly sold over 100,000 copies, and in 1948, Alpha was awarded a state prize. One city donated to him a beautiful villa furnished at considerable expense. A useful writer in a people's democracy cannot complain of a lack of attention.

The Party dialecticians knew perfectly well that Alpha's hero was not a model of the "new man." That he was a Communist could be divined only from the author's assurances. He appeared on the pages of the book prepared to act, but not in action. Alpha's old hero had merely traded his priest's cassock for the leather jacket of a Communist. Although Alpha had changed the language of his concepts, the residue of tragedy and metaphysics remained constant. And even though the old Communist did not pray, the readers would not have been surprised to hear his habitually sealed lips suddenly utter the lamentations of Jeremiah, so well did the words of the prophet harmonize with his personality. Alpha, then, had not altered subjectively since his pre-war days; he still could not limit himself to a purely utilitarian ethic expressed in rational acts. Faust and King Lear did penance within his hero. Both heaven and earth continued to exist. Still one could not ask too much. He did not belong to the Party, but he showed some understanding. His treatment of the terrorist youth even more than his portrayal of the old Communist demonstrated that he was learning. It was too early to impose "socialist realism"; the term was not even mentioned lest it alarm the writers and artists. For the same reason, the peasants were assured that there would be no collective farms in Poland.

The day of decision did not come for Alpha until a few years after he had published his novel. He was living in his beautiful villa, signing numerous political declarations, serving on committees and traveling throughout the country lecturing on literature in factory auditoriums, clubs and "houses of culture." For many, these authors' trips, organized on a large scale, were a painful duty; but for him they were a pleasure, for they enabled him to become acquainted with the life and problems of the working-class youth. For the first time, he was really stepping out of his intellectual clan; and better still, he was doing so as a respected author. As one of the top-ranking writers of the people's democracies he could feel himself, if not a cardinal, then at least an eminent canon.

In line with the Center's plan, the country was being progressively transformed. The time came to shorten the reins on the writers and to demand that they declare themselves clearly for the New Faith. At writers' congresses "socialist realism" was proclaimed the sole indicated creative method. It appears that he lived through this moment with particular pain. Showing incredible dexterity the Party had imperceptibly led the writers to the point of conversion. Now they had to comply with the Party's ultimatum or else rebel abruptly and so fall to the foot of the social ladder. To split one's loyalties, to pay God in one currency and Caesar in another, was no longer possible. No one ordered the writers to enter the Party formally; yet there was no logical obstacle to joining once one accepted the New Faith. Such a step would signalize greater courage, for admission into the Party meant an increase in one's responsibilities.

As the novelist most highly regarded by Party circles, Alpha could make but one decision. As a moral authority he was expected to set an example for his colleagues. During the first years of the new order he had established strong bonds with the Revolution. He was, at last, a popular writer whose readers were recruited from the masses. His highly praised pre-war novel had sold scarcely a few thousand copies; now he and every author could count on reaching a tremendous public. He was no longer isolated; he told himself he was needed not by a few snobs in a coffee-house, but by this new workers' youth he spoke to in his travels over the country. This metamorphosis was entirely due to the victory of Russia and the Party, and logically one ought to accept not only practical results but also the philosophical principles that engendered them.

That was not easy for him. Ever more frequently he was attacked for his love of monumental tragedy. He tried to write differently, but whenever he denied something that lay in the very nature of his talent his prose became flat and colorless; he tore up his manuscripts. He asked himself whether he could renounce all effort to portray the tragic conflicts peculiar to life in a giant collective. The causes of the human distress he saw about him daily were no longer the same as in a capitalist system, but the sum total of suffering seemed to grow instead of diminish.

Alpha knew too much about Russia and the merciless methods dialecticians employed on "human material" not to be assailed by waves of doubt. He was aware that in accepting the New Faith he would cease to be a moral authority and become a pedagogue, expressing only what was recognized as useful. Henceforth, ten or fifteen dialectical experts would weigh each of his sentences, considering whether he had committed the sin of pure tragedy. But there was no returning. Telling himself that he was already a Communist in his actions, he entered the Party and at once published a long article about himself as a writer. This was a self-criticism; in Christian terminology, a confession. Other writers read his article with envy and fear. That he was first everywhere and in everything aroused their jealousy, but that he showed himself so clever—so like a Stakhanovite miner who first announces that he will set an unusually high norm—filled them with apprehension. Miners do not like any of their comrades who are too inclined to accumulate honors for having driven others to a speed-up.

His self-criticism was so skillfully written that it stands as a classic declaration of a writer renouncing the past in the name of the New Faith. It was translated into many languages, and printed even by Stalinist publications in the West. In condemning his previous books he resorted to a special stratagem: he admitted openly what he had always secretly thought of the flaws in his work. He didn't need dialectics to show him these flaws; he knew them of old, long before he approached Marxism, but now he attributed his insight to the merits of the Method. Every good writer knows he should not let himself be seduced by high-sounding words or by emotionally effective but empty concepts. Alpha affirmed that he had stumbled into these pitfalls because he wasn't a Marxist. He also let it be understood that he did not consider himself a Communist writer, but only one who was trying to master the Method, that highest of all sciences. What was remarkable about the article was the sainted, supercilious tone, always Alpha's own, in which it was written. That tone led one to suspect that in damning his faults he was compounding them and that he gloried in his new garb of humility.

The Party confided to him, as a former Catholic, the function of making speeches against the policy of the Vatican. Shortly thereafter, he was invited to Moscow, and on his return he published a book about the "Soviet man." By demonstrating dialectically that the only truly free man was the citizen of the Soviet Union, he was once again reaching for the laurels of supremacy. His colleagues had always been more or less ashamed to use this literary tactic even though they knew it was dialectically correct. As a result, he came to be actively disliked in the literary ghetto. I call this a ghetto because despite the fact that they were lecturing throughout the country and reaching an ever larger public the writers were now as securely locked up in their collective homes and clubs as they had been in their pre-war coffee-houses. Alpha's fellow-authors, jealous of the success his noble tone had brought him, called him the "respectable prostitute."

It is not my place to judge. I myself traveled the same road of seeming inevitability. In fleeing I trampled on many values that may determine the worth of a man. So I judge myself severely though my sins are not the same as his. Perhaps the difference in our destinies lay in a minute disparity in our reactions when we visited the ruins of Warsaw or gazed out the window at the prisoners. I felt that I could not write of these things unless I wrote the *whole* truth, not just a part. I had the same feeling

about the events that took place in Nazi-occupied Warsaw, namely that every form of literature could be applied
to them except fiction. We used to feel strangely ashamed,
I remember, whenever Alpha read us his stories in that
war-contaminated city. He exploited his subject matter
too soon, his composition was too smooth. Thousands of
people were dying in torture all about us; to transform
their sufferings immediately into tragic theater seemed to
us indecent. It is sometimes better to stammer from an
excess of emotion than to speak in well-turned phrases.
The inner voice that stops us when we might say too
much is wise. It is not improbable that he did not know
this voice.

Only a passion for truth could have saved Alpha
from developing into the person he became. Then, it is
true, he would not have written his novel about the old
Communist and demoralized Polish youth. He had allowed himself the luxury of pity, but only once he was
within a framework safe from the censors' reproaches.
In his desire to win approbation he had simplified his
picture to conform to the wishes of the Party. One compromise leads to a second and a third until at last, though
everything one says may be perfectly logical, it no longer
has anything in common with the flesh and blood of
living people. This is the reverse side of the medal of dialectics. This is the price one pays for the mental comfort dialectics affords. Around Alpha there lived and continue to live many workers and peasants whose words are
ineffectual, but in the end, the inner voice they hear is not
different from the subjective command that shuts writers'
lips and demands all or nothing. Who knows, probably
some unknown peasant or some minor postal employee
should be placed higher in the hierarchy of those who
serve humanity than Alpha the moralist.

CHAPTER V

Beta, The Disappointed Lover

WHEN I met Beta in 1942, he was twenty years old. He was a lively boy with black, intelligent eyes. The palms of his hands perspired, and there was that exaggerated shyness in his behavior that usually bespeaks immense ambition. Behind his words one felt a mixture of arrogance and humility. In conversation he seemed inwardly convinced of his own superiority; he attacked ferociously yet retreated immediately, bashfully hiding his claws. His ripostes were full of pent-up irony. Probably, though, these characteristics were most pronounced when he spoke with me or with other writers older than he. As a beginning poet, he felt he owed them a certain respect, but actually he believed they were none too deserving of it. He knew better; in him lay the promise of a truly great writer.

In 1942 in Warsaw, we were living without hope, or rather on a hope we knew to be a delusion. The empire which had absorbed our country was so mighty that only an incorrigible optimist could believe in the possibility of a totally vanquished Germany. Nazi plans in regard to our nation were perfectly clear: to exterminate the educated class, to colonize, and to deport a segment of the population to the East.

Beta was one of the young people who started writing

during the War, in the language of slaves. He supported himself by various odd jobs. It is hard to define exactly how people earn a living in a city completely outside the law. Usually they took half-fictitious posts in an office or factory that supplied them with a work-card plus the opportunity to operate a black market or to steal, which was not regarded as immoral because it injured the Germans. At the same time, he studied in the underground university and shared the exuberant life of the resistance youth. He went to meetings where he and the other young people drank vodka, argued heatedly about literature and politics, and read illegal publications.

But he smiled scornfully at his comrades; he saw things more clearly than they. He found their patriotic zeal for battle against the Germans a purely irrational reflex. Battle—yes, but in the name of what? None of these young people believed any longer in democracy. Most of the countries of Eastern Europe had been semi-dictatorships before the War; and the parliamentary system seemed to belong to a dead era. There was no question as to how one came into power; whoever wanted to take over authority had only to seize it by force, or else create a "movement" to exert pressure on the government for admittance into a coalition. This was an age of nationalist "movements," and Warsaw youth was still very much under their influence even though, obviously, it had no sympathy for either Hitler or Mussolini. Its reasoning was confused. The Polish nation was oppressed by the Germans; so, one had to fight. When Beta declared that they were merely countering German nationalism with Polish nationalism, his comrades shrugged their shoulders. When he asked what values they wanted to defend or on what principles Europe was to be built in the future, he got no reply.

Here indeed was a well of darkness: no hope of liberation, and no vision of tomorrow. A battle for battle's sake. A return to the pre-war status quo, bad though it had been, was to be the reward for those who might live to see the victory of the Anglo-Saxons. This lack of any sort of vision led him to see the world as a place in which nothing existed outside of naked force. It was a world of decline and fall. And the liberals of the older generation, mouthing nineteenth-century phrases about respect for man—while all about them hundreds of thousands of people were being massacred—were fossil remains.

Beta had no faith, religious or other, and he had the courage to admit it in his poems. He ran off his first volume of verse on a mimeograph machine. No sooner had I received his book and pried apart its sticky pages than I realized that here was a real poet. The reading of his hexameters was not, however, a joyous undertaking. The streets of occupied Warsaw were gloomy. Underground meetings in cold and smoky rooms, when one listened for the sound of Gestapo boots on the stairs, were like grim rituals conducted in catacombs. We were living at the bottom of a huge crater, and the sky far up above was the only element we shared with the other people on the face of the earth. All this was in his verse—grayness, fog, gloom, and death. Still his was not a poetry of grievance but of icy stoicism. The poems of this entire generation lacked faith. Their fundamental motif was a call to arms and a vision of death. Unlike young poets of other epochs, they did not see death as a romantic theme but as a real presence. Almost all these young writers of Warsaw died before the end of the War either at the hands of the Gestapo or in battle. None of them, however, questioned the meaning of sacrifice to the same degree as did he. "There will remain after us only scrap-iron and the hollow, jeering laughter of generations," he wrote in one of his verses.

His poetry had in it none of that affirmation of the
world that is present in the sympathy with which the artist
portrays, for example, an apple or a tree. What his verse
disclosed was a profoundly disturbed equilibrium. One
can divine a great deal from a work of art, e.g. that the
world of Bach or of Breughel was ordered, arranged hierarchically. Modern art reflects the disequilibrium of modern society in that it so often springs from a blind passion
vainly seeking to sate itself in form, color, or sound. An
artist can contemplate sensual beauty only when he loves
all that surrounds him on earth. But if all he feels is loath-
ing at the discrepancy between what he would wish the
world to be and what it is in reality, then he is incapable
of standing still and beholding. He is ashamed of reflexes
of love; he is condemned to perpetual motion, to a rest-
less sketching of discontinued, broken observations of
nature. Like a sleep-walker, he loses his balance as soon
as he stops moving. Beta's poems were whirlpools of fog,
saved from complete chaos only by the dry rhythm of
his hexameters. This character of his poetry must be attributed at least in part to the fact that he belonged to an
ill-fated generation in an ill-fated nation, but he had thousands of brothers in all the countries of Europe, all of
them passionate and deceived.

Unlike his comrades who acted out of loyalty to their
fatherland, on Christian or vague metaphysical grounds,
he needed a rational basis for action. When the Gestapo
arrested him in 1943, it was rumored in our city that he
was taken as the result of an "accident" to one of the left-
wing groups. If life in Warsaw was little reminiscent of
paradise, then Beta now found himself in the lower circle
of hell: the "concentration universe." In what was then
the normal order of events, he spent several months in
jail before being shipped off to Auschwitz. Incredibly, he

managed to survive there for two years. When the Red
Army drew near, he and the other prisoners were transported to Dachau, and there they were eventually set free
by the Americans. We learned of all this only after the
War, when he published a volume of stories recounting his
experiences.

Immediately after his release he settled in Munich. It
was there in 1946 that the book, *We Were in Auschwitz*,
written by him and two of his fellow-prisoners, appeared.
It was dedicated to "The American Seventh Army which
brought us liberation from the Dachau-Allach concentration camp." On his return to Poland, he published his
volume of short stories.

I have read many books about concentration camps,
but not one of them is as terrifying as his stories because
he never moralizes, he relates. A special social hierarchy
comes into being in a "concentration universe." At the top
stand the camp authorities; after them come prisoners
trusted by the administration; next come the prisoners
clever enough to find means of getting sufficient food to
keep up their strength. At the bottom stand the weak and
clumsy, who daily tumble lower as their undernourished
organisms fail to bear up under the work. In the end they
die, either in the gas chamber or from an injection of
phenol. Obviously this hierarchy does not include the
masses of people killed immediately upon their arrival,
i.e. the Jews, except for those who were single and especially fit for work. In his stories, Beta clearly defines his
social position. He belonged to the caste of clever and
healthy prisoners, and he *brags* about his cunning and
agility. Life in a concentration camp requires constant
alertness; every moment can decide one's life or death. In
order to react appropriately at all times, one must know
where danger lies and how to escape it: sometimes by

blind obedience, sometimes by calculated negligence, sometimes by blackmail or bribery. One of his stories consists of an account of a series of dangers he dodges in the course of a single day:

1. A guard offers him some bread. To get it he has to jump a ditch that constitutes the line of watch. Guards, under orders to shoot prisoners who cross it, receive three days' leave plus five marks for everyone they kill beyond this limit. Beta, understanding the guard's intentions, refuses the bait.

2. A guard overhears him telling another prisoner the news of the fall of Kiev. Beta forestalls a report of the offense by giving the guard, through an intermediary, an old watch as a bribe.

3. He slips out of the hands of a dangerous camp overseer, or kapo, by a quick execution of an order. The fragment I quote below concerns some Greek prisoners who were too weak to march properly. As a punishment, sticks were tied to their legs. They are supervised by a Russian, Andrej.

I leap back, struck from behind by a bicycle. I whip off my cap. The Unterscharführer, a landlord from Harmenze, jumps off the bicycle red with irritation.

"What's happening in this crazy unit? Why are those people walking around with sticks tied to their legs? It's time for work!"

"They don't know how to walk!"

"If they don't know how to walk, kill them! And you, do you know another goose has disappeared?"

"Why are you standing there like a dumb dog?" the kapo screamed at me. "Tell Andrej to settle with them. Los!"

I ran down the path . . .

"Andrej, finish them off! Kapo's orders!"

Andrej seized a stick and struck with all his might. The

Greek shielded himself with his arm, howled, and fell. Andrej put the stick across his throat, stepped on it and rocked himself. I went on my way quickly.

His day is filled not only with escapes from danger, but also with the intricate game waged between him and his Russian co-prisoner Ivan. Ivan has stolen a piece of soap from him. He decides to avenge himself and patiently seeks his opportunity. He observes that Ivan has stolen a goose; an artfully arranged report (so that he won't be stigmatized as an informer) occasions a search. The goose is found and Ivan is beaten by an SS man. The score is settled.

He is proud to succeed when others, less clever, perish. There is no small amount of plain sadism in his repeated emphasis of the fact that he is well-dressed, well-fed, and healthy.

"They keep moving to avoid a beating; they eat grass and slimy mud so they won't feel hungry; they walk dejectedly, still-living corpses," he says of his fellow-inmates. But of himself: "It's good to work after one has eaten a breakfast of a rasher of bacon with bread and garlic, and washed it down with a can of condensed milk." A detail concerning his · clothes (all about him are half-naked wretches): "I go into the shade and place my jacket under me *so that I won't soil my silk shirt* [the italics are mine, C. M.] and settle down comfortably to sleep. Each of us rests however he can afford to." And here is a scene of "class" contrast. Beker, another prisoner, is to be burned in the crematorium because he is too weak to be useful.

At that moment, a huge gray skull emerged out of the depths, over the edge of the wooden bunk and embarrassed, blinking eyes peered at us. Then Beker's face appeared, crumpled and more aged than ever.

"Teddy, I have something to ask you."

"Talk," I said, leaning down to him.

"Teddy, I'm going to the chimney."

I leaned down a little more, and looked into his eyes at close range. They were calm and empty.

"Teddy, I've been hungry for so long. Give me something to eat. For this last evening."

Kazik slapped me on the knee.

"Do you know this Jew?"

"It's Beker," I answered softly.

"You, Jew, get up there on the bunk and stuff yourself. When you're full, you can take the rest with you to the chimney. Go on! I don't sleep there so you can take along your lice."

"Teddy," he took me by the arm, "come. In the barrack I've got a wonderful apple pie, straight from my mother."

The strong and clever were used by the camp authorities for special work, which gave them the opportunity to procure food and clothing. One of the most sought-after jobs was that of unloading the box-cars that brought Jews from all the cities of Europe to Auschwitz. These Jews brought suitcases full of clothes, gold, jewels, and food with them because they had been told they were leaving for "re-settlement." When the train entered the gates of the camp, the frightened crowd was immediately chased out of the cars. Those who were young and strong enough to work were separated out, while old people and women with children were sent at once to the gas chambers and crematoriums. The work of the prisoners was to carry out the baggage that was destined to enrich the Reich and the camp administration. Beta describes his work around the transport. He has gotten into this brigade through a French friend, Henri.

In the abundant literature of atrocity of the twentieth century, one rarely finds an account written from the

point of view of an accessory to the crime. Authors are
usually ashamed of this role. But collaboration is an empty
word as applied to a concentration camp. The machine is
impersonal; responsibility shifts from those who carry out
orders to those higher, always higher. Beta's stories about
the "transport" should, I believe, be included in all anthologies of literature dealing with the lot of man in totalitarian society, if ever such anthologies are compiled.

The arrival of a "transport" is spread out, like a play,
over several acts. A few quotations will give a better picture of his literary method than any amount of description:

PROLOGUE, *or anticipation of the "transport"*

Greeks are sitting around us, moving their jaws voraciously
like huge inhuman insects, greedily eating moldy clods of
bread. They are uneasy; they don't know what they'll be doing. Rails and planks worry them. They don't like heavy haul-
ing.

"Was wir arbeiten?" they ask.

"Niks. Transport kommen, alles Krematorium, compris?"

"Alles verstehen," they answer in crematorium esperanto.
They calm down; they won't be loading rails on trucks, or
carrying planks.

ACT I, *or the arrival of the "transport"*

A striped crowd lay near the tracks in the long strips of
shade. It breathed heavily and unevenly, spoke lazily in its own
tongues and gazed indifferently at the majestic people in green
uniform, at the green of the trees, near and unattainable, at the
steeple of a distant little church which at that moment was
tolling a late angelus.

"The transport is coming," someone said, and everyone stood
up in expectation. Freight cars appeared around the curve as
the train backed in. The trainman standing in the caboose

leaned out, waved his hand, whistled. The locomotive screeched, wheezed and the train trundled slowly along the station. Behind the tiny barred windows one could see human faces, pale, crumpled, disheveled, as if they were sleepy—frightened women, and men who, exotically, had hair. They passed slowly, gazing at the station in silence. Then something started to boil inside the wagons and to beat against their wooden walls.

"Water! Air!" Despairing, hollow cries burst out.

Human faces pressed to the windows, lips desperately gasping for air sucked in a few gulps, vanished; others struggled into their place, then they too vanished The shrieks and moans grew steadily louder.

ACT II, *or the segregation* (a few scenes will suffice)

Here comes a woman walking briskly, hurrying almost imperceptibly yet feverishly. A small child with the plump, rosy face of a cherub runs after her, fails to catch up, stretches out its hands, crying, "Mama, mama!"

"Woman, take this child in your arms!"

"Sir, it isn't my child, it isn't mine!" the woman shouts hysterically, and runs away covering her face with her hands. She wants to hide; she wants to reach those who won't leave in a truck, who will leave on foot, who will live. She is young, healthy, pretty, she wants to live.

But the child runs after her, pleading at the top of its voice, "Mama, mama, don't run away!"

"It's not mine, not mine, not . . . !"

Until Andrej, the sailor from Sevastopol, overtook her. His eyes were troubled by vodka and the heat. He reached her, knocked her off her feet with a single powerful blow and, as she fell, caught her by the hair and dragged her up again. His face was distorted with fury.

"Why you lousy fucking Jew-bitch! Jebit twoju mat'! You'd run away from your own child! I'll show you, you whore!" He grabbed her in the middle, one paw throttling her throat which wanted to shout, and flung her into the truck like a heavy sack of grain.

"Here! Take this with you, you slut!" And he threw her child at her feet.

"Gut gemacht. That's how one should punish unnatural mothers," said an SS man standing near the van.

A pair of people fall to the ground entangled in a desperate embrace. He digs his fingers into her flesh convulsively, tears at her clothes with his teeth. She screams hysterically, curses, blasphemes until, stifled by a boot, she chokes and falls silent. They split them apart like a tree; and herd them into the car like animals.

Others are carrying a young girl with a missing leg; they hold her by her arms and by her one remaining leg. Tears are streaking down her face as she whispers sadly, "Please, please, it hurts, it hurts . . ." They heave her into a truck, among the corpses. She will be burned alive, together with them.

ACT III, *or the conversation of the witnesses*

A cool and starry evening falls. We are lying on the tracks. It is infinitely silent. Anemic lamps burn on high poles behind the circles of light.

"Did you exchange shoes?" Henri asks me.

"No."

"Why not?"

"Man, I have enough, absolutely enough!"

"Already? After the first transport? Just think, me—since Christmas maybe a million people have passed through my hands. The worst are the transports from Paris: a man always meets friends."

"And what do you say to them?"

"That they're going to take a bath, and that we'll meet later in the camp. What would you say?"

EPILOGUE (many trains came to Auschwitz that evening.
          The transport totaled 15,000 people)

As we return to the camp, the stars begin to fade, the sky
becomes ever more translucent and lifts above us, the night
grows light. A clear, hot day announces itself.

From the crematoriums, broad columns of smoke rise steadily
and merge above into a gigantic, black river that turns exceedingly slowly in the sky over Birkenau and disappears beyond the forests, in the direction of Trzebinia. The transport is
already burning.

We pass an SS squad, moving with mechanized weapons to
relieve the guard. They march evenly, shoulder to shoulder,
one mass, one will.

"Und Morgen die ganze Welt . . ." they sing at the top of
their lungs.

Beta is a nihilist in his stories, but by that I do not mean
that he is amoral. On the contrary, his nihilism results from
an ethical passion, from disappointed *love* of the world and
of humanity. He wants to go the limit in describing what
he saw; he wants to depict with complete accuracy a
world in which there is no longer any place for indignation. The human species is *naked* in his stories, stripped
of those tendencies toward good which last only so long
as the habit of civilization lasts. But the habit of civilization is fragile; a sudden change in circumstances, and
humanity reverts to its primeval savagery. How deluded
are those respectable citizens who, striding along the streets
of English or American cities, consider themselves men
of virtue and goodness! Of course, it is easy to condemn a woman who would abandon her child in order
to save her own life. This is a monstrous act. Yet a woman
who, while reading on her comfortable sofa, judges her
unfortunate sister should pause to consider whether fear

would not be stronger than love within her, if she too were faced with horror. Perhaps it would, perhaps not—who can foretell?

But the "concentration universe" also contained many human beings who spurred themselves to the noblest acts, who died to protect others. None of them figure in Beta's stories. His attention is fixed not on man—man is simply an animal that wants to live—but on "concentration society." Prisoners are ruled by a special ethic: it is permissible to harm others, provided they harm you first. Beyond this unwritten contract, every man saves himself as best he can. We would search in vain for pictures of human solidarity in Beta's book. The truth about his behavior in Auschwitz, according to his fellow-prisoners, is utterly different from what his stories would lead one to suppose; he acted heroically, and was a model of comradeship. But he wants to be *tough;* and he does not spare himself in his desire to observe soberly and impartially. He is afraid of lies; and it would be a lie to present himself as an observer who judged, when in reality he, though striving to preserve his integrity, felt subjected to all the laws of degradation. As narrator, he endows himself with the qualities which pass as assets in a concentration camp: cleverness and enterprise. Thanks to the element of "class" war between the weak and the strong, wherein he did not deviate from the truth, his stories are extraordinarily brutal.

Liberated from Dachau, he became acquainted with the life of refugees in Western Germany. It was like an extension of the life in the camp. Demoralization, thievery, drunkenness, corruption—all the evil forces set loose in man by the years of Hitlerism continued to triumph. The callous policy of the occupying powers toward the millions of recent slaves aroused his anger. Here, then, was the dreamt-of end of the war: again the law of the jungle prevailed; again the strong, this time mouthing the slogans of democracy and freedom, trod upon the weak or treated them with cruel indifference.

Beta had a keen eye, but it was focussed on all that was absurd, infamous, and vile in those about him. Pitiless and intolerant, he was one open wound. Perhaps he would have been less bitter had he been able, after these years of suffering, to *stand still* at one point for one moment and see an *individual* man instead of a society shaken by the great paroxysm of the end of the War. He was in constant inner motion; his face was perpetually distorted into a grimace of rage and irony. He continued to see the mass of humanity in whose midst he was living as *naked* and ruled by a few primitive impulses. For him, who had to aim toward something, such a world was unbearable. He felt he could no longer remain in a state of undirected fury and revolt.

Like many ex-prisoners, he had to choose between return to his native country and self-imposed exile. His wartime Marxist sympathies were vaguely rooted in a feeling that Marxism treats man realistically. His convictions could be reduced to the simple maxim that man is not governed by his good intentions, but solely by the laws of the social order in which he is placed. Whoever wants to change man must, first of all, change social conditions. Still, like all Poles, he was suspicious of the powerful Russian state. The violence of his style brought him closest to such writers as Zola or, among contemporaries, Hemingway, whom he read avidly; and thus he was one of those artists known in Russia as "the slime of the West." Nothing evokes such horror in the land of dialectics as a writer who depicts man in terms of elementary forces of hunger and love.

He hesitated for a long time. Finally, after literary publications appearing in Poland began to filter through to him, he made up his mind to go back. Two major factors determined his decision. He had great literary ambitions, but he was a beginner and unknown. Where, outside his own country, could he find readers of books written in his native tongue? Besides, a revolution was in progress in Poland. That was the place for a man torn by fury; that was where he could find the opportunity to remake the world.

He said good-bye to his friends, and returned to a Warsaw whose inhabitants were living in the cellars of demolished houses. With their own hands they were clearing away the heaps of rubble and loading them on shoddy little horse-carts. Thus was the rebuilding of the town begun. But books and magazines were instantly snatched up throughout Poland. The government spared no expense in its support of literature. Unlimited possibilities opened before any writer who had the slightest bit of talent. Beta's career began at the tempo of a blitz. By publishing in the best reviews, and collecting large royalties, he was getting only his due. He had a fine mastery of the language; his style was terse and biting. Because his experiences were those of many of his countrymen, his subject matter was universally near and understandable. No wonder, then, that his book of stories about the "concentration universe" was hailed as a literary event of first importance.

Fortunately for him, socialist realism was not yet obligatory, for his book was in the most blatant opposition to Soviet writing techniques. According to the canons imposed on writers by the Center, it was practically a crime. Obviously, the subject itself was politically irreproachable. Descriptions of the bestiality of Hitlerism were eminently desirable, especially since the average Pole hated the Russians just about as much as he hated the Germans. Concentrating the readers' attention upon German atrocities channeled their hatred into a single direction and so contributed to the "psychological preparation" of the country. Hence the growing number of books about the Gestapo, partisan warfare, or concentration camps.

Official tolerance went so far that one was free to write sympathetically about the Polish army's fight against the Germans in 1939, even though that army had defended a "lordly" Poland that was like a cinder in the Soviet Union's eye. Still, a politically correct theme would not have saved him from the critics' attack had they wanted to apply orthodox criteria, because he described the concentration camp as he personally had seen it, not as one was *supposed* to see it. In this lay his transgression. How was one supposed to see a concentration camp? It is not hard to enumerate: 1) the prisoners should have banded together in secret organizations; 2) the leaders in these organizations should have been Communists; 3) all the Russian prisoners appearing on the pages of the book should have distinguished themselves by their moral strength and heroic behavior; 4) the prisoners should have been differentiated according to their political outlook. None of this is true of his stories. The Party noticed this and even though it did not consider Polish writers ripe for socialist realism, its critics upbraided him for his chief sins. They proclaimed that his work resembled depraved, or American, literature; that it was pessimistic; and that it lacked the element of "conscious struggle," i.e. struggle in the name of Communism. But these criticisms were uttered in a persuasive tone. He was young and needed educating, yet he had in him the makings of a real Communist writer. Observing him carefully, the Party discovered in him a rare and precious treasure: true hatred.

Beta was receptive. The more he read of Leninist-Stalinist theory, the more he convinced himself that this was exactly what he was looking for. His hatred was like a torrential river uselessly rushing ahead. What could be simpler than to set it to turning the Party's gristmills. What a relief: useful hatred, hatred put to the service of society!

At the root of his hatred was the same reaction that Sartre called "la nausée," namely, disgust with man as a *physiological* being determined by the laws of nature and society, and subject to the destructive effects of time. Man should somehow break these shackles, and rise even if he had to hoist himself up by his own bootstraps. Had Beta been French, perhaps he might have become an existentialist; probably, though, that would not have satisfied him. He smiled contemptuously at mental speculation, for he remembered seeing philosophers fighting over garbage in the camp. Human thought had no significance; subterfuges and self-deceptions were easy to decipher; all that really counted was the movement of matter. He absorbed dialectical materialism as a sponge soaks up water. Its materialistic side appeased his hunger for brutal truth; its dialectical side permitted a sudden leap *above* the human species, to a vision of humanity as the material of history.

In a very short while, he published a new book. Its title alone was symbolic of his attitude, *The Stony World*—stony, therefore merciless and bare. The book comprised extremely short stories devoid of almost all action, no more than sketches of what he had seen. He was a master at the art of using material details to suggest a whole human situation. The "stony world" was Central Europe after the defeat of Hitler and the end of the Second World War. Since he had spent some time in the American zone of Germany, he had an ample store of subjects—people of all nationalities and social positions, ex-Nazis, ex-prisoners, the German bourgeoisie baffled by what had happened, American soldiers and officers, etc. Under his temperate words lurked an immensity of bitterness against a civilization whose fruit was Hitlerism. He set up equations: Christianity equals capitalism equals Hitlerism. The theme of the book was the *finale* of civilization. Its tone can be summed up in a single protest: "You told me about culture, about religion, about morality; and look what they led to!"

For Beta, as for many of his companions, the reign of Hitler was the culmination of the capitalist era in Europe. Its collapse announced the victory of the Revolution on a world scale. The future might mean further striving, but the turning point was passed. Almost all the books written in the early post-war years by young men like him developed the theme of man's impotence against the laws of History: even people with the best of intentions had fallen into the machine of Nazi terror and been converted into frightened cave men. The reading public was faced with a dilemma, a choice between the old civilization which had taken its evilness out on their hides, or the new civilization which could arise only through the victorious might of the East. So powerful is the hold success has over man's imagination that it seems not to result from human design plus favorable circumstances, but to reflect the highest law of the age. (Yet Russia and her seemingly invincible order had been merely a hair's-breadth away from defeat in the Second World War.)

The Stony World was the last book in which Beta tried to employ artistic tools, like restraint, hidden irony, masked anger, etc., recognized as effective in Western literature. He quickly realized that all his concern about "art" was superfluous. On the contrary, the harder he stepped down on the pedal, the more he was praised.

Loud, violent, clear, biased—this is what his writing was expected to be. As Party writers (he entered the Party) began to outbid each other in an effort to be accessible and simple, the boundary between literature and propaganda began to fade. He started to introduce more and more direct journalism into his writing. He discharged his venom in attacks on capitalism, i.e. on all that was happening outside the sphere of the Imperium. He would take an item from the news about warfare in Malaya or hunger in India, for example, and turn it into something halfway between an article and a snapshot.

I saw him for the last time in 1950. He had changed a great deal since the days before his arrest by the Gestapo. His former shyness and artificial humility were gone. Whereas once he had walked with a slight stoop and a lowered head, he was now a straight-backed man with an air of self-assurance. He was dry, concentrated on his work. The bashful poet had become a thorough *homo politicus*. At that time he was already a well-known propagandist. Every week one of his malignant articles appeared in a government weekly. He visited Eastern Germany frequently to gather news stories. No reporter can serve a cause as well as an author with a period of disinterested writing in his background; and Beta used all his knowledge of the writer's trade in his poisonous articles against America.

Looking at this esteemed nihilist, I would often think how like a smooth slope any form of art is, and of the amount of effort the artist must expend in order to keep from sliding back to where the footing is easier. The inner command that forces him to this effort is, at the core, irrational. By refusing to recognize disinterested art, the New Faith destroys this inner command. Beta was a real writer in his stories about the concentration camp;

though he questioned all man's inner imperatives, he counterfeited nothing, he did not try to please anybody. Then he introduced a single particle of politics and, like a supersaturated solution, his writing crystallized, became thereafter transparent and stereotyped. But one must not oversimplify. Many great authors, among them Swift, Stendhal, Tolstoi, wrote out of political passion. One might even say that political conviction, an important social message a writer wants to communicate to his readers, adds strength to his work. The essential difference between the great writers who criticized the political institutions of their day and people of Beta's type seems to lie in the total non-conformity of the former. They acted in opposition to their environment; he, writing, listened for the applause of his Party comrades.

For all their violence and precision of language, his articles were so dull and one-dimensional that this debasement of a gifted prose-writer stirred my curiosity. He was certainly intelligent enough to understand that he was wasting his talent. In conversation with several literary authorities whose word determines a writer's place in the official hierarchy, I asked why such measures were being applied to him. Surely the interests of the Party did not require it to reduce him to a rag. He was certainly more useful as a writer of stories and novels; to force him to write articles meant bad management of available artistic resources. "No one makes him write articles," came the reply, "that's the whole misfortune. The editor of the weekly can't drive him away. He himself insists on writing them. He thinks there is no time, today, for art, that you have to act on the masses more directly and elementally. He wants to be as useful as possible." This was a somewhat hypocritical answer. The Party constantly stresses its desire for good literature; at the same time, it creates such a tense atmosphere of propaganda that writers feel compelled to resort to the most primitive and over-simplified literary techniques. Yet it was true that Beta *himself* wanted to devote all his time to journalism; although he was a highly qualified specialist, he seized upon work that was easy for the most ordinary drudge. His mind, like that of so many Eastern intellectuals, was impelled toward self-annihilation.

The psychological process that is set into motion as soon as such an intellectual takes up his pen is fairly complex. Let us imagine he is about to describe a certain event in international politics. He sees that phenomena are inter-related functionally rather than causally. Therefore, to present the event honestly, he would have to penetrate the motives of the opposing forces and the necessities which govern them—in short, to analyze it from every side. Then anger comes to his rescue, introducing order into the tangle of interdependencies and releasing him from the obligation to analyze. This anger against the *self-deception* that anything at all depends on man's will is, simultaneously, a fear of falling prey to one's own naïveness. Since the world is brutal, one must reduce everything to the simplest and most brutal factors. The author understands that what he is doing is far from accurate: people's stupidity or people's good intentions influence events no less than do the necessities of the economic struggle. But he takes his vengeance upon mankind (upon others and upon himself) by demonstrating that man is dominated by a few elementary laws; at the same time, he feeds his sense of superiority and proves himself acute and strong enough to dispense with "prejudices."

In his political articles, just as in his concentration camp stories, Beta's urge to simplify, to strip off all illusions, to present everyone and everything nakedly

was always predominant. But if one continues to follow this urge one reaches a point at which the intellect
has nothing more to say. Words become a war-cry, an
imperfect substitute for a clenched fist. Beta did arrive
at the stage where words no longer satisfied him; he could
not write novels or stories because they would last through
time and so could not answer his need for a cry to battle.
The movement to which he was subjected went on acceler-
ating: faster and faster, greater and greater doses of hatred
and of dizziness. The shapes of the world became simpler
and simpler, until at last an individual tree, an individual
man, lost all importance and he found himself not among
palpable things, but among political concepts. His feverish
addiction to journalism is not hard to explain. The writing of articles acted on him like a narcotic. When he put
down his pen he felt he had accomplished something. It
didn't matter that there wasn't a single thought of his
own in these articles; it didn't matter that thousands of
second-rate journalists from the Elbe to the Pacific were
saying exactly the same thing. He was active in the sense
that a soldier marching in formation is active.

"Und Morgen die ganze Welt" sang the SS guards moving against the background of the black smoke pouring
out of the crematoriums of Auschwitz. Nazism was collective insanity; yet the German masses followed Hitler
for profound psychological reasons. A great economic and
social crisis gave birth to Nazism. The young German of
that day saw all about him the decay and chaos of the
Weimar Republic, the degradation of millions of unemployed, the disgusting aberrations of the cultured elite,
the prostitution of his sisters, and the fight of man against
man for money. When the hope of socialism vanished, he
accepted the other philosophy of history that was offered
him, a philosophy that was a parody of Leninist-Stalinist

doctrine. It is possible that the German who locked Beta
into the concentration camp was, like him, a disappointed
lover of the world who longed for harmony and purity,
discipline and faith. He despised those of his countrymen
who refused to join in the joyous march. Pitiful remnants
of humanitarianism, they mumbled that the new movement violated moral principles. Here, immediate and in
sight, was the salvation of Germany and the reconstruction of the world. And in this unique moment—a moment that occurs once in a thousand years—these whining
believers in that miserable Jesus dared to mention their
trifling moral scruples! How hard it was to fight for a new
and better order—if among one's own people one still
encountered such infantile prejudice!

Beta also could see a new and better order within his
grasp. He believed in, and demanded, earthly salvation.
He hated the enemies of human happiness and insisted
that they must be destroyed. Are they not evil-doers
who, when the planet enters a new epoch, dare to maintain that to imprison people, or to terrify them into professions of political faith, is not quite nice? Whom do we
imprison? Class enemies, traitors, rabble. And the faith
we force on people, is it not true faith? History, History, is with us! We can see its living, explosive flame!
Small and blind, indeed, are the people who, instead of
comprehending the whole of the gigantic task, squander
their time on worry about insignificant details!

Despite his talent and intelligence, Beta did not perceive
the dangers inherent in an exciting march. On the contrary, his talent, intelligence, and ardor drove him to action while ordinary people temporized and rendered unto
an unloved Caesar only so much as was absolutely necessary. He willingly shouldered responsibility. He did not
pause to consider what a philosophy of historic change be-

comes once it sets out to conquer the world by the might of armies. "And tomorrow the world!"

A few months after I wrote this portrait, I learned of Beta's death. He was found one morning in his home in Warsaw. The gas jet was turned on. Those who observed him in the last months of his feverish activity were of the opinion that the discrepancy between what he said in his public statements and what his quick mind could perceive was increasing daily. He behaved too nervously for them not to suspect that he was acutely aware of this contrast. Moreover, he frequently spoke of the "Mayakovski case." Numerous articles appeared in the press written by his friends, writers of Poland and Eastern Germany. His coffin, draped with a red flag, was lowered into the grave to the sound of the "Internationale" as the Party bid farewell to its most promising young writer.

CHAPTER VI

Gamma, the Slave of History

IN speaking of Gamma, I must evoke a picture of the town in which I went to school and later to the University. There are certain places in Europe which are particularly troublesome to history and geography teachers: Trieste, the Saar Basin, Schleswig-Holstein. Just such a sore-spot is the city of Vilna. In the last half-century it belonged to various countries and saw various armies in its streets. With each change, painters were put to work repainting street and office signs into the new official language. With each change, the inhabitants were issued new passports and were obliged to conform to new laws and injunctions. The city was ruled in turn by the Russians, Germans, Lithuanians, Poles, again the Lithuanians, again the Germans, and again the Russians. Today it is the capital of the Lithuanian Soviet Socialist Republic, a fancy title designed to conceal the blunt fact that Russia is effectively carrying out the precepts of the Tsars in regard to territorial expansion.

During my school and university years the city belonged to Poland. It lies in a land of forests, lakes, and streams, concealed in a woody dale. Travelers see it emerge unexpectedly from behind the trees. The steeples of its scores of Catholic churches, built by Italian architects in the baroque style, contrast in their gold and white with the blackness of the surrounding pines. Legend tells us that a certain Lithuanian ruler, hunting in the wilds, fell asleep by a fire and had a prophetic dream. Under the spell of his dream, he constructed a city on the spot where he had slept. Throughout the many centuries of its existence, Vilna never ceased to be a city of the forests. All about it lay an abandoned province of Europe whose people spoke Polish, Lithuanian, and Byelorussian, or a mixture of the three, and retained many customs and habits long since forgotten elsewhere. I speak in the past tense because today this city of my childhood is as lava-inundated as was Pompeii. Most of its former inhabitants were either murdered by the Nazis, deported to Siberia, or re-settled by the Russians in the western territories from which the Germans were expelled. Other people, born thousands of miles away, now walk its streets; and for them, its churches, founded by Lithuanian princes and Polish kings, are useless.

Then, however, no one dreamt of mass murder and mass deportations. And the life of the town unfolded in a rhythm that was slower and less subject to change than are forms of government or borders of kingdoms. The University, the Bishops' Palace, and the Cathedral were the most esteemed edifices in the city. On Sundays, crowds filled the narrow street leading to the old city gate upon which, in a chapel, was housed the picture of the Virgin known for its miraculous powers. Vilna was a blend of Italian architecture and the Near East. In the little streets of the Jewish quarter on a Friday evening, through the windows one could see families seated in the gleam of candlelight. The words of the Hebrew prophets resounded in the ancient synagogues, for this was one of the most important centers of Jewish literature and learning in

Europe. Great fairs on Catholic holidays attracted peasants from neighboring villages to the city, where they would display their wooden wares and medicinal herbs on the ground. No fair was complete without *obwarzanki* (hard, round, little cakes threaded on a string); and no matter where they were baked, they always bore the name of the little town whose only claims to fame were its bakeries and its one-time "bear academy," an institution where bears were trained. In the winter, the steep streets were filled with boys and girls on skis, their red and green jerkins flashing against a snow that became rosy in the frosty sun.

The University building had thick walls and low, vaulted classrooms. The uninitiated were bound to get lost in the labyrinth of its shaded courtyards. Its arcades and halls might just as easily have been located in Padua or Bologna. Once Jesuits used to teach the sons of the nobility in this building; but at the time when I was studying there, lay professors were teaching young people whose parents were for the most part small landholders, tenant-farmers, or Jewish merchants.

It was in that building that I met Gamma. He was an ungainly, red-faced boy, coarse and boisterous. If Vilna itself was provincial, then those who left their backward villages to come there to study were doubly so. Muddy country roads made communication practically impossible in spring and autumn; peasants' horses were seized by fits of terror at the sight of an automobile; in many villages, homes were still lit by twig torches. Home handicrafts and lumbering were the only occupations, outside of farming, that the people knew. Gamma came from the country. His father, a retired officer of the Polish army, had a farm. The family had lived in those regions for generations, and its name can be found in the registers of the lower nobility of that land. Gamma's mother was Russian and he grew up bi-lingual. Unlike the majority of his companions who were Catholic, he was Orthodox, a faith he inherited from his mother.

Our first conversations did not portend a close understanding between us. True, we were bound by a common interest in literature, but I was offended by his behavior, by his piercing voice—he just did not know how to speak in a normal tone—and by the opinions he uttered. He always carried a heavy cane of the type that was the favorite weapon of young people given to anti-Semitic extravagances. His violent anti-Semitism was, in fact, his political program. As for myself, I despised such nationalists; I thought them dangerous blockheads who, in order not to think, were raising a loud hue and cry, and stirring up mutual hatreds in various national groups. There are certain conversations that stick in one's memory; and sometimes what one remembers, even more than the actual words, is what one was looking at then. When I recall our talk about racism, I see his legs, the round paving stones of the street, and his cane leaning against the gutter. He spoke of blood and earth, and of how power should be vested not in the whole of the citizenry regardless of race or native tongue, but in the dominant national group, who should take measures to safeguard its blood against contamination. Perhaps his nationalist zeal was an effort to compensate for his own deficiencies; his mixed, half-Russian origin and his Orthodox faith must surely have caused him much unpleasantness at the hands of his provincial and primitive schoolmates. His voice rang out, belligerent and permeated by a sense of his own superiority. My arguments against racist theories awakened a profound disgust in him; he considered me a person whose thinking was an obstacle to action. As for him, he wanted action. This was the year 1931. We were both very young, very poor, and unaware of the unusual events we were to be thrust into later.

I visited him in 1949 in one of the capitals of Western Europe where he was the ambassador of Red Poland, and a trusted member of the Party. His residence was guarded by a heavy wrought-iron gate. A few minutes after one rang, an eye would appear at the aperture, hinges would rattle, and one would see the big courtyard with a few shining cars in it.

To the left of the entrance stood the sentry-box of the chauffeur on duty, who was armed with a pistol against any eventuality. Standing in the middle of the courtyard, one perceived the proportions of the façade and the wings. This was one of the most beautiful palaces in that beautiful capital. A certain eighteenth-century aristocrat had built it for his mistress. The interior retained its former character; the big rooms, their walls covered with gilded wainscoting, contained furniture, rugs and Gobelin tapestries of that century. Gamma received me in the midst of gilt and marble; he was cordial; the years had worn the roughness off his gestures, and injected a slightly artificial sweetness into his manner. In this palace he had his apartment, reception salons, and offices. Many of the most eminent representatives of Western art and science visited him frequently. A well-known English scholar called him a charming man, liberal and free of fanaticism. This opinion was shared by many members of the intellectual elite, among them Catholics, liberals, and even conservatives. As for the luminaries of Western Communist literature, they admired him both because he was an emissary of the East they worshipped, and because he was extremely acute in his Marxist appraisal of literary problems. Obviously, they did not know his past nor the price one pays in order that an unseasoned youth, raised in one of the most forsaken corners of Europe, may become the master of an eighteenth-century palace.

Gamma felt fine in this Western capital. He loved to visit night spots and cabarets and was so well-known in them that whenever he entered, the maître d'hôtel would lead him ceremoniously to the best table. Seeing that non-chalant man watching people through narrowed eyes from behind champagne bottles ranged in ice buckets, one could easily have mistaken him for an English squire who had managed to salvage something of his fortune. Tall, slightly stooped, he had the long, ruddy face of a man who has spent much time with guns and dogs. He looked very much like what he really was: a member of the lower Polish nobility, which once hunted passionately, drank passionately, fulfilled its political duties by delivering orations plentifully interspersed with Latin, and quelled opposition by a choral shout of protest or, when necessary, by fencing duels amid overturned benches and tables. The freedom of his gestures was the freedom of a man conscious of his privileges. Toward his subordinates who, as part of their job, often accompanied him on his nocturnal expeditions, he behaved with benevolent disdain. In the office he would at times, out of an excess of high spirits, pull the noses of the embassy secretaries or give them a resounding slap on the behind. But he was also prone to attacks of unbridled anger. Then his ruddy face would turn purple, his blue eyes would become bloodshot, and his voice recapture its former piercing, savage note. No wonder that Western diplomats, scholars, and artists considered him a none too psychologically-complicated *bon viveur*. Even his tactlessness seemed to stem from a broad, open nature that offended at times out of excessive sincerity but that was, in any case, free of guile. The lack of embarrassment with which he spoke of matters considered touchy by other Communists won the confidence of his listeners. This was no Communist—they would agree after a visit to the embassy—or if he was, then how broad and civilized his outlook! What they thought was naturalness was for him sheer artifice. Conscious of his resemblance to a country squire, he used his simple, good-natured mannerisms with deliberate skill. Only those who knew him very intimately saw the cold calculation that lay beneath his feigned effusiveness. In his bosom he carried an invisible dagger with which he could strike unexpected and treacherous blows. But at the same time, this dagger, from which he was never parted either by day or by night, chilled his heart. He was not a happy man.

Wearing his most enchanting smile, he convinced diplomats suspected of not wanting to return behind the iron curtain of his personal benevolence toward them. He thundered against the idiots in Warsaw who did not understand how matters had to be handled in the West. After which he proposed a joint excursion to Warsaw by air, for a few days, to explain to those fools how to settle some question that had occasioned the exchange of numerous telegrams. The delinquent reflected: Gamma's good will was obvious; every trip to Warsaw was a proof of loyalty toward the government and so prolonged one's stay abroad; and, as far as he could see, no risk was involved. In a festive mood, exchanging little jokes with Gamma, the diplomat boarded the plane. No sooner had he reached the airfield in Warsaw than he realized that he had fallen into a trap. Having accomplished his mission, Gamma took the first plane going in the other direction. To supervise the consciences of his personnel was not the least of his duties; it was, in fact, an honor, a sign of trust. His dagger always worked best whenever the talents of a psychologist were required, that is, in cases normally assigned to the political police.

But let me return to the past. Then, he did not know the taste of champagne. Faithful to ancient tradition, the University cafeteria in which we ate bore, as did many institutions of the University, a Latin name, *mensa*. The meals cost very little, but were as bad as they were cheap. Consequently they were the favorite subject of satiric verse which sang the unparalleled hardness of the meat balls and the wateriness of the soups. Amid the smoke of bad cigarettes, we used to sit there discussing poetry and reciprocally meting out laurels that interested no one but ourselves. Still, our group of beginning writers was to interest many people in the future and to play an important role in the history of our country. While our comrades were concerned with their studies or with winning good jobs in the future, we longed for fame and dreamt of reshaping the world. As so often happens, what intelligence and talent we had was paid for by a disturbance of our internal balance. In each of us were deep wounds dating from our childhood or adolescence, different in each of us but identical in one basic element, in something that made it impossible for us to live in harmony with others of our age, something that made us feel "different" and hence drove us to seek compensations. The subjective motives that breed immoderate ambition are not easy to track down. Gamma was, I believe, extremely sensitive about his family. Another factor that might have affected him deeply was something that occurred when he was a schoolboy: he accidentally killed a friend while hunting. The feeling of guilt that arose as a result of this accident probably helped to mold his future decisions.

Perhaps even more important was a disturbance of our

social equilibrium. We were all in revolt against our environment. None of us was of the proletariat. We derived from the intelligentsia, which in that part of Europe was a synonym for the impoverished nobility or the lower middle class. Gamma's father was, as I said, a retired officer; George, a poet, was the son of a provincial lawyer; Theodore, a poet (later shot by the Polish underground as a Party propagandist), bore an aristocratic name although his mother was an employee in a bank; Henryk, an orator, writer, and politician (later shot by the Germans), was the son of a railroad engineer who prided himself on bearing one of the most well-known names in Poland; Stefan, a poet who later became a prominent economist, came of an unsuccessful, half-German mercantile family; my family belonged to the Lithuanian nobility, but my father had migrated from the country to the city to become an engineer. The revolt against one's environment is usually *shame* of one's environment. The social status of all of us was undefined. Our problems were those of the twentieth century, but the traditions of our families bound us to concepts and customs we thought ridiculous and reactionary. We were suspended in a void, and in this we were no exceptions. The country had never experienced a real industrial revolution; the middle class was weak; the worker was for some people a brutal dirty-faced creature who worked hard or drank hard, and for others a myth, an object of worship. Our society was divided into an "intelligentsia" as opposed to the "people." To the latter belonged the workers and peasants. We were of the "intelligentsia," but we rebelled against it because it was oriented toward the past rather than the future. One could compare our situation, in some respects, to that of the sons of impoverished first families of the South in the United States. We were adrift, and we could find no place to anchor. Some people called us the "intellectuals' club" in an effort to oppose the intellectuals to the "intelligentsia."

These were years of acute economic crisis. Unemployment spread throughout wide spheres of the population. The university youth, living without money and without hope of finding work after finishing his studies, was of a radical temper. This radicalism took two forms. Some, like Gamma, at the beginning of his stay at the University, became intensely nationalistic. They saw the answer to all difficulties in a vaguely defined "national revolution." In practice, this meant a hostile attitude toward their Jewish comrades, who as future lawyers and doctors would be their professional competitors. Against these nationalists emerged the "left" whose program, depending on the group, vacillated between socialism and a variation on the New Deal. During annual elections to "The Fraternal Aid," which was something in the nature of an autonomous student government that administered student houses, the *mensa,* etc., these two camps waged battles with words and sometimes with fists.

Both the Communists and the government tried to win over the "left," if I may use this term to describe a conglomeration of differing groups. Pilsudski's mild semidictatorship, lacking a clear-cut program, timidly courted the favor of the young people in an effort to recruit new leaders. Seeing the growing radicalism of the universities, it wooed the "left" by promising reforms. For a certain time, our group was the mainstay of the government's attempts to consolidate its position among the university youth. Our friends, Stefan and Henryk, were considered the most promising of the young "government" politicians in the country. But these attempts ended in failure. "The most promising young politicians" broke with the government and went further to the left; whereas the mechanism of events pushed the government ever more to the right. Nationalism—if not downright totalitarianism in a local edition—began to gain ever greater victories. The government abandoned its support of the patchwork "government left" and started to flirt with the nationalists.

Let this suffice as a general picture of pre-war politics in the now lava-deluged city of Vilna. My account covers many years. During that time, every spring just when we had to study for exams the trees would turn green; and ever since, nowhere else has the green seemed so joyous to me. On the river, little boats appeared taking trippers out to nearby beaches, and long logs floated out of the forests down to the sawmills. Young couples, holding hands, strolled under the arcades of the University. To rise before daybreak, take a kayak at the landing stage and, in the light of the rising sun, paddle on the river whose swift waters pushed between sandy cliffs and clumps of pines —that was pure joy. We often made excursions to nearby lakes in whose midst whole archipelagos of islands thrust up like big bouquets. The grass on the islands was buoyant, untouched by human feet; nightingales shouted in the willows. We would swarm into the water and swim out, troubling the reflections of clouds and trees on its smooth surface; or we would float on our backs in the water, look up at the sky and sing happy, inarticulate songs. We lived through betrayals of love, sorrows over failed exams, mutual intrigues and envies. Our articles and poems appeared in print. Over the hard meat balls in the *mensa,* the topics of conversation changed. Disputes over the significance of metaphor in poetry yielded to discussions of the theories of Georges Sorel, and later Marx and Lenin.

Gamma parted with the nationalists rather quickly; still, he had little sympathy for the "government left" or for the Catholic left. He wrote poetry which was printed in magazines issued by our group; but his poems, unlike those written by Theodore, George, or myself, were the object of neither attack nor praise. The critics received them in silence. He had that mastery of technique that modern poetry requires, but what he wrote was lifeless. Those he envied wrote, I believe, stupidly; but their style was individual, their rhythmic incantations expressed the authors' feelings, their fury and sarcasm irritated the readers, but caught their attention. Gamma's poems were studied arrangements of carefully selected metaphors that said nothing.

Our group became more and more radical. After the collapse of the "government left," the question arose: what "left"? Social democracy in our country shared the faults of all the social democratic parties of the continent—it was weak and willing to compromise. Russia began to figure in our conversations ever more frequently. We lived less than a hundred miles from the borders of the Soviet Union, yet we had no more knowledge of it than did the inhabitants of Brazil. The border was hermetically sealed. We were situated on the peripheries of a world that differed from the East as much as if it were another planet. That Eastern world, which we knew only from books, seemed to us like a world of progress when we compared it with conditions we could observe at first hand. Weighing the matter rationally, we were convinced that the future lay with the East. Our country was in a state of paralysis. The masses had no say in the government. The social filter was so contrived that the peasants' and workers' youth had no access to secondary schools and universities because the expenses, though low, were never-

theless beyond their means. Infinitely complicated national minority problems (and our country had a high
percentage of minorities) were resolved in the most chau-
vinistic spirit. The nationalist movement, supported by
the petty bourgeoisie and the penniless intelligentsia, drove
the government to ever sharper discrimination. The country was heading toward a variation on what was happening in neighboring Germany, the same Germany that
threatened war and the destruction of Poland. Can one
wonder that we looked to Russia as the country where
a solution had been found to all the problems that beset
us, as the country which alone could save us from the
misfortunes which we could so easily visualize as we listened to Hitler's speeches over the radio?

Still, it was not easy to become a Communist, for Communism meant a complete revision of one's concepts of
nationality. For centuries Poland had been in a state of
permanent war with Russia. There was a time when
Polish kings had led their troops to the very gates of the
"Rome of the East." Then the scale tipped in favor of
Moscow until at last, throughout the whole nineteenth
century, the greater part of Poland was under Tsarist rule.
In accepting Communism, one agreed to consider those
old conflicts between the two nations to have been conflicts between their ruling classes only. It was necessary
to forget the past. One conceded that Poland—after its
short period of independence resulting from the Ver-
sailles peace—would, in the event of the victory of Communism, become once again a province of Russia. Poland's eastern territories, and the city in which we lived,
were to be incorporated directly into the Soviet Union
because Moscow regarded them as part of the Byelorussian
and Ukrainian republics. As for the rest, that obviously
would become one more republic in the Union. Polish

Communists made no attempt to conceal that such was the Party program.

To renounce loyalty towards one's country and to eradicate patriotic feelings inculcated in school and in the University—this was the price of entrance upon the road of progress. Not everyone was prepared to pay this price. Our group disintegrated. "The most promising young government politicians," Stefan and Henryk, became Stalinists; George and I withdrew. Those who crossed the line thought the rest of us weak poets, bookworms incapable of action. Perhaps their opinion was not far from the truth. I am not sure, however, that cast-iron consistency is the greatest of human virtues.

Gamma became a Stalinist. I think he felt uneasy writing his passionless poetry. He was not made for literature. Whenever he settled down before a sheet of paper he sensed a void in himself. He was incapable of experiencing the intense joys of a writer, either those of the creative process or those of work accomplished. The period between his nationalism and his Stalinism was for him a limbo, a period of senseless trials and disillusionment.

The Communist Party was illegal in our country. Membership in it was punishable under a paragraph of the law that defined any attempt to deprive Poland of any part of her territory as a criminal offense. Party leaders, realizing they had nothing to gain at the time from illegal activity, tried to reach and sway public opinion through sympathizers not directly involved in the Party. A number of publications appeared in Poland which followed the Party line, adapting it to the level of unwary readers. The group in which Gamma found himself started to edit one such periodical. Contacts with Party messengers took place in secret, often on trips to the neighboring forests. By now, most of the members of our original group had completed their course of studies. This was the period of war in Spain and of the Communist front "in defense of culture," when the Party was trying to rally all the forces of liberalism under a popular slogan.

Gamma wrote articles, spoke at meetings, marched in May Day parades. He acted. When the authorities closed down the periodical, arrested the editors and put them on trial, he, together with the others, found himself in the dock. The trial created a great sensation in the city; it was a considerable blow to the government because it showed that this youth, on which it had counted most, had rapidly evolved toward Communism. Many liberals were incensed by the severity of the authorities toward these university graduates, these young doctors of law or philosophy. The best lawyers in the city defended them. The accused argued and lied convincingly and often; they were mentally better trained than the prosecutor, nor did they yield to him in knowledge of the law. They received mild sentences. Gamma was acquitted for lack of evidence.

During the years that immediately preceded the outbreak of the Second World War, Gamma worked at his profession, doing literary research. He wrote a book on the structure of the short story which in no way betrayed his political convictions. It would have been equally difficult to discover any particularly revolutionary notions in the two volumes of verse that he published. He married, and a daughter was born to him. His life was a constant struggle against financial troubles. Because he was known to be a Communist, he could not hope for a government position, so he supported himself by occasional literary jobs. From time to time, he published a temperate article about literature in leftist publications. He awaited his hour.

That hour came shortly. Hitler attacked Poland, and

his march was swift. The Red Army moved to meet him and occupied, in accordance with the Molotov-Ribbentrop pact, those territories which the Party program had always openly proclaimed should be joined to the Union. The effect of these attacks was like that of a fire in an anthill. Thousands of hungry and frightened people clogged the roads: soldiers of the beaten army trying to get home, policemen getting rid of their uniforms, women searching for their husbands, groups of men who had wanted to fight but who had not found arms. This was a time of universal migration. Throngs of people fled from the East to German occupation in the West; similar throngs fled from the Germans to the East and Soviet rule. The end of the State was marked by a chaos that could occur perhaps only in the twentieth century.

Gamma was mobilized but he spent only a few days in the army, so quickly did defeat come. The Soviet Union magnanimously offered the city of Vilna to Lithuania, which was to enjoy the friendship of its mighty neighbor for a year before it was finally swallowed up. Gamma, craving action, moved to Lvov, the largest city under Soviet occupation. There he met other pro-Stalinist writers, and they quickly organized. With the support of the new authorities, they acquired a house in which they set up a canteen and living quarters; and there they went to work on the new type of writing—which consisted mostly of translations from Russian, or else not overly fastidious propaganda.

In these new circumstances Gamma very quickly won the trust of the literary specialists who had been sent from Russia to supervise the "cultural clean-up" of the newly acquired territories. Many of his companions, although theoretically Communist, were torn by internal conflicts. The misfortunes of their fatherland were reducing them to a state of nervous breakdown. The savagery of the conquerors and their enmity toward all Poles filled them with fear. For the first time, they were in contact with the new and ominous world which, until now, they had known only from embellished accounts. But Gamma showed no doubt; his decision was made. I am tempted to explain this on the basis of his voice and his dry, unpleasant laugh, which could lead one to suspect that his emotional life was always rather primitive. He knew anger, hatred, fear, and enthusiasm; but reflective emotion was alien to him—in this lay the weakness of his talent.

Condemned to purely cerebral writing, Gamma clung to doctrine. All he had to say could have been shouted at a meeting or printed in a propaganda leaflet. He could move forward without being swayed by any affective complications; he was able to express himself in a single tone. His success (not as a writer but as a literary politician, which is the most important type of literary success in the Stalinist system) was also promoted by his fluent knowledge of Russian. He was, after all, half-Russian, and so he could arrive more easily than others at an understanding with the new rulers. He was regarded as one of the "surest."

But most people in the newly acquired areas were not so well off. They trembled with fright. The first arrests told them to expect the worst; and their fears were well-founded for the worst came quickly, in the form of mass deportations. At dawn, agents of the NKVD knocked at the doors of houses and huts; they allowed little time for the arrested families to gather together even the most essential articles; they advised them to dress warmly. Bolted cattle cars carried away the prisoners, men, women, and children. Thousands upon thousands ebbed away to the East. Soon the number was tens of thousands, and finally hundreds of thousands. After many weeks or months of travel, the human transports arrived at their destinations: forced labor camps in the Polar regions, or collective farms in Asia. Among the deportees were Gamma's father, mother, and teen-aged sisters. The father—it is said—cursed his unnatural son who could write eulogies of the rulers who were the cause of his countrymen's sufferings. The father died somewhere in those vast expanses where a thousand miles seems a modest distance, but the mother and daughters lived on as slaves. At the time, Gamma was delivering inflammatory speeches about the great joy it was to live and work in this new and best of orders that was turning man's dreams into reality. Who can guess what he felt then? Even if he had tried to defend his family, he could not have saved them; and besides, although he was in the good books of the NKVD, he was afraid.

The Russians distrust Communists of other nationalities; and most of all, Polish Communists, as specific examples from the years 1917–39 demonstrate. Many active Polish Communists fleeing to the Soviet Union in fear of persecution were there accused of imaginary crimes and liquidated. That happened to three well-known Polish Communist poets: Wandurski, Standé, and Bruno Jasieński. Their names are never mentioned today; their works will never be re-edited. Yet once Jasieński's novel *I Burn Paris* appeared serially in France's *L'Humanité*, and he had the same international fame that Communist poets like Nazim Hikmet and Pablo Neruda enjoy today. He died in a slave labor camp near the Arctic Circle.

The wave of arrests did not by-pass the little group of "sure" individuals. Polish Communists were always suspected of nationalist tendencies. The discovery that they suffered over the plight of their nation was sufficient cause for repression. Suddenly one day, the NKVD started house-cleaning in the circle that Gamma belonged to. One of the men arrested was the famous poet W. B. If Communist authorities in France were to arrest Aragon, or if American Communists were to imprison Howard Fast, the effect on the public would be more or less the same as that created by W. B.'s arrest. He was a revolutionary poet worshipped by the entire left and too respected by everyone, even his political adversaries, to be prevented from publishing his verse. Consequently, he held an exceptional position in our country. Fleeing from German-occupied Warsaw, he had taken refuge in the Soviet zone.

After the arrest of his colleagues, Gamma succumbed to a violent attack of fear. Never before in his life had he been so frightened. He assumed that this was just the beginning and that on the next round all the writers who were still at liberty would find themselves under lock and key. Feverish and wild-eyed, he ran to his fellow Communists with a proposal for immediate preventive measures. He wanted to issue a public manifesto condemning the arrested, among them W. B., as fascists. He argued that such a manifesto, signed by scores of names, would constitute a proof of orthodoxy. But his colleagues were reluctant to make a public statement denouncing their friends as fascists. This was, in their opinion, too drastic a step. They were experienced Communists and explained to him that such a move would be politically unwise. It could only prove harmful to those who signed because it was dictated so transparently by cowardice. Besides, it was hard to foresee the shape events would take in the future. Caution was indicated. The manifesto was not issued.

At that time Gamma was just beginning his career and had not yet mastered the canons of complicated political strategy. His reactions were uncontrolled. He had yet to learn how to act with true cunning.

. . .

Then Hitler attacked Russia, and in a few days his army reached Lvov. Gamma could not remain in the city; he was too well-known as a Communist writer and speaker. In the general panic that accompanied the hasty evacuation of offices, NKVD men, and the fleeing army, he succeeded in hopping a train bound for the East. He left his wife and daughter in the city. To tell the truth, the married life of this couple left much to be desired. The wife disliked the new order, as did nearly everyone who had occasion to watch it operate. She disapproved of her husband's new career. They parted, and their separation was to prove definitive.

Gamma found himself in Russia. His years there were years of education. Many Poles who had arrived in bolted cattle cars were scattered throughout Russia at that time. Their number, including the interned soldiers and officers of the Polish army, amounted to some one and a half millions. Moscow regarded them as a hostile element and treated them accordingly. The Kremlin never, even at the time of its military setbacks, abandoned its far-sighted plans for the new Poland that was to arise in the future. Poland was the most important country in the Kremlin's calculations because it was a gangplank to Europe. Since the "cadres" of the new Poland could not be recruited from among the deportees, the Party had to use the little group of "sure" Communist intellectuals. In Russia Gamma met the university colleagues with whom he had once stood trial; and it was they, together with a few others, who founded a society nobly christened the Union of Patriots. This society became the nucleus of the government that rules in Warsaw today.

Even before the war the members of the Union of Patriots had agreed to renounce independence for their country in the name of the logic of History. While in Russia, they began to pay this price in practice, for they were not free to show any solidarity with the masses of Polish prisoners and slave laborers. The deportees (among them were not only former landowners, manufacturers, and government functionaries, but mostly poor people—peasants, woodsmen, policemen, small Jewish merchants, etc.) were nothing but human pulp. Their thinking was branded with the stamp of noble and bourgeois Poland; they invoked pre-war days as a lost paradise. What else could one do with them except keep them in labor camps or on remote collective farms? The members of the Union of Patriots could sympathize with them as people, but their sympathy was not to be permitted to influence their political decisions. In any case, typhus, hunger, and scurvy were destroying this human material so effectively that in a few years it would cease to exist as a problem.

Gamma, whose family was among the deportees, understood why they thought of pre-war Poland as a lost paradise. Their lot, though not very different materially from that of millions of Soviet citizens, was particularly hard because they were unaccustomed to hunger and a severe climate. When the London government-in-exile concluded a pact with Moscow that called for the formation of a Polish army within the Soviet Union and an amnesty for Polish political prisoners, masses of people poured out of the northern slave labor camps and rushed to the south. The corpses of these ragged beggars littered the streets of the cities of southeastern Russia. Out of the totally exhausted, half-dead people who survived the trek, an army was formed that took its orders from the exile government in London. For Gamma, as for the Russian rulers, this was the army of the class enemy; like the English and Americans, it was only a temporary ally.

The Polish command was seeking officers. Several thou-

sand Polish officers had been interned in conformance
with the Molotov-Ribbentrop pact. Now they could not
be found. Gamma knew that the London Poles' search
would not be crowned with success. This was a delicate
matter. Civilized nations do not, in general, kill interned
members of the military forces of countries they are not
even at war with; still, the logic of History sometimes demands such measures. Polish officers were the "cadre"
of the old order in Poland. Most of them were reserve officers; in civilian life they were teachers, lawyers, doctors,
government officials, in short, the intelligentsia, whose ties
to the past obstructed the way of the revolution that was
to be imposed on Poland. Considering that the Germans,
on their part, were doing an excellent job in that country
of wiping out its intelligentsia, a cadre of over ten thousand constituted an impressive number, and one was not
completely unjustified in using drastic methods to get rid
of them. Whenever they heard of the London government's fruitless efforts to find some trace of the internees,
Gamma and the other members of the Union of Patriots
exchanged ironic glances.

One of the interned officers was a young professor from
the University where Gamma and I had studied. The professor was a liberal who had commiserated with Gamma
and his comrades over their arrest. He was, however, the
author of several economic studies which presented the
Soviet Union in a none too flattering light. Somewhere in
the security files in Moscow his name had been written
down. It took a number of months before NKVD authorities identified him in a camp. Their discovery came just
in time: the telegram demanding his immediate transfer
to a prison in Moscow arrived at the railroad station where
the transports of internees were actually in the process of
being unloaded, preparatory to their being taken into the

nearby forests and shot. The professor did not share this fate because, as bureaucracy would have it, complicated cases must be studied with special diligence. After the amnesty he got out of Russia.

Many Poles who observed life in the Soviet Union at first hand underwent a change of heart. After a sojourn in prisons or labor camps, former Communists entered the army of the London government. One of those released as a result of the amnesty was the poet W. B. When the Polish army was evacuated from Russia to the Near East (later to take part in the battles in Italy), W. B. was happy to leave the country of hopes unrealized after thirty years. Yet after the end of the War, he could not bear to remain an exile. He returned to a Poland ruled by Gamma and others like him. He forgave. Today every school child learns his *Ode to Stalin* by heart.

Despite any internal vacillations or moments of despair, Gamma and his comrades in the Union of Patriots persevered. They played for high stakes, and their expectations were fulfilled. The tide of victory swung in Russia's favor. A new Polish army started to form in the Soviet Union. It was to enter Poland with the Red Army and to serve as a mainstay of the new pro-Soviet Polish government. Gamma was among the first organizers of this army. Since there were no Polish officers, the higher ranks were filled by Russians. But one could not complain of a lack of soldiers. Only a small number of the deportees had managed to make their way to Persia together with the London army. For those who were left behind the only remaining chance of salvation, that is of escape outside the borders of the Soviet Union, was enlistment in the new army politically supervised by the NKVD and the Union of Patriots.

The summer of 1944 arrived. The Red Army, and with

it the new Polish army, set foot on Polish soil. How the years of suffering, humiliation, and clever maneuvering were repaid! This was what came of betting on a good horse! Gamma joyously greeted the little towns ravaged by artillery fire, and the narrow plots of land which were a relief for the eyes after the monotonous expanses of Russian collective farms. His jeep carried him over roads bordered by the twisted iron of burnt-out German tanks toward power and the practical embodiment of what had hitherto been theoretic discussions full of citations from Lenin and Stalin. This was the reward for those who knew how to think correctly, who understood the logic of History, who did not surrender to senseless sentimentality! It was they, and not those tearful fools from London, who were bringing Poland liberation from the Germans. The nation would, of course, have to undergo a major operation; Gamma felt the excitement of a good surgeon entering the operating room.

Gamma, now a political officer with the rank of major, brought with him from Russia a new wife, a Polish soldier-wife. In uniform, wearing heavy Russian boots, she looked as if she might be of any age. In reality she was very young, but she had lived through many hardships in Russia. She was barely in her teens when she, her sister, brother, and mother were arrested and deported from the center of Europe to the Asiatic steppes. Summers there are as hot as they are in tropical countries; winters so severe that the tears that flow from the cold are instantly transformed into icicles. A loaf of bread is a small fortune; hard work breaks the strength of undernourished bodies. Police supervision and the vastness of the Asiatic continent kill all hope of escape. The young girl, a daughter of a middle-class family, was not accustomed to hard, physical toil, but she had to support her family. She succeeded after a while in entering a course on tractor driving, and after completing it she drove huge Russian tractors on the steppes of Kazakhstan. Her sympathy for the Stalinist system, after these experiences, was not great. In fact, like almost all the soldiers of the new Polish army, she had come to hate it. At last, however, she found herself in Poland, and the game for high stakes that Gamma was playing was also her game.

The Red Army reached the Vistula. The new government, which was as yet known only as the Liberation Committee, began to function in the city of Lublin. Great tasks and great difficulties faced the Union of Patriots. There was little fear that the Western allies would cause any trouble. The obstacles were of an internal nature; they sprang from the hostile attitude of the people. Once again the old conflict between two loyalties flared up. In the territories now held by the Russians large units of partisans, the so-called Home Army, affiliated with the London Government-in-Exile, had operated against the occupying Germans. Now these units were disarmed, their members drafted into the new Polish army or else arrested and deported to Russia. Gamma humorously recounted what happened in Vilna, the city of our youth. An uprising against the Germans broke out, and detachments of the Home Army entered the city simultaneously with the Russian troops. Then the Soviet command gave a magnificent banquet to which it invited the officers of the Home Army. This was, as Gamma said, a feast in the ancient Slavonic manner, a sumptuous repast during which, according to legend, midst friendly embraces, toasts, and song, invited kinsmen were quietly poisoned. In the course of the banquet, the officers of the Home Army were arrested.

From Lublin, Gamma observed that much the same

thing, but on an incomparably larger scale, was happening in Warsaw. At that time the Red Army stood on the line of the Vistula, with Warsaw on the opposite side of the river. The radio of the Liberation Committee urged the inhabitants of the capital to revolt against the Germans. Yet once the uprising broke out, the radio, receiving new instructions, began to heap abuse on the leaders. Of course: they were acting on orders from the Soviet Union's rival in the struggle for power. A feast in the Slavonic tradition was an inadequate measure in this instance; Warsaw itself, a center of opposition to the Russians just as much as to the Germans, had to be destroyed. The officers of the Red Army gazed through their binoculars at the street fighting on the other side of the river. Smoke obscured their field of vision more and more. Day after day, week after week, the battle went on, until at last the fires merged to form a wall of flame. Gamma and his friends listened to awkward accounts of what was happening in this hell, from the lips of insurgents who managed to swim across the river. Indeed, the price one had to pay to remain true to the logic of History was terrible. One had to behold passively the death of thousands, take on one's conscience the torture of women and children transformed into human torches. Who was guilty? The London Government-in-Exile because it wanted to use the uprising as a trump card in its play for power? The Kremlin because it refused to aid the stricken city out of its conviction that national independence is a bourgeois concept? Or no one?

Leaning over a table, Communist intellectuals dressed in heavy wool uniforms listened to the tale of a young girl, one of those who had succeeded in swimming the river. Her eyes were crazed, she was running a high fever as she spoke. "Our unit was smashed and pushed to the river. A few succeeded in joining other units. All of those who remained on the bank were wounded. At dawn the SS would attack. That meant that all of us would be shot. What was I to do? Remain with my wounded comrades? But I couldn't help them. I decided to swim. My chances of getting across were small because the river is lit by floodlights. There are German machine-gun nests everywhere. On the shoals in the middle of the river I saw lots of corpses of people who had tried to swim across. The current carries them to the sandbanks. I was very weak. It was hard for us to find food, and I was sick. The current is very strong. They shot at me, so I tried to swim under water as much as possible."

After two months of battle, the Germans were masters of the ruins of the city. But Communist intellectuals had too much work before them to have time to brood over the misfortunes of Warsaw. First of all, they had to set the printing presses into motion. Because Communism recognizes that rule over men's minds is the key to rule over an entire country, the word is the cornerstone of this system. Gamma became one of the chief press organizers in the city of Lublin.

In the course of these years, he became a better writer than he had been before the war. He thrived on a strict diet of the doctrine, for "socialist realism" strengthens weak talents and undermines great ones. His primitivism, of which he had long since ceased to be ashamed, now lent the semblance of sincerity to his works. His true voice, which he had once tried to smother, now spoke in his verse, sharp and clamorous. He also wrote a number of orthodox stories about the War and Nazi atrocities, all of them modeled on the pattern that was to produce thousands of pages of Russian prose.

In January 1945, the Red Army began its offensive,

crossed the Vistula and swiftly neared Berlin. Gamma also moved to the west. The Party directed him to Cracow, the city in which the greatest number of writers, scholars and artists had sought refuge after the fall of Warsaw. There he tasted the delights of dictatorship. Strange creatures dressed in remnants of furs, belted peasant jerkins and clumsy rope-laced boots began to swarm out of holes in old houses, indeed from beneath their very floors. Among them were the intellectuals who had survived the years of German occupation. Many remembered Gamma as a young pre-war poet whose works they had ignored. Now they knew he was all-powerful. On his word depended the possibility of their obtaining a chance to publish, a house, an income, a job with a newspaper, magazine, or publishing firm. They approached him apprehensively. Neither before the war nor in their underground activity were they Communist. But the new government was a fact. Nothing could prevent events from evolving as Moscow, as well as Gamma and his friends, desired. With a broad smile of friendship, he pressed the extended hands of these people and amused himself. Some were recalcitrant; some tried not to show how much his favor meant to them; some were openly servile. In a short time, he was surrounded by a court of yes-men who frowned when he frowned or guffawed loudly whenever he deigned to tell a joke.

Possibly he would not have become such a popular figure so quickly had he behaved as impetuously and brutally as before. But years of schooling stood him in good stead. Observation of life in Russia and long hours spent discussing Stalinist strategy and tactics prepared him and his companions for the work that awaited them. The first and most important maxim was not to frighten people, to appear liberal, helpful, and to give men an opportunity to earn a living while posing only minimal demands. Most people were not ready for diamat; their mentality still resembled that of the fools in the West. It would be a criminal mistake to create points of psychological resistance. The process of re-education had to be gradual and imperceptible. His second principle was to side immediately and indignantly with anyone who rebelled against the drastic methods of the government, the censors, or the political police. His third precept was to accept everyone who could be useful regardless of his political past, with the exception of confirmed fascists or Nazi collaborators.

By adhering faithfully to these principles, he brought many captives into the government camp. They became followers of the government not because they wanted to, nor even because of their public statements, but because of stern facts. The government took possession of all the printing shops and all the larger publishing firms in the country. Every writer or scholar had many manuscripts dating from the War when printing houses were inactive, and everyone was anxious to publish. From the moment his name appeared on the pages of a government-controlled periodical, from the moment his book was printed by a government-owned firm, the writer could not assert that he was hostile to the new authorities. In time, concessions were made to a few Catholic publications and to a certain number of small private publishers, but they were carefully kept as parochial as possible so as not to attract the best writers.

Not too much pressure was exerted; no great demands were made on anyone. National flags flew in the cities, and the arrests of members of the Home Army were carried out quietly. There was a determined effort to grant sufficient outlets for patriotic sentiment. The catchwords were freedom and democracy. Following Lenin's tactics, the government proclaimed a division of the landed estates among the peasants. Whoever dared to speak of collectives at that time was punished as an enemy of the people for spreading alarm and slandering the government.

Obviously, the landowners whose property was confiscated were not content. Still, most of the estates, like the factories and mines, had been placed under compulsory German management during the Nazi occupation and their owners had been, in effect, dispossessed. The peasants' class hatred of the manor was not violent in our country so the expelled proprietors were not harmed. City-dwellers felt no particular sympathy for that feudal group of landholders; in fact, no one was upset by their loss of power. As for the intellectuals, they thought it just that factories and mines should become the property of the state. We must remember that five and a half years of Nazi rule had obliterated all respect for private property. A radical agricultural reform also seemed, in general, justified. The intellectuals were concerned about something else, about the boundaries of freedom of speech. At the time, they were rather broad. One thing was certain: one was not free to write anything that might cast aspersion on the institutions of the Soviet Union. The censors made sure that this rule was strictly enforced. However, praise of Russia was not, as later, obligatory; one could remain silent on the subject. Outside this sphere, writers were given considerable freedom.

In spite of everything, the entire country was gripped by a single emotion: hatred. Peasants, receiving land, hated; workers and office employees, joining the Party, hated; socialists, participating nominally in the government, hated; writers, endeavoring to get their manuscripts published, hated. This was not their own government; it owed its existence to an alien army. The nuptial bed prepared for the wedding of the government with the nation was decked with national symbols and flags, but from beneath that bed protruded the boots of an NKVD agent.

The people who fawned on Gamma also hated. He knew it, and this was the source of not the least of his pleasures. He would hit sore-spots, and then observe the reactions of his listeners. The terror and fury that appeared on their faces would give way, in an instant, to an ingratiating smile. This was as it should be. He held these people in his hand. A stroke of his pencil could remove their articles or poems from the page proofs of a magazine; his word could cause their books to be rejected by a publishing house. They had to behave themselves. Yet even as he played with them, he was friendly and helpful; he allowed them to earn a living, he watched over their careers.

I met him in Cracow. Many years had elapsed since our discussions in the *mensa*—during one I had deliberately thrown a box of matches into his soup and since he was subject to attacks of rage, the incident had ended in fisticuffs. In the intervening years I had completed my studies in Paris, and later lived in Warsaw. I left our university city because I was thrown out of my job at the request of the city administration. I was suspected of Communist sympathies (it seems that differentiation between the Stalinist and anti-Stalinist left presents insurmountable difficulties to all the police in the world) and of being too well-disposed toward the Lithuanians and Byelorussians. The latter suspicion was completely justified. Now I was a refugee from Warsaw. My fortune consisted of the work-clothes I was wearing plus a hemp sack which contained my manuscripts, shaving kit and a two-penny edition of Gay's *The Beggar's Opera*. From the point of view of the Soviet Union's interests, I did not deserve anything for what I had done during the War; on the contrary, I had committed certain sins. Nevertheless, now I was needed and useful; my record from the period of German occupation was not so bad; my pen could be of value to the new order.

My meeting with Gamma was almost friendly. Two dogs—rather stiff, yet courteous. We were on our guard lest we bare our teeth. He remembered the literary rivalry between us which had formerly caused him so much vexation; he also remembered my open letter against the Stalinists, which had placed me more or less in the position of present-day Western dissidents. Still he had a sentimental attachment—as did I—toward his former university comrades. This helped to break the ice. That meeting was the first move in a game between us that was to last a long time.

This game was not limited to the two of us. All the intellectuals who had remained in Poland during the Nazi occupation were teamed against the group that had returned from the East. The division was clear. Much more important matters than mere personal rivalry were at stake. After the experiences of the War, none of us, not even former nationalists, doubted the necessity of the reforms that were being instituted. Our nation was going to be transformed into a nation of workers and peasants and that was right. Yet the peasant was not content even though he was given land; he was afraid. The worker had not the slightest feeling that the factories belonged to him, even though he worked to mobilize them with much self-denial, and even though the propaganda assured him that they were his. Small contractors and merchants trembled at the knowledge that they were destined to be exterminated as a group.

This was, indeed, a peculiar Revolution; there was not

even a shadow of revolutionary dynamics in it; it was carried out entirely by official decree. The intellectuals who had spent the War in Poland were particularly sensitive to the temper of the country. Gamma and his friends glibly ascribed the mood of the people to a "survival of bourgeois consciousness," but this formula failed to encompass the truth. The masses felt that *nothing* depended on them, and that nothing ever would. Henceforth all discussion would serve merely to justify the Center's decisions. Should one resist? But in a system in which everything gradually becomes the property of the state, sabotage strikes at the interests of the entire population. Only mental opposition was possible; and the intellectuals, at least the majority of them, felt very deeply that this was their duty. By publishing articles and books they satisfied the fisherman. The fish swallowed the bait and, as we know, when that happens one should slacken the line. The line remained slack; and until the fisherman resolved to pull out the fish, certain valuable cultural activities went on that were impossible in such countries, for example, as the Baltic states which were directly incorporated into the Union. The question was how long this state of affairs could continue. It might easily last five, ten, or even fifteen years. This was the only game that was possible. The West did not count, and the political emigration mattered even less.

Certain personal factors, however, entered into the game between Gamma and me. His solicitude toward the members of our old group was not motivated entirely by fond memories of our university days. He could never free himself of a feeling of guilt that dated back to his childhood; and only by converting those of us who were not Stalinists could he feel that his past actions were at last justified. The trouble was that he was deeply pessimistic about the future of mankind, whereas those whom he tried to convert were not. Loyal to the Center, he voiced official optimism, while in reality, after the years he had spent in Russia, he was convinced that History is the private preserve of the devil, and that whoever serves History signs a satanic pact. He knew too much to retain any illusions and despised those naïve enough to nourish them. To bring new damned into the fold was his one means of reducing the number of internally free people, who, by the mere fact of their existence, judged him.

Nor was our game played only within the confines of Poland. With Gamma's assistance, George, who became a Catholic poet, was sent to France as a cultural attaché; and I was appointed cultural attaché to the United States. A sojourn abroad presented important advantages. From that distance, I could publish impudent articles and poems whose every word was an insult to the Method. Whenever I felt that the line was too taut, I would write something that could be interpreted as a sign of approaching conversion. Gamma wrote me warm, lying letters. Both of us committed errors. He knew that the risk of my defecting was not great. Almost more than anyone else, I felt tied to my country. I was a poet; I could write only in my native tongue; and only in Poland was there a public—made up chiefly of young people—with which I could communicate. He knew that I was afraid to become an exile, afraid to condemn myself to the sterility and the vacuum that are proper to every emigration. But he overestimated my attachment to a literary career. On the other hand, I knew that his letters were false, but I could not renounce the idea that there was at least an iota of sincerity in his professions of friendship. I also believed that he was sufficiently intelligent not to expect me to sign the pact as he did. But I was wrong, for the day came when he decided to convert me by both trickery and force. His dagger missed me, which is why I am free to write this portrait.

Gamma, too, went abroad. He left Poland after the initial post-war disorder had been mastered. A period of relative stability was in sight. The Peasant Party had to be eliminated and the Socialist Party absorbed, but these operations did not promise to be too troublesome. In general this was to be the era of the NEP. Liberalism was the word in cultural matters. Gamma, believing he needed a bit of peace after the nervous tension of the last years, took a post in the diplomatic service.

He sent his new wife to school in Switzerland to learn foreign languages and proper manners. In a very short time she was transformed from a soldier-bride wearing clumsy Russian boots into a doll with bleached hair and long, painted eyelashes. She became very chic, and dressed in the finest Paris fashions. He, meanwhile, devoted much of his time to writing. He wrote a novel about the trial of the group of young Stalinists in our university city, the trial in which he himself had been a defendant. It was published at once, and favorably reviewed. Still, it was not so warmly praised as one might have expected. "Socialist realism" had not yet made Polish prose sterile; whereas his book was one of those ideological exercises called novels in Russia.

When we were young, Vilna was an unusually picturesque city, not only because of its architecture or its setting amidst forests and hills, but also because of the number of languages and cultures that co-existed there. None of this found its way into his novel. Colorless, unable to evoke tangible things, his prose was merely a tool with which to etch in events and people. Events and people did not fare very well, however. Recognizing real persons in his heroes, I could see how inaccurately he drew his characters. A novelist often modifies the people he has known; he concentrates his colors, selects and stresses those psychological traits which are most characteristic. When a writer strives to present reality most faithfully he becomes convinced that untruth is at times the greatest truth. The world is so rich and so complex that the more one tries not to omit any part of the truth, the more one uncovers wonders that elude the pen.

Gamma's inaccuracy was of a different order. In accordance with the Method, he created abstract political types. Into these prefabricated forms he tried to squeeze living people; if they did not fit, he unhesitatingly chopped off their legs or their heads. Stefan and Henryk, his heroes, were reduced to the sum total of their political activity. But knowing them well, I know how complicated their personalities were. Henryk, who died before a German firing squad, was an unhappy man, internally at war with himself; he was the most glaring and tragic example of a Polish Communist torn between two loyalties. Stefan, who after his return from Moscow became one of the dictators of Poland's economy, was always a riddle to me. Now a heavy-set, sullen man, a perfect prototype of the Soviet official, he had changed completely from the days when he had hesitated about embracing Stalinism. I knew him when he used to write poems and intelligent literary essays. Then, he was a young Faust—drunk with the beauty of the world, ironic, brilliant, and rapacious. Gamma's novel was entitled *Reality*, but there was little reality in it. It was a travesty on pre-war Poland that attempted, unsuccessfully, to present as demons the rather inefficient police and the sluggish judges of that time.

After completing his novel, Gamma began to feel somewhat bored. He started to travel. He visited many European countries, he went to Africa. Once, as we debated in the *mensa,* we used to dream of traveling. Our doubts as to whether we would ever realize our dreams turned out to have been unnecessary; we were to come to know this type of diversion all too well. The pleasures he got out of traveling were not, it seems, overly refined. He had little appreciation for architecture and art; he had no great curiosity about patterns of life in different civilizations. Had it been otherwise, he would have been a better writer. Travel for him was a pleasant way of killing time and of satisfying the youthful ambitions of a former provincial.

Outside of travel, his greatest pleasure was to play games with foreigners. Their conviction that he was basically "liberal" was not too far from the truth. The outrage with which he stormed against certain overly brutal methods of Stalinism cannot be described as completely false. He considered himself a servant of the devil that ruled History, but he did not love his master. By rebelling against him he not only eased his own internal tension, but won a good opinion for himself in the West. His demon-lord was lenient, granting him the delights of sporadic mutiny —just so long as it was useful. Gamma, observing the faces before him, smiled at people's credulity.

Whenever he was not busy with diplomatic duties, receptions, or the political training of his personnel, he gave bridge parties. He was an excellent, and a fanatic bridge player. He complained that he was too tired after work to do anything except play cards, that diplomacy kept him from writing. Actually, this was not quite true. At an early age he had already reached the summit of his career. Had he so wished he could have become a minister of state in a country where a minister is ruled by the decisions of the Central Committee of the Party. He was a member of the Central Committee. What next? During his stay in the lovely Western capital, he took stock and discovered he had nothing. Well might he cry, "Qu'as-tu fait, toi que voilà, de ta jeunesse?" What, indeed, had he done with his youth? Where was there something he could call his own and not just the product of historic determinism? He was nearing forty, and he was clear-sighted. The old feeling of literary defeat was returning. He felt as empty as a sieve with a wind blowing through it. That wind of historic necessity swept all the meaning out of literature. One more astute ideological equation, several more pages of doctrinal prose! Why write when everyone knew in advance exactly what was to be said? He played bridge in his gilded and mirrored salon not because he was tired but because he was afraid to find himself alone before a sheet of blank paper.

Gradually he grew accustomed to this mode of life. But the Party does not like comfort to become a habit. Changes were occurring in Poland. At last strict orthodoxy was required of all writers. Gamma was needed on the spot. He left his eighteenth-century palace and the beautiful Western capital with sorrow. He knew that Eastern world to which he was returning much too well. Fierce battles and intrigues, constant dread of Moscow's frown awaited him. Sorrow was pointless; he had to go.

The position he received upon his return was higher than the rank of ambassador to a major Western country. He became, this time officially, the political overseer of all the writers, the keeper of their consciences. It was his duty to make certain that Polish literature developed in harmony with the Party line. The government had just offered the Writers' Union a newly constructed building in Warsaw that housed a huge modern amphitheatre, conference rooms, offices, a restaurant, and living quarters for writers. That was where he officiated, attending numerous conferences with writers, publishers, security police, and representatives of kindred unions.

He was given an apartment in a government building reserved for higher dignitaries. Admission to this block of apartments is possible only after a previous arrangement by telephone. But these telephone numbers are not listed in the directory; they are issued only to trusted individuals. The member of the security police at the entrance telephones upstairs to verify whether the meeting was actually agreed upon; after which he takes the guest's personal papers and permits him to enter.

Gamma was right in foreseeing a period of intrigue. In general, he had little to fear from other writers because he was, hierarchically speaking, their superior; although even among them there were certain dangerous individuals who were stronger in dialectical materialism than he, and more rabbinical in their mentality. The real struggle for power was waged higher up, in the top brackets of the Party. There he had many enemies. Despite his long years of training, the fiery squire in him would still fall into a rage whenever someone crossed him. In such moments, he treated people as he would servants in his private manor. As ambassador, he could permit himself such brutality without fear of reprisal, but now it caused him trouble. Besides, the line had stiffened so much in Poland that a single sincere word, even if it was uttered only to win converts, could give rise to fatal consequences. Shortly after his return, he made one of the gravest blunders of his political career. This occurred at a meeting which took place directly after the outbreak of the war in Korea. Gamma, replying to "whispered propaganda," shouted heatedly, "Yes, we attacked first, because we are stronger."

It took a lot of work to patch up the damage caused by his unfortunate outburst. As we know, according to the official line, North Korea was attacked.

He also had to settle down seriously to his writing. Only an "active" writer can be a member of the Writers' Union. Every author is compelled to publish under threat of expulsion from the Union and consequent loss of all his privileges. The obligation to keep active is doubly binding on the bosses.

Someone in Warsaw said of Gamma, "He fights this war against imperialism and Western propaganda in the cause of peace, but he dreams of one thing: war. For if the war broke out, then there would be speeches, airplane flights, news reports from the front; and he wouldn't have to sit down every day behind his desk and torture himself over a novel. But just for spite, there will be peace; and he'll have five desks in that elegant apartment of his, and on each one, the beginning of a novel. And every day he'll howl with despair knowing that everything he writes is as dead as a stone."

One cannot envy this man his choice. Looking at his country, he knows that an ever greater dose of suffering awaits its people. Looking at himself, he knows that not one word he pronounces is his own. I am a liar, he thinks, and makes historical determinism responsible for his lies. But sometimes he is haunted by the thought that the devil to whom men sell their souls owes his might to men themselves, and that the determinism of History is a creation of human brains.

ΛΛΛΛΛΛΛΛΛΛΛΛΛΛΛΛΛΛΛΛΛΛΛΛΛ

CHAPTER VII

Delta, the Troubadour

IN Central and Eastern Europe, the word "poet" has a somewhat different meaning from that which it has in the West. There a poet does not merely arrange words in beautiful order. Tradition demands that he be a "bard," that his songs linger on many lips, that he speak in his poems of subjects of interest to all the citizens. Every period of history has understood the poet's obligations differently. Probably Delta would have been happiest in the days when kings and nobles assured the poet a place at their table in exchange for a song or a jest. Even the dress of former ages would have suited his appearance better than the business suit of our century; and only long hair and a lute in his hand could have created a picture in keeping with his character.

Delta had dark, gypsy coloring, was freckled, not tall, and when he laughed his thick mouth was distorted by a jocular grimace. He brushed his hair back from a high forehead. His head was so disproportionately big for his short body that he looked somehow like a dwarf or jester, as one sees them in court paintings. He wore his neckties in a loose, big knot and otherwise betrayed a penchant for eccentric clothes. Often, those who resort to superficial quirks to identify themselves as members of the artistic clan are second-rate artists. But his "artiness" was part of his over-all act. With every gesture, every intonation of his voice, he played, so to speak, with the world; he accented the difference between his own rhythm and that of his environment. His rhythm was suggestive. He recited his verse magnificently in huge halls filled with people. He was a good actor; he dominated the audience, and he knew how to key his listeners up to a climax without once letting the mounting tension drop. He imposed his poems slowly, pausing between words; and though he was speaking, he sang. At such times, he was a living rhythmic incantation; he changed, he grew in stature.

No one knows his origins. He altered his biography to fit the needs of the moment. Once his father was a sexton; once, a restaurant owner. At times his family was Czech; at times it had Muscovite connections. The boundaries between fantasy and truth did not exist for him.

How he came by his knowledge of foreign languages was another mystery. It would be hard to imagine him sitting down to a dictionary and a grammar. Yet he cited copiously from Latin, English, French, and German poets. For a short while he studied at the University, where he became famous for writing an essay on a seventeenth-century English poet who never existed. After giving an extensive biography of the poet, the essay went on to a detailed analysis of the circumstances in which his individual works appeared. A charlatan, a hoaxer—this is what he wanted to be then, and always, enjoying himself mightily when his pedantic professor found himself in trouble, overwhelmed by such obvious proof of erudition.

Delta was an inveterate alcoholic, usually in cycles that lasted several days. Alcohol brought him to a state of hallucination marked by actions which rarely occur to other drunkards. In a travel bureau he would order a glass of beer. He would hire a hack, order it to stop at a main intersection and, after delivering a speech to an astonished crowd, he would throw off his coat and phlegmatically relieve himself on it. Or he would come to his friends complaining that he had had trouble in finding their homes because, as he said, "his people," whom he had stationed throughout the city to point him the way, had so disguised themselves that he could not recognize them. Such extravagances indicated that alcohol plunged him into the world of Hoffmann or Edgar Allan Poe. He became a legendary figure whose latest escapades were the talk of the literary cafés.

Delta's poetry was an added source of legend. It was unlike anything written in Europe in the first half of the twentieth century. No literary school influenced him. He dwelt in the aura of the Italo-Latin civilization whose mark was still deeply graven on our country. The accessories he borrowed from the poetry of the past he then put together in a manner reminiscent of his drunken fantasies. His poetry was a kaleidoscope of chubby baroque angels, magicians carried off through the window by some unknown power (they are retained, at the last moment by a wifely bite on the ear), falconry, astrologists prophesying the end of the world. Interspersed in it were phonograph records playing the music of Bach or Mozart, potatoes in the soil dreaming of the vodka that would be made of them, planets in the shape of young women dressed in blue pants, and folk dances in the suburbs. His poetry was tragic and comic, senseless yet full of sense. This alogical hodgepodge of disparate elements differed from confessedly decadent types of modern poetry in one respect: despite the peculiar assemblage of images it presented, it was not unintelligible. The reader surrendered to its musical charm, swallowed portions of abstraction that annoyed him in other poets, laughed at the sudden twists of the author, in short, unsuspectingly entered a realm ruled by laws unlike those of everyday life.

He published much humorous verse, signing it with a variety of pseudonyms. His inventiveness in finding subjects seemed inexhaustible. Among other things, he wrote a cycle entitled *Little Songs of the Chief of the Office of Graves*. He liked to include a fictitious list of his works in each book; I remember such a title as "An Introduction to Cannibalism—stenographed university lectures: Troilus Drug Store, Publisher, out of print." Because he was popular with the readers, he never lacked offers from publishers and the radio. His pen, which was his sole means of support, could have earned him a good living; but he constantly needed money because he immediately drank up his fees.

When he was sober, no one could have guessed that he was the author of poems that made the public laugh. Taciturn, gloomy, sly, he became animated only at the sight of money. In bargaining, he was inexorable. Once he named a sum, no argument could induce him to make a concession. What was worse, he demanded payment at once, which posed a terrible dilemma for his editors. They wanted his poems; but giving him money involved the risk that he would begin his drinking cycle and forget his commitments. Some editors found a solution: they would give him the money, then refuse to leave him for a single second until he handed them a manuscript. Such transactions often occurred in coffee-houses. The banknote would lie on the table between the two contracting parties. Delta, after fruitless efforts to soften his opponent, would take out his pen, write the poem (which, depending on his mood, might be excellent or mediocre), and picking up his note go off to drink.

Sometimes he landed in a sanatorium for alcoholics. The results of the "cures" were not good. His victories in his battles against the medical profession were widely recounted. In one of the sanatoriums, story has it, his triumph was so absolute that both patients and doctors, equally drunk, held bicycle races through the corridors.

Charlatan, drunkard—and yet he was an outstanding and, despite appearances, tragic poet. He began his literary career in years of economic crisis. Unemployment, universal hopelessness, the growth of Nazism in neighboring Germany all shaped the character of his writing. He was rightly called the "king of nonsense." Yet readers who were not deceived by his superficial buffoonery saw in his poetry an ominous vision of the end of civilization, of an approaching "iron age," of catastrophe. He spoke as if everything were lost years before Europe plunged into darkness and cruelty. The dread and beauty of past ages lived again in his work, but there was no hope of rest in them. The concepts and images he used had the consistency of dreams; they chased one another with the speed of a hurtling train. The Madonna who often figured in his poems was not the Madonna of the pious but merely a stylistic ornament. Fascists and Communists killed each other off in his verse with the gory ardor of actors in the Grand Guignol, while he mockingly cried: "O reality! O my sweet mother! For you killing flies is the same kind of bother!" He defined himself exactly when he said: "Braced on my Waterman/ I go off to the abyss/ of eternal doubt."

The End of the World is his title for a poem in which scholars and politicians, revolutionists, lovers and drunkards, canaries and cats are all swept away in the end by a cosmic catastrophe—to the satisfaction of the author, and the fulfillment of the "vanity of vanities" theme of *Ecclesi-*

astes. And all this is described by a pen that is playing. In another of his poems, *Folk Fair,* there are carrousels, young pairs sitting on the grass, lawns littered with empty bottles, seesaws. Suddenly the sky clouds over, rain begins to fall, and the darkened heavens—in a manner that is a secret of Delta's art—merge into a sad eclogue by Virgil punctuated by the bark of machine-guns.

His most unusual poem was *Solomon's Ball.* Why does King Solomon give a ball? Why is he living in the twentieth century? Perhaps it is not King Solomon after all, simply Solomon? Why do the unemployed enter the ballroom selling butterflies? Who keeps singing Persian songs about Gulistan, the garden of roses? Where do the hordes of policemen come from who suddenly start performing wild dances? It is pointless to pause over such questions. The special logic of the dream does exist, but only such a poet as he can use it freely. "In the room the women come and go talking of Michelangelo" was T. S. Eliot's expression for nonsense. Delta raised the conversations that took place at Solomon's ball one degree higher, into the realm of delirium and "eternal doubt."

The world as reflected in his poetry was oppressive; yet his poems—and here is one more inner contradiction of this queer man—were free of sadness and despair. On the contrary, they said a vigorous "yes" to life. With every word he praised the world as he saw it, a tangle of absurd pleasures, drives, words, and wars. He loved his phantasmagory. He loved carrousels, dancing gypsies, crowded Sunday excursion boats on the Vistula, his wife to whom he addressed his odes, cats sleeping on parapets, blooming apple trees. He loved enthusiasm and joyousness for their own sake. Whatever he touched changed into a scene of movement, color, and music. Subjects were merely a pretext for him. Like a silkworm, he spun out of himself a

fine thread which he wrapped around whatever he encountered. He could compose songs and hymns on any
topic.

Never displaying any political inclinations, he had always distributed his mockery evenly over all the groups
that were vying for power. That is why his conversion,
in 1937, to extreme nationalism was received with some
amazement. The editor of an important rightist weekly
had long tried to capture him, and at last he succeeded in
purchasing him as the exclusive property of the periodical.
The magazine on whose pages his poems now began to
appear was violently anti-Semitic. Its large circulation figures resulted from the spread of nationalist convictions in
our country, particularly among the youth. The liberal
public could hardly believe this new phase of his shenani-
gans: he lauded the marching "falangists," prophesied a
"night of long knives," a new St. Bartholomew's Eve for
the Jews, liberals, and the left. Still, it was obviously a fact;
such articles and poems did appear, signed by his name
and bearing all the traits of his style.

Why did he write them? Racial questions were of supreme indifference to him. He had many Jewish friends,
and the very day he published his racist statements, he
would come to these friends (naturally he was drunk by
then) and, falling on his knees, would declare his love for
them and beg their forgiveness. The causes of his union
with the right must be sought elsewhere than in his political tastes. Delta, buffoon and troubadour, did not lack professional principles. He respected his poetic trade; but his
respect was not for what he wrote about. How and for
whom—that was important. He scorned esoteric literary
schools that catered to a small cluster of connoisseurs. He
ridiculed poets whose words could be understood only by
a smattering of intellectuals. Solitary meditations that had

no hope of finding readers were not for him. Like troubadours of yore, he longed for a lute and a throng of admirers. It would be hard to find a better example of a writer revolting against the isolation of the intellectual in the twentieth century.

Delta's hostility toward the Jews had no racial roots; he confined it to Jewish writers who, in general, were particularly given to celebration of literary "values" and "refinements." It sprang from his battle against, and struggle to escape from, the literary cafés. Besides, as I have said, he was for enthusiasm. The crowd marched, the crowd brandished canes; this was health, strength, primitiveness, a great popular festival. Where my readers go, there go I; what my readers want, I give them—this is what he confirmed in every poem. As the nationalist "movement" began to take on mass proportions, he moved to keep in stride with the masses. He told with pride of the thousands of young people who knew his verses by heart. His pride was justified. The poets of the sophisticated "avantgarde," isolated as they were, took pride in their craft; but he beat them even on their own ground. Nor did they dispose over such a range of artistic media as he did. Last of all, we must consider that in order to live he needed a patron, a person who would force him to write, fight his drunkenness and, in short, control and care for him.

The War broke out. He was mobilized as a private. His unit was stationed in eastern Poland, on the borders of the Soviet Union. When the Reds moved to meet the German army, he was captured by the Russians. But along with a number of other disarmed Polish soldiers, Delta was turned over to the Germans. He spent the next five and a half years in a POW camp in the Reich. As a prisoner he was used for various types of work, chiefly agricultural. His qualifications for physical labor were slight. It is hard even to imagine a man less prepared for a mode of life in which the most important and almost unsolvable problem was how to fill one's stomach. Still, he survived, this strange court dwarf in tatters, wielding a shovel as he recited Horace. Undoubtedly, his fluent knowledge of German came to his assistance.

Meanwhile, terror ruled in Warsaw. Those who only a short while before had used the Germans as a model now became hunted prey. The rightist editor who had been Delta's patron became one of the most active workers in the Underground. He was a fanatical patriot. I still remember him as I saw him for the last time, in the coffeehouse that was the base of his underground group and of the publication he issued. His thin Jewish face (like many anti-Semites in our country, he was half-Jewish) was undermined with fury, fever burned in his eyes, his tight lips urged immediate action. Shortly thereafter, the Gestapo came upon the trail of his organization. The entire personnel of the café, made up of his closest co-workers, was arrested; the editor himself spent a long time in prison in Warsaw before a heavily guarded van carried him away for his last ride. He was shot in the woods near Warsaw: sand, pines, words of command. Still, his was a kindly form of death. He would have fared worse had he shared the lot of the three million Jews of Poland among which he, as a half-Jew, could have been counted. In that case, he would have found himself in the ghetto that was created in Warsaw in 1940 by order of the occupying authorities. From there, he would certainly have been sent, like the others, to the gas chamber.

The nationalist "movement," marching columns, the excited crowd! The crushing defeat of 1939 frustrated all this, leaving only the bitter memory of human insanity. The Nazis carried the anti-Semitic program into practice.

but no longer as a boycott of Jewish stores or an annoyance of Jewish vendors, nor even as literary bouts like Delta's. To write of the tragedy of the Warsaw ghetto, to which I was an eyewitness, is hard for me. The vision of the burning ghetto is too welded into all I lived through in my adult years for me to speak of it quietly. But I should like to describe one incident. Often, as I am sitting on the terrace of a Paris café or walking through the streets of a large city, I succumb to a certain obsession. I look at the women who pass, at their luxuriant hair, their proudly lifted chins, their slender throats whose lines awaken delight and desire—and then I see before my eyes always the same young Jewish girl. She was probably about twenty years old. Her body was full, splendid, exultant. She was running down the street, her hands raised, her chest thrust forward. She cried piercingly, "No! No! No!" The necessity to die was beyond her comprehension—a necessity that came from outside, having nothing in common with her unprepared body. The bullets of the SS guards' automatic pistols reached her in her cry.

The moment when bullets pierce the flesh is a moment of amazement for the body. Life and death mingle for a second, before a bloody rag falls to the pavement and is kicked aside by an SS boot. This girl was not the first nor the last of the millions who were killed in the period when the life-force within them was at its height. But the obstinacy with which this image returns—and always when I am drunk with the beauty of being alive amidst living human beings—merits some reflection. This is perhaps a matter that belongs to the same sphere as do the collective sex orgies of some primitive tribes. At such times, this or another object of desire are the same, all women and men are fused by a great feeling of communion through which everyone belongs to all. Monogamy can give no outlet to such urges. In other words, this is a profound basis for love of mankind, a love one cannot really conceive of if, looking at a group of laughing women, one does not recall this young Jewish girl as *one of them,* as identical and ever present. One of the best poems Delta wrote about his stay in Germany was on the death of a young Venetian girl, arrested and deported to the Reich. This was an erotic poem; the Venetian girl appeared in it not as an individual but as the beauty of youth, as the charm of breasts, arms, hands, thighs destroyed by death.

In 1945 he and his fellow prisoners welcomed the arrival of the British troops. Since they were accompanied by units of the London Polish army, he entered upon a round of encounters, drinking, and song. Having dried up those springs of money and alcohol, he set out for France. Once again, as in 1939, this was an era of universal wandering. All of Europe was on the road; millions of forced laborers, prisoners, and slaves were returning to their homes; other millions were fleeing or being expelled from their native lands. Delta met large numbers of Poles everywhere. He wrote patriotic and anti-Russian poems that harmonized perfectly with the mood of his audience. He squeezed money out of every variety of émigré committee. His pre-war admirers, rejoicing that he had survived, did everything they could for him.

Gradually, however, his life in Paris and Brussels lost its charm. The possibilities of publishing were small; the public was dispersed over various countries; and there was ever less money. He felt he was becoming an ordinary impoverished exile whose buffoonery, personal and poetic, passed unnoticed. Gloomy, bitter emigration, a void, and a taste of disaster. Where was the mass of people which could give him back warmth and friendship? It was in his native land. There, too, was his wife, who had lived through the German occupation working as a waitress in Warsaw restaurants. Publications that came from Poland persuaded him that the trend was liberal. The envoys of the Warsaw government assured him that he would be received warmly and that his pre-war rightist sins would be forgotten.

His return to Poland was accomplished with every prescribed scandal. From the moment he left the boat, he was in a state of alcoholic and patriotic euphoria. He sent telegrams to his wife from every railroad station. When at last he showed up in Cracow (where his wife had gone after the fall of Warsaw), in the company of a girl friend he had brought from Brussels, his wife immediately instituted sharp repressive measures and threw out the girl. His wife came of a Georgian émigré family. She was small, thin, and black-haired; she had oriental features, a slightly humped prominent nose, and fiery black eyes. She liked to wear silver bracelets on her fine wrists. In all, she looked like a Caucasian madonna. Though she was passive and female, she had a good head for business and a gift for keeping her husband in hand.

Delta's return was convenient for those who directed literature and propaganda. He was a popular poet. That he was known as a rightist only enhanced his value. He was a considerably greater asset to the new regime than many overly zealous leftists.

He had always needed a patron; now he found one who was really munificent, the state. His became a truly golden pen; its every motion—he wrote in big, decorative letters on long scrolls of paper—brought him larger fees than he had ever earned before. Moreover, his verbal enthusiasm, without which he could not live, now rested on a solid foundation. There were no longer "falangists" nor crowds excited against racial minorities; but there was the rebuilding of the country and the placating of national honor through the acquisition of territories in the West which originally belonged to Germany. His poems were always sunny no matter what he wrote about. That was good. Now he filled them with optimistic subject matter, with pictures of reconstruction and of the happy future; and that was even better. Since he had no trouble in finding remuncrative outlets, he went wild. Odes, satiric verse, humorous prose, dialogues flowed from his workshop in an unbroken torrent. One magazine gave him a whole column in which, every week, he lodged his "theatrical pieces." These were short, little scenes from what he called the "smallest theater in the world," the *Green Goose*. In no other language have I read such pure absurdity. The heroes of the *Green Goose* were people, animals, and objects. The readers who attended these weekly performances of his cabaret were a little ashamed of their liking for these oddities, but they pounced on every issue of the magazine.

His activity was the subject of much controversy. Those who wanted to be considered "sure" and those who took their Marxism seriously were indignant. How could one, they asked, permit this clown to run riot as if he were in a Parisian existentialist café? He was a petty bourgeois who had gone mad. Why print his poems on the front pages of leading magazines; why allow him to have a career? Everybody remembered his anti-Semitic days, when he threatened his colleagues with a "night of long knives"! Now, no one was so well off as he. Wasn't this disgraceful?

Experienced members of the Party quieted the outraged puritans, smiling indulgently at their naïveness. Delta was needed and useful *at that stage*. He had many followers; everything he wrote helped create an atmosphere of patriotism. It was politic to show that even rightists and Catholics had joined forces with the government. The reading public was not as yet ready for serious, sensible literature. At the moment, Delta's farces best suited its taste. All this was a game, for a time; and then—off with his head.

When Poland was at last obliged to pass from restrained worship of Russia to outright idolatry, he let no one outdo him. He wrote of the heroism of Soviet soldiers, of the gratitude every Pole should feel toward Russia, of Lenin, of Komsomol youth. He adhered to the Communist line in every respect. As an eminent author, he received a Soviet visa and spent some time in Moscow, sending back enthusiastic reports in prose and verse. In one he announced that the magnificence of Moscow was marred by but a single flaw: it was too much like Taormina; people ate just as many oranges there, and he didn't like oranges.

His correspondence from Moscow drove the puritans crazy. They knew that Moscow was a gloomy and rather forbidding city. His raptures bore all the traits of derision. They seemed to say: "You want me to sing praises; very well, I'll sing praises till they come out of your ears." Still, it was not easy to guess his real intentions. It was impossible to tell whether he was lying or telling the truth. Normal criteria did not apply to him. He moved in a different dimension. Like a prestidigitator, he always pulled the proper number of rabbits out of his hat, and all of them rabbits of the required color. He invariably transformed everything into *opéra bouffe*. Because he constantly used exaggeration as his artistic tool, his opponents could prove nothing against him. He neither mocked nor spoke the truth; he performed tricks, he practiced art for art's sake.

He was never "serious." And as we know, this is the

basic requirement of socialist realism. After the writers' congresses at which socialist realism was proclaimed the sole creative method allowed, the partisans of gravity began their action against him, sure now that they could take their revenge. Analyzing his poetry, they proved that the world for him was nothing but a toy to play with. Once, before the war, he had written *An Elegy on the Death of a Butterfly Run Over by a Freight Van*. Despite its long title, the elegy consisted of four lines which concluded that the thoughtless butterfly richly deserved its fate. Now he found himself under the wheels of the van. The period of austerity and precision was beginning. He could write on every subject, from the Madonna to Lenin and Moscow, just so long as his master demanded his services. Yet his poems never lacked spontaneity. They were always exuberant; but we must add that in them the Madonna as well as Lenin and Moscow became something unreal, a kind of theater in the clouds. Now, however, "the struggle against the spontaneity of the creative process" had become the slogan, which meant that it was no longer enough to write on prescribed subjects; one had to write in a prescribed manner.

Delta wanted to serve his lord. In order to exist as a poet he needed a genial, amused *seigneur* who believed that neither his government nor anything in heaven or on earth deserves to be taken too seriously, that song—half serious, half scoffing—matters more. But such princes have long since ceased to be. The lord who held him in thrall tolerated him for a while not because his songs were pleasing, for song is merely a means to an end. It was when his songs no longer served the desired end that his master knit his brows in anger. Publishers were instructed to print only those of his poems in which he demonstrated that he had reformed. The puritans rubbed their hands in glee. At last they had wrung his neck. They knew that no matter how he tried he could not reform. Deprived of their former exuberance, his poems no longer differed from verse ground out by second-rate rhymesters.

Thus he entered the realm of living shadows. Nothing should be wasted, however, in a socialist economy. Men who have fulfilled their role can find work enough for their capacities. Delta's existence was assured; a state publishing house commissioned him to do a translation of *A Midsummer Night's Dream*.

Some two years after his fall from grace he has been given another chance. At this writing, all his past sins are being discussed openly in the leading literary weekly. This is a sort of trial, with a favorable verdict prepared in advance. Delta will return to favor once more; but once more, it will be only for a time.

CHAPTER VIII

Man, This Enemy

WHOEVER reads the public statements of the four writers discussed in the previous chapters might say that they sold themselves. The truth is, however, more involved. These men are, more or less consciously, victims of a historic situation. Consciousness does not help them to shed their bonds; on the contrary, it forges them. At the very best, it can offer them the delights of Ketman as a consolation. Never before has there been such enslavement through consciousness as in the twentieth century. Even my generation was still taught in school that reason frees men.

In the people's democracies, a battle is being waged for mastery over the human spirit. Man must be made to understand, for then he will accept. Who are the enemies of the new system? The people who do not understand. They fail to understand because their minds work feebly or else badly.

In every capital of Central and Eastern Europe the windows in the Central Committee buildings are illuminated late into the night. Behind their desks sit men well-versed in the writings of Lenin and Stalin. Not the least of their tasks is to define the position of the enemy. As the situation changes, this military staff pins another little flag on the battle map. Data from each country then aid the supreme command in Moscow to establish an over-all strategy.

Different groups of people are the main object of study. The least important is the propertied class which was dispossessed by the nationalization of factories and mines and by the agricultural reform. Their number is insignificant; their way of thinking amusingly old-fashioned. They are no problem. In time they will die off—if need be, with a little help.

The petty bourgeoisie, that is the small merchants and craftsmen, cannot be taken so lightly. They constitute a powerful force, one that is deeply rooted in the masses. Hardly is one clandestine workshop or store liquidated in one neighborhood or city than another springs up elsewhere. Restaurants hide behind a sliding wall of a private house; shoemakers and tailors work at home for their friends. In fact, everything that comes under the heading of speculation sprouts up again and again. And no wonder! State and municipal stores consistently lack even the barest essentials. In the summer, one can buy winter clothes; in the winter, summer wear—but usually of the wrong size and of poor quality. The purchase of a spool of thread or a needle is a major problem, for the one state store in the town may not carry them for a year. Clothes that are given to be mended are held by the local crafts' cooperative for six months. The inns ("Points of Collective Nourishment") are so crowded that people lose the desire to drink with their friends. They know they will have to sit down at a table with strangers and wait, sometimes as long as an hour, before the waiter appears.

All this creates a field for private services. A worker's wife goes to a nearby town, buys needles and thread, brings them back and sells them: the germ of capitalism.

The worker himself of a free afternoon mends a broken bathroom pipe for a friend who has waited months for the state to send him a repair man. In return, he gets a little money, enough to buy himself a shirt: a rebirth of capitalism. He hasn't time to wait in line on the day that the state store receives a new shipment of goods, so he buys his shirt from a friend. She has cleverly managed to buy three, let us say, through her friendship with the salesgirl and now she resells them at a small profit. She is speculating. What she earns as a cleaning-woman in a state factory is not enough to support her three children since her husband was arrested by the security police. If these manifestations of human enterprise were not wiped out it is easy to guess what they would lead to. A worker would set up a plumbing repairs shop. His neighbor, who secretly sells alcohol to people who want to drink in relative privacy, would open a café. The cleaning-woman would become a merchant, peddling her goods. They would gradually expand their businesses, and the lower middle class would reappear. Introduce freedom of the press and of assembly, and publications catering to this clientele would spring up like mushrooms after the rain. And there would be the petty bourgeoisie as a political force.

What is worse, this matter involves the peasant problem. Peasants, who make up the majority of the population of the country, have a middle-class mentality. They are more deeply attached to their few little hectares of field than the storekeepers are to their little shops. As late as the nineteenth century they were still living in bondage. They oppose collectivization because they see it as a return to a state their fathers found unbearable. To leap out of bed at the signal of an official on a collective farm is just as hateful as to do so at the sound of a gong rung by the overseer of an estate. The peasants' blind hatred worries the

Party. Its more sensitive members secretly bow to the necessity of making concessions. They believe that collectivization should be preceded by cooperative use of machinery on private fields, and that it can come only after a long introductory phase of education, extending possibly over decades. This temporizing spirit breeds trouble; that is why the whispered slogans of the "national Communists" are always so popular. But the Center exacts a certain tempo. The structure of every dependent country must be brought to resemble that of Russia as quickly as possible.

This problem, in turn, affects the cities. Peasants are divided into three categories—"poor," "middle," and "kulak"—in an effort to break their solidarity by engendering mutual antagonisms. A peasant's wealth is rated not only by the amount of land he holds, but by how many horses, cows, and pigs he owns, how he lives, eats, and dresses. Lest he fall into an uncomfortable classification, he drops farming and flees to the city; or else he keeps only a minimum amount of livestock and pretends to be poor. As a result, the city suffers from a lack of provisions.

But the peasants are not dangerous. They may beat up a Party boss or even kill him in a burst of desperation, but nothing more. When the state is the sole buyer of their produce, and when they cannot voice their protest at the amount of tribute the state demands of them, they are powerless. The security police can easily handle recalcitrants, especially since it can complain of no lack of informers, now that informing has become an excellent means of saving oneself. The peasants are a leaderless mass. History shows few instances when they seriously threatened the rulers. The term "peasant revolt" sounds nice in textbooks and has a certain propaganda value, but only for the naïve. In reality, the peasants have almost always served as a tool; their leaders, most often of non-peasant origin, have used them for their own ends. The power of the peasants lies in their number; it is a power only when a man like Lenin comes along and throws the weight of their numbers into the scale of events. Obviously, peasants can cause trouble in such moments of upheaval as wars. As long as a private peasant economy exists it acts as a natural base for partisan operations. A peasant hut is the ideal place for partisans to eat, sleep, and work out plans of action. Therefore, a collective farm, where a man's every step is easy to trace, guarantees a degree of control that is indispensable if one wants to preclude hostile underground activity.

Workers are far more important than peasants. Most of them are antagonistic to the new system. That is understandable. They resent the norms they must fill. Those norms are constantly rising. Though the "solidarity of the workers" makes a fine slogan, it does not mean that the solidarity of the crews in a factory is to be tolerated. Their ranks are split by the institution of "shock-workers" which is fostered by an appeal to ambition and enforced by pressure from members of the Party cell. A man may at first refuse to become a shock-worker. But gradually he learns it does not pay to be stubborn; because when workers are being chosen for a course in bookkeeping, for instance, his application is rejected, or when his turn comes for a free vacation he is declared ineligible, etc.

The attitude of the workers toward the regime is ambivalent. On the one hand, they prize its positive contributions. Unemployment is a thing of the past; in fact, there is a constant lack of skilled labor. Not only the head of a family but most of its members are employed. This accumulation of wages means that a family would be able to live better than ever before if only the stores were fairly well stocked; but given the shortage of food and consumer goods, this is rarely, if ever, the case. For workers' children, social advancement is easy because the Party must recruit the cadres of the new intelligentsia from their ranks. The worker can educate himself by attending countless evening courses. If he stands in good favor with the Party he can enjoy a vacation in a rest home, all expenses paid. On the other hand, he cannot defend himself against exploitation by his employer, the state. His trade union representatives are Party tools. They team together with the factory managers for one purpose: to raise production. Workers are told that a strike is a crime. Against whom are they to strike? Against themselves? After all, the means of production belong to them, the state belongs to them. But such an explanation is not very convincing. The workers, who dare not state aloud what they want, know that the goals of the state are far from identical with their own.

Central and Eastern Europe produce in order to raise the military and economic potential of the Center and to compensate for the industrial backwardness of Russia. Workers and their needs have no influence on production plans. Most of the goods produced ebb away to the East. Besides, every product of a worker's hands is the object of innumerable bookkeeping operations. A whole staff of functionaries sits in every factory, counting, writing reports, compiling statistics; the same thing happens on every rung of the state hierarchy, right through to the state wholesale houses and retail stores. If, at last, the article reaches the consumer, it is very expensive; into its cost are counted the salaries of the swarms of bureaucrats through whose hands it must pass. Factory machines are over-aged; there is a scarcity of essential spare parts. So workers are ordered to replace broken parts by whatever homemade means they can devise. Production comes first, even at the price of using up the machines. Discipline is severe; negligence or even a few minutes' lateness are strictly punished. No wonder, then, that the bad side of the system outweighs the good in the worker's mind. Still, he dares not complain. If he betrays any signs of discontent the security police, whose secret agents are his co-workers and sometimes his friends, takes care of him.

The wildcat strikes that break out from time to time are no threat in themselves, for peace returns quickly after mass arrests of all participants. They are, however, ominous signs that discontentment has reached a tension that can find release only in desperate acts. A strike requires a certain minimum of organization. That is why nothing else makes Party dialecticians so uneasy. The workers are the only class capable of organized action—that Marxist principle has never been forgotten. No action, however, is possible without leaders. If the leaders reason correctly, that is, if they understand the necessities of the historic process, then the workers as a mass will be unable to protest.

Everything, thus, takes us back to the question of mastery over the mind. Every possible opportunity for education and advancement is offered to the more energetic and active individuals among the workers. The new, incredibly extensive bureaucracy is recruited from among the young people of working-class origin. The road before them is open, open but guarded: their thinking must be based on the firm principles of dialectical materialism. Schools, theaters, films, painting, literature, and the press all shape their thinking.

We should also call attention to a new institution, the "club," whose significance is comparable to that of the chapel in the middle ages. It exists in every factory, ev-

ery school, every office. On its walls hang portraits of
Party leaders draped with red bunting. Every few days,
meetings following pre-arranged agendas take place, meetings that are as potent as religious rites. The Catholic
Church wisely recognized that faith is more a matter of
collective suggestion than of individual conviction. Collective religious ceremonies induce a state of belief. Fold-
ing one's hands in prayer, kneeling, singing hymns *pre-
cede* faith, for faith is a psycho-physical and not simply
a psychological phenomenon. Edward Gibbon, describing the effects of Theodosius's decrees forbidding pagan
rites (*The Decline and Fall of the Roman Empire*, Chapter XXVIII), says: "The devotion of the poet, or the philosopher, may be secretly nourished by prayer, medita-
tion, and study; but the exercise of public worship appears
to be the only solid foundation of the religious sentiments
of the people, which derive their force from imitation and
habit. The interruption of that public exercise may con-
summate, in the period of a few years, the important work
of a national revolution. The memory of theological opinions cannot long be preserved, without the artificial helps
of priests, of temples, and of books. The ignorant vulgar,
whose minds are still agitated by the blind hopes and
terrors of superstition, will be soon persuaded by their
superiors to direct their vows to the reigning deities of the
age; and will insensibly imbibe an ardent zeal for the support and propagation of the new doctrine, which spiritual
hunger at first compelled them to accept." The Party has
learned this wise lesson from the Church. People who attend a "club" submit to a collective rhythm, and so come
to feel that it is absurd to think differently from the collective. The collective is composed of units that doubt; but
as these individuals pronounce the ritual phrases and sing
the ritual songs, they create a collective aura to which they

in turn surrender. Despite its apparent appeal to reason, the "club's" activity comes under the heading of collective magic. The rationalism of the doctrine is fused with sorcery, and the two strengthen each other. Free discussion is, of course, eliminated. If what the doctrine proclaims is as true as the fact that 2×2 equals 4, to tolerate the opinion that 2×2 equals 5 would be indecent.

From his first day in school, the young citizen receives an education based on this truth. There is a great difference between schools in the people's democracies and schools in the West, for example the schools I attended in pre-war Poland. My friends and I were exposed to a dual system of values. Mathematics, physics, and biology taught us scientific laws, and inculcated respect for a materialistic outlook inherited from the nineteenth century. History and Letters seemed to elude scientific laws, while the history of the Catholic Church and Apologetics cast doubt, though often naïvely, on what physics and biology taught. In the people's democracies, the materialistic outlook of the nineteenth century has been extended consistently to every subject; history and every branch of human creativity are presented as governed by unshakeable and *already known* laws.

In the nineteenth century, with the rise of literacy, brochures popularizing scientific theories made their appearance. Regardless of the intrinsic worth of these theories, we must grant that from the moment they take on a popular form they become something other than what they were as hypotheses of scientific research. For example, the simplified and vulgarized version of Darwin's theory of the origin of species and the struggle for existence is not the same concept that it was for Darwin or for his scholarly opponents. It takes on emotional coloration, and changes into an important sociological element.

The leaders of the twentieth century, like Hitler for instance, drew their knowledge from popular brochures, which explains the incredible confusion in their minds. Evidently, there is no place in such digests for the humble remarks of true scientists who assure us that the laws discovered are hypothetical and relative to the method chosen and the system of symbols used. Vulgarized knowledge characteristically gives birth to a feeling that *everything* is understandable and explained. It is like a system of bridges built over chasms. One can travel boldly ahead over these bridges, ignoring the chasms. It is forbidden to look down into them; but that, alas, does not alter the fact that they exist.

Once the science of nature taught that a forest was a collective of trees governed by a few elementary laws. It seemed that if one cut out the forest and replanted it, after a definite period of years a new forest, exactly like the old, would appear. Today we know this is not so; a forest is an organism arising out of complicated interactions of mosses, soil, fungi, trees, and grasses. The moment these mosses and fungi are destroyed by the cutting out of the forest, the symbiotic pattern is disturbed and the new forest is a completely different organism from what might be expected by someone who ignored the sociology of plants. Stalinists have no knowledge of the conditions human plants need in order to thrive. Forbidding any research in this direction because such study contradicts orthodoxy, they bar mankind from the possibility of acquiring fuller knowledge of itself.

Dialectical materialism, Russian-style, is nothing more than nineteenth-century science vulgarized to the second power. Its emotional and didactic components are so strong that they change all proportions. Although the Method was scientific at its origins, when it is applied to humanistic disciplines it often transforms them into edifying stories adapted to the needs of the moment. But there is no escape once a man enters upon these convenient bridges. Centuries of human history, with their thousands upon thousands of intricate affairs, are reduced to a few, most generalized terms. Undoubtedly, one comes closer to the truth when one sees history as the expression of the class struggle rather than a series of private quarrels among kings and nobles. But precisely because such an analysis of history comes closer to the truth, it is more dangerous. It gives the illusion of *full knowledge;* it supplies answers to all questions, answers which merely run around in a circle repeating a few formulas. What's more, the humanities get connected with the natural sciences thanks to the materialistic outlook (as, for example, in theories of "eternal matter"), and so we see the circle closing perfectly and logically. Then, Stalin becomes the crowning point of the evolution of life on our planet.

The son of a worker, subjected to such an education, cannot think otherwise than as the school demands. Two times two equals four. The press, literature, painting, films, and theater all illustrate what he learns, just as the lives of saints and martyrs serve as illustrations of theology. It would be wrong to assert that a dual set of values no longer exists. The resistance against the new set of values is, however, emotional. It survives, but it is beaten whenever it has to explain itself in rational terms. A man's subconscious or not-quite-conscious life is richer than his vocabulary. His opposition to this new philosophy of life is much like a toothache. Not only can he not express the pain in words, but he cannot even tell you which tooth is aching.

Thanks to excellent means of vulgarization, unprepared people (i.e., those whose minds work feebly) are taught to reason. Their training convinces them that what is happening in the people's democracies is necessary, even if temporarily bad. The greater the number of people who "participate in culture"—i.e. pass through the schools, read books and magazines, attend theaters and exhibitions—the further the doctrine reaches and the smaller grows the threat to the rule of philosophers.

But some people, even with sufficient education, reason "badly." They are impervious to the influence of Hegelian philosophy. A chicken cannot be taught to swim; just so, those who belong to the social groups condemned to disappear cannot be convinced of the truth of dialectics. According to the Party, if these people were clearly aware of their situation, they would have to confess that there is no hope for them. Therefore they look for mental subterfuges. Those people are enemies. They must be ejected to the margins of society not because of what they do, but because of what they *are*. Despite the fact that their intentions may be subjectively good, their guilt has an *objective* character.

Dialecticians have to know the enemy's mentality. Studying the reactionary as a social type, they establish certain features by which he can be recognized. The reactionary, they argue, even though he be an educated man, is incapable of grasping the concept of the interdependence of phenomena. Therefore his political imagination is limited. A man who has been trained sociologically can deduce a whole line of reasoning as to the causes and consequences of every phenomenon. Like a paleontologist, he can divine a whole formation from a single fossil. Show him the verse of a poet from any country, a picture, even an item of clothing and he immediately fits it into a historical context. His line of reasoning may be false; nonetheless he sees everything within the sphere of a given civilization as a symptom, not an accident. The reactionary, incapable of this type of thinking, sees the world as a series of unrelated, parallel occurrences.

Thus, Nazism was for the reactionary merely the result of the activity of Hitler and his clique; revolutionary movements are the effects of Moscow's machinations, etc. All the changes occurring in the people's democracies seem to him to resolve themselves into a question of superior force; if some miraculous accident were to remove this force, everything would return to "normal." He is like a man whose garden has been inundated by a raging river, and who expects to find his old flower beds intact after the waters subside. But a flooding river does not merely *exist;* it tears up and carries away whole banks of soil, fells trees, piles up layers of mud, overturns stones, until the garden of old becomes nothing more than a given number of square meters of unrecognizable land. The reactionary cannot grasp movement. His very language is static; his concepts, unchangeable, never renewed by observation. Laurel and Hardy once made a film in which Laurel, an American soldier in the First World War, is ordered to remain in the trench at his machine-gun post when the company moves to attack. Immediately thereafter the Armistice is signed, and in the resultant confusion he is forgotten. They find him twenty years later, his trench surrounded by a mountain of empty cans. He is still at his post, shooting at every commercial airplane that flies by. The reactionary, like Laurel, knows he must shoot, and he cannot realize that the plane is no longer what it was when he got his orders.

No matter how many books the reactionary reads about the dialectical method, he cannot understand its essence. Some little spring is missing in his mind. As a result he cannot properly evaluate human psychology. Dialecticians work on the premise that a man's mental and emotional life is in constant motion, that it is senseless to treat individuals as if they retained a certain stable, innate character in all circumstances. They know that by changing living conditions they change people's beliefs and reflexes. The reactionary is amazed by the changes people undergo. He awkwardly explains his friends' gradual conversion to the system as "opportunism," "cowardice," "treachery." Without such labels he feels lost. Reasoning on the principle of "either—or," he tries to divide the people about him into "Communists" and "non-Communists"; but such a differentiation loses all meaning in a people's democracy. Where dialectics shapes life whoever tries to resort to old-world logic must feel completely out of his depth.

Such misfortune always befalls the reactionary. The content suddenly flees from his concepts, and all he has left are empty words and phrases. His friends, who only a year ago used these words and phrases fondly, have rejected them as too general, too ill-defined, too remote from reality. He despairingly repeats "honor," "fatherland," "nation," "freedom," without comprehending that for people living in a changed (and daily changing) situation these abstractions take on a concrete and totally different meaning than before.

Because they so define a reactionary, dialecticians consider him a mentally inferior, and therefore not very dangerous, creature. He is no match for them. Once the propertied class is liquidated, the old intelligentsia (which was reactionary in these terms) can be brought to heel with no great difficulty. Its more vigorous representatives cross over to new ideological positions, while the rest lag further and further behind the transformations occurring all about them and so sink ever lower both socially and mentally.

The new and the old intelligentsia no longer speak a common language. Reactionary tendencies exist in the peasants and the former petty bourgeoisie, but they are unexpressed. The masses are being educated by their new living conditions, and though they are discontented, with every month the mental distance between them and the program of the reactionaries increases. Émigré politicians help greatly to facilitate the work of the government. Ninety per cent of them are, according to the above definition, reactionaries. Their appeals and radio talks resemble poor Laurel's barrages at the airplanes. Their listeners are not displeased to hear them abuse a government they, too, dislike; still they cannot treat their formulations seriously. The discrepancy between these politicians' favorite words and the real situation is too clear; the superiority of the dialecticians, whose reasoning is always adapted to actuality, is too obvious. The reactionaries always lose by such comparison; the people's instinctive judgment is tinged with something like embarrassment, with shame that those who oppose dictatorship are not mentally up to its stature. Because man instinctively senses weakness, the people become ever more reluctant to side with the reactionaries. Thus, the feeling of fatalism grows stronger.

Rule over the minds of the masses, therefore, is not seriously threatened. Wherever it appears, intellectual energy can find only one outlet. It is a different matter, however, when one considers the emotional life of the masses and the terrible hatred that dominates it. This hatred cannot be explained on purely economic grounds. The Party senses that in this realm, which Marxism has studied least, surprises and real threats lie hidden.

Above all, there exists the question of religion. This problem still persists despite the many weak points in

Christianity that can be attacked successfully. Not without reason did the Catholic Church defend the feudal structure against nascent capitalism during the Reformation. Capitalism created scientific thinking and dealt a powerful blow to religion in Europe by removing the best minds from the confines of theology. Modern society reveals how swiftly ideas that were at first the property of the intellectual few can spread; to discover along what lines society will develop, it is sometimes useful to trace the trend in the thinking of a small number of clearsighted sensitive people. What is on the surface at a given moment, e.g. a literary style, gives way to new elements, though it may survive for a long time on a second or third level. (Revivals are, of course, possible.) This is what happened to theology in Europe. The Church lost its top-level position when, during the industrial upheavals, it lost the intellectuals and failed to win the new class of workers. And these are the two groups to which the Party attaches most importance. Today, the intellectual life of Christianity grows on the outer fringes of the Church, in little circles that are trying to adapt Christian philosophy to the new needs of the century.

Still, religious needs exist in the masses and it would be a mistake, from the Party's point of view, to deny them. Perhaps they will disappear once the entire population has been transformed into workers; but no one knows when that will happen. We are dealing here with imponderable elements. Mysterious, indeed, is the instinct which makes man revolt against a reasonable explanation of all phenomena. Christianity's armor is so thin in the twentieth century, a child in school is so deeply immersed in the new way of thinking, and yet the zone of shadow eludes the light of reason. We suddenly stumble upon puzzles. Professor Pavlov, who originated the theory of conditioned reflexes, was a deeply religious man. Moscow caused him no trouble over this because he was an eminent scientist and because he was old. The creator of the theory of conditioned reflexes—the very theory that constitutes one of the strongest arguments against the existence of some sort of constant called "human nature"! The defenders of religion maintain that this "human nature" cannot change completely; that gods and churches have existed over thousands of years and in all kinds of civilizations, and that one can expect this to be true of the future as well. What went on in Professor Pavlov's head if two systems of concepts, one scientific and one religious, existed simultaneously there?

The Party teaches that "existence shapes consciousness," that circumstances alter men. But it matters little whether religious drives result from "human nature" or from centuries of conditioning; they exist. During the war against Hitler, the Soviet Union had to dust off its priests as well as appeal to nationalistic feelings. When imminent death brings that moment of absurd revelation that *everything is senseless,* dialectical materialism suddenly discloses its mathematical structure. Man falls from the industriously built bridges. He prefers to surrender to the magic of icons.

In its own fashion, the Party too is a church. Its dictatorship over the earth and its transformation of the human species depend on the success with which it can channel irrational human drives and use them to its own ends. No, logical arguments are not enough. "Club" ceremonies, poetry, novels, films are so important because they reach deeper into the stratum on which the emotional conflict rages. No other church can be tolerated; Christianity is Public Enemy No. 1. It fosters all the skepticism of the masses as to the radical transformation of mankind. If, as the Gospel teaches, we must not do harm unto others, then perhaps we must not harm kulaks? If the highest glory does not belong to man, then perhaps worship of Lenin and Stalin is idolatry?

I have known many Christians—Poles, Frenchmen, Spaniards—who were strict Stalinists in the field of politics but who retained certain inner reservations, believing God would make corrections once the bloody sentences of the all-mighties of History were carried out. They pushed their reasoning rather far. They argue that history develops according to immutable laws that exist by the will of God; one of these laws is the class struggle; the twentieth century marks the victory of the proletariat, which is led in its struggle by the Communist Party; Stalin, the leader of the Communist Party, fulfills the law of history, or in other words acts by the will of God; therefore one must obey him. Mankind can be renewed only on the Russian pattern; that is why no Christian can oppose the one—cruel, it is true—idea which will create a new kind of man over the entire planet. Such reasoning is often used by clerics who are Party tools. "Christ is a new man. The new man is the Soviet man. Therefore Christ is a Soviet man!" said Justinian Marina, the Rumanian patriarch.

In reality, such Christians (even omitting men like Marina) perpetuate one of the greatest lies of all centuries. They renounce their faith but are ashamed to admit it. The contradiction between Christianity and Stalinist philosophy cannot be overcome. Christianity is based on a concept of *individual* merit and guilt; the New Faith, on *historical* merit and guilt. The Christian who rejects individual merit and guilt denies the work of Jesus, and the God he calls upon slowly transforms himself into History. If he admits that only individual merit and guilt exist, how can he gaze indifferently at the suffering of people whose only sin was that they blocked the path of "historical processes"? To lull his conscience he resorts to the thesis that a reactionary cannot be a good man.

Who is the reactionary? Everyone who opposes the inevitable historical processes, i.e. the Politburo police. The thesis of the "sin of the reactionary" is argued very cleverly: every perception is "oriented," i.e. at the very moment of perceiving we introduce our ideas into the material of our observations; only he sees reality truly who evaluates it in terms of the interests of the class that is the lever of the future, i.e. the proletariat. The writings of Lenin and Stalin teach us what the interests of the proletariat are. Whoever sees reality otherwise than as the proletariat sees it falsely; in other words, his picture of reality is deformed by the pressure of the interests of classes that are backward and so destined to disappear. Whoever sees the world falsely necessarily acts badly; whoever acts badly is a bad man; therefore the reactionary is a bad man, and one should not feel sorry for him.

This line of reasoning has at least one flaw—it ignores the facts. The pressure of an all-powerful totalitarian state creates an emotional tension in its citizens that determines their acts. When people are divided into "loyalists" and "criminals" a premium is placed on every type of conformist, coward, and hireling; whereas among the "criminals" one finds a singularly high percentage of people who are direct, sincere, and true to themselves. From the social point of view these persons would constitute the best guarantee that the future development of the social organism would be toward good. From the Christian point of view they have no other sin on their conscience save their contempt for Caesar, or their incorrect evaluation of his might.

The assertion that historical guilt is individual guilt *per se* is nothing more than the subterfuge of a guilty and lying conscience. This does not mean that one can put off the problem of historical guilt with easy generalizations. Stupidity, i.e. inability to understand the mechanism of events, can cause tremendous suffering. In this sense, the Polish commanders who gave the order to start the Warsaw uprising in 1944 are guilty of stupidity, and their guilt has an individual character. Another individual guilt, however, weighs upon the command of the Red Army which refused to aid the insurgents—not out of stupidity, but on the contrary out of a full understanding of "historical processes," i.e. a correct evaluation of power.

One more example of guilt through stupidity is the attitude of various societies toward thinkers, writers, or artists whose vision reached into the future and whose works were largely incomprehensible to their contemporaries. The critic who denied the value of these works might have acted in good faith, but by his stupidity he condemned men of incomparably greater worth than himself to poverty, even persecution. The specific trick of the Christian-Stalinists is to lump these two concepts of guilt, individual and historical, together, while it is only in a few instances that these concepts coincide.

Catholics who accept the Party line gradually lose everything except the phraseology of their Christian metaphysics. The true content of their faith becomes the Method by a psychological process well-known to Christians in the people's democracies. The existence of a large number of loyal half-Christians in the subjugated part of Europe could have a tremendous effect on the Imperium's political plans. Toleration and even support of these "Christian-patriots," as they are called, enables the Center to avoid a dangerous conflict. The transition from Chris-

Man, This Enemy   211

tianity to a cult of History takes place imperceptibly. Without doubt, the greatest success of the Imperium would come if it could install a Party-line pope in the Vatican. A mass in the Basilica of St. Peter in Rome performed by such a pope, with the assistance of dignitaries from those subjugated countries which are predominately Catholic, would be one of the most important steps toward the consolidation of the world empire.

Christians who serve the Eastern Imperium ingeniously resolve the problem posed by Jesus' words "Render therefore unto Caesar the things that are Caesar's; and unto God the things that are God's." Until now the contrast between the ordinary man and Caesar has never been effaced. Christianity guaranteed this division by teaching that every man had his own history, distinct from the history of the social group or the nation to which he belonged. If, as is taught today from the Elbe to Vladivostok, the history of every man is nothing more than the reflection of the history of his class, and if his class is personified in Caesar, then it is clear that the man who rebels against Caesar rebels against himself. Christians who agree to this thesis prove they no longer believe in God's judgment of each man's acts. Fear that History will damn them eternally motivates their submission.

The Party knows that the conflict between true Christianity and the Revolution is fundamental. The Revolution aims at the highest goal the human species has ever set for itself on earth, the end of "man's exploitation of man." To do this, it must replace man's desire for profit with a feeling of collective responsibility as a motive for action. This is a distant and honorable goal. Probably it will not be reached quickly; and probably, too, for a long period it will be necessary to maintain a constant terror in order to instill that feeling of responsibility by force.

But Christianity contains a dual set of values; it recognizes man to be a "child of God" and also a member of society. As a member of society, he must submit to the established order so long as that order does not hinder him in his prime task of saving his soul. Only by effacing this dualism, i.e. raising man as a purely social creature, can the Party release the forces of hatred in him that are necessary to the realization of the new world.

The masses in highly industrialized countries like England, the United States, or France are largely de-Christianized. Technology, and the way of life it produces, undermines Christianity far more effectively than do violent measures. The erosion of religious beliefs is also taking place in Central and Eastern Europe. There, the core of the problem is to avoid galvanizing the forces of Christianity by some careless misstep. It would be an act of unforgivable carelessness, for example, to close the churches suddenly and prohibit all religious practice. Instead, one should try to split the Church in two. Part of the clergy must be compromised as reactionaries and "foreign agents"—a rather easy task, given the utterly conservative mentality of many priests. The other part must be bound to the state as closely as the Orthodox Church is in Russia, so that it becomes a tool of the government. A completely submissive Church—one that may on occasion collaborate with the security police—loses authority in the eyes of the pious. Such a Church can be preserved for decades, until the moment when it dies a natural death due to a lack of adherents.

So there are measures that can be taken even against the Church, this last stronghold of opposition. Nevertheless, the masses in the people's democracies behave like a man who wants to cry out in his sleep and cannot find his voice. They not only dare not speak, they do not know *what* to say. Logically, everything is as it should be. From the philosophical premises to the collectivization of the farms, everything makes up a single closed whole, a solid and imposing pyramid. The lone individual inevitably asks himself if his antagonism is not wrong; all he can oppose to the entire propaganda apparatus are simply his irrational desires. Should he not, in fact, be ashamed of them?

The Party is vigilantly on guard lest these longings be transmuted into new and vital intellectual formulas adapted to new conditions and therefore capable of winning over the masses. Neither the reaction nor the Church are as great a menace as is *heresy*. If men familiar with dialectics and able to present dialectical materialism in a new light appear, they must be rendered harmless at once. A professor of philosophy who clings to obsolete "idealistic" concepts is not particularly dangerous. He loses his lectureship, but he is allowed to earn a living by editing texts, etc. Whereas a professor who, using the names of Marx and Engels, permits himself departures from orthodoxy sows seeds from which alarming crops may grow.

Only the bourgeois persists in thinking that nothing results from these nuances of thought. The Party knows that much can come of them: there was a time when the Revolution was merely a nuance in the thinking of a little group of theoreticians led by Lenin, quarreling around a café table in Switzerland. The most neuralgic points of the doctrine are philosophy, literature, the history of art, and literary criticism; those are the points where man in his unfortunate complexity enters the equation. The difference of a tiny fraction in the premises yields dizzying differences after the calculation is completed. A deviation from the line in the evaluation of some work of art may become the leaven of a political upheaval. The Party rightly and logically condemned the foremost Marxist literary scholar of the twentieth century, the Hungarian professor Lukacs. Deep, hidden reasons lay behind the enthusiasm his works aroused in the Marxists of the people's democracies. They saw in him the harbinger of a new philosophy and a new literature. The dislike of "socialist realism" that he betrayed corresponded to the belief, prevalent in the first years after the Second World War, that in the people's democracies the science of Marx and Engels would blaze new paths, unknown in Russia. Because Lukacs expressed this belief in his books, the Party had no course but to stigmatize him.

When one considers the matter logically, it becomes obvious that intellectual terror is a principle that Leninism-Stalinism can never forsake, even if it should achieve victory on a world scale. The enemy, in a potential form, will *always* be there; the only friend will be the man who accepts the doctrine 100 per cent. If he accepts only 99 per cent, he will necessarily have to be considered a foe, for from that remaining 1 per cent a new church can arise. The explanation Stalinists often advance, that this is only a *stage* resulting from "capitalist encirclement," is self-contradictory. The concept of a *stage* presupposes planning from the top, absolute control now and always. Eastern rulers are aware of this contradiction. If they were not, they would not have to present forced participation in clubs and parades, forced voting for a single list, forced raising of production norms, etc. as spontaneous and voluntary acts. This is a dark, unpleasant point for even the most passionate believers.

This way of posing the problem discloses the madness of the doctrines. Party dialecticians know that similar attempts on the part of other orthodoxies have always failed. In fact, History itself exploded one after another the formulas that have been considered binding. This time, however, the rulers have mastered dialectics so, they assert, they will know how to modify the doctrine as new necessities arise. The judgments of an individual man can always be wrong; the only solution is to submit unreservedly to an authority that claims to be unerring.

But what can the doctrine do about the unformulated longings of men? Why does a good Communist, without any apparent reason, suddenly put a pistol to his head? Why does he escape abroad? Isn't this one of those chasms over which the scientifically constructed bridges pass? People who flee from the people's democracies usually give as their chief motive the fact that life in these countries is psychically unbearable. They stammer out their efforts to explain: "The dreadful sadness of life over there"; "I felt I was turning into a machine." It is impossible to communicate to people who have not experienced it the undefinable menace of total rationalism.

To forestall doubt, the Party fights any tendency to delve into the depths of a human being, especially in literature and art. Whoever reflects on "man" in general, on his inner needs and longings, is accused of bourgeois sentimentality. Nothing must ever go beyond the description of man's behavior as a member of a social group. This is necessary because the Party, treating man exclusively as the by-product of social forces, believes that he becomes the type of being he pictures himself to be. He is a social monkey. *What is not expressed does not exist.* Therefore if one forbids men to explore the depths of human nature, one destroys in them the urge to make such explorations; and the depths in themselves slowly become unreal.

I should like to clear up in advance a possible misunderstanding. Personally, I am not in favor of art that is too subjective. My poetry has always been a means of checking on myself. Through it I could ascertain the limit beyond which falseness of style testifies to the falseness of the artist's position; and I have tried not to cross this line. The war years taught me that a man should not take a pen in his hands merely to communicate to others his own despair and defeat. This is too cheap a commodity; it takes too little effort to produce it for a man to pride himself on having done so. Whoever saw, as many did, a whole city reduced to rubble—kilometers of streets on which there remained no trace of life, not even a cat, not even a homeless dog—emerged with a rather ironic attitude toward descriptions of the hell of the big city by contemporary poets, descriptions of the hell in their own souls. A real "wasteland" is much more terrible than any imaginary one. Whoever has not dwelt in the midst of horror and dread cannot know how strongly a witness and participant protests against himself, against his own neglect and egoism. Destruction and suffering are the school of social thought.

Yet, if the literature of socialist realism is useful, it is so only to the Party. It is supposed to present reality not as a man *sees* it (that was the trait of the previous realism, the so-called "critical"), but as he *understands* it. Understanding that reality is in motion, and that in every phenomenon what is being born and what is dying exist simultaneously—dialectically speaking, this is the battle between the "new" and the "old"—the author should praise everything that is budding and censure everything that is becoming the past. In practice, this means that the author should perceive elements of the class struggle in every phenomenon. Carrying this reasoning further, the doctrine forces all art to become didactic. Since *only* the Stalinists have the right to represent the proletariat, which

is the rising class, everything that is "new" and therefore
praiseworthy results from Party strategy and tactics. "Socialist realism" depends on an identification of the "new"
with the proletariat and the proletariat with the Party. It
presents model citizens, i.e. Communists, and class enemies. Between these two categories come the men who
vacillate. Eventually, they must—according to which
tendencies are stronger in them—land in one camp or the
other. When literature is not dealing with prefabricated
figures of friends and foes, it studies the process of metamorphosis by which men arrive at total salvation or absolute damnation in Party terms.

This way of treating literature (and every art) leads to
absolute conformism. Is such conformism favorable to
serious artistic work? That is doubtful. The sculptures of
Michelangelo are completed acts that endure. There was a
time when they did not exist. Between their non-exist-
ence and existence lies the creative act, which cannot be
understood as a submission to the "wave of the future."
The creative act is associated with a feeling of freedom
that is, in its turn, born in the struggle against an apparently invincible resistance. Whoever truly creates is
alone. When he succeeds in creating, many followers and
imitators appear; and then it seems that his work con-
firms the existence of some sort of "wave of history." The
creative man has no choice but to trust his inner command
and place everything at stake in order to express what
seems to him to be true. This inner command is absurd
if it is not supported by a belief in an order of values that
exists beyond the changeability of human affairs, that is by
a metaphysical belief. Herein lies the tragedy of the twentieth century. Today, only those people can create who
still have this faith (among them are a certain number of
Stalinists who practice Ketman), or who hold a position

of lay stoicism (which, after all, is probably another form of faith). For the rest there remains the sorry lie of a safe place on the "wave of the future."

This is the framework within which life develops in the people's democracies; but it is a life that moves at a frenzied tempo. "Socialist construction" is not merely a slogan; it is taken in a quite literal sense. The observer's eye meets scaffolding everywhere; new factories, offices, and government buildings spring up almost overnight; production curves rise; the masses change character with unheard-of rapidity; more and more persons become state functionaries and acquire a certain minimum of "political education." The press, literature, films, and theater magnify these attainments. If a man from Mars, knowing nothing of earthly affairs, were to judge the various countries of the world on the basis of Soviet books, he would conclude that the East is inhabited by rational, intelligent beings, while the West is peopled by dwarfs and degenerates. Small wonder that so many intelligent Westerners, for whom the Soviet Union and its satellites are the legendary isles of happiness, arrive at a similar conclusion.

The citizen of the people's democracies is immune to the kind of neurosis that takes such manifold forms in capitalist countries. In the West a man subconsciously regards society as unrelated to him. Society indicates the limits he must not exceed; in exchange for this he receives a guarantee that no one will meddle excessively in his affairs. If he loses it's his own fault; let psychoanalysis help him. In the East there is no boundary between man and society. His game, and whether he loses or wins, is a public matter. He is never alone. If he loses it is not because of indifference on the part of his environment, but because his environment keeps him under such minute scrutiny. Neuroses as they are known in the West result, above all, from man's aloneness; so even if they were allowed to practice, psychoanalysts would not earn a penny in the people's democracies.

The torment of a man in the East is, as we have seen, of a new, hitherto unknown variety. Humanity devised effective measures against smallpox, typhus, syphilis; but life in big cities or giant collectives breeds new diseases. Russian revolutionists discovered what they claimed were effectual means of mastering the forces of History. They proclaimed they had found the panacea for the ills of society. But History itself repays them in jeers.

The supreme goal of doing away with the struggle for existence—which was the theoretician's dream—has not been and cannot be achieved while every man fears every other man. The state which, according to Lenin, was supposed to wither away gradually is now all-powerful. It holds a sword over the head of every citizen; it punishes him for every careless word. The promises made from time to time that the state will begin to wither away when the entire earth is conquered lack any foundation. Orthodoxy cannot release its pressure on men's minds; it would no longer be an orthodoxy. There is always some disparity between facts and theories. The world is full of contradictions. Their constant struggle is what Hegel called dialectic. That dialectic of reality turns against the dialectic fashioned by the Center; but then so much the worse for reality. It has been said that the twentieth century is notable for its synthetic products—synthetic rubber, synthetic gasoline, etc. Not to be outdone, the Party has processed an artificial dialectic whose only resemblance to Hegel's philosophy is purely superficial. The Method is effective just so long as it wages war against an enemy. A man exposed to its influence is helpless. How can he fight a system of symbols? In the end he submits; and this is the secret of the Party's power, not some fantastic narcotic.

There is a species of insect which injects its venom into a caterpillar; thus inoculated, the caterpillar lives on though it is paralyzed. The poisonous insect then lays its eggs in it, and the body of the caterpillar serves as a living larder for the young brood. Just so (though Marx and Engels never foresaw this use for their doctrine), the anaesthetic of dialectical materialism is injected into the mind of a man in the people's democracies. When his brain is duly paralyzed, the eggs of Stalinism are laid in it. As soon as you are a Marxist, the Party says to the patient, you *must* be a Stalinist, for there is no Marxism outside of Stalinism.

Naïve enemies of the poison may think that they can rid themselves of the danger by locking up the works of Marx and Engels in burglar-proof safes and never allowing anyone to read them. They fail to consider that the very course of history leads people to think about the subject matter of these works. Those who have never personally experienced the magnetic attraction and force of the problems posed in these books can count themselves lucky. Though that does not necessarily mean that they should feel proud of themselves.

Only the blind can fail to see the irony of the situation the human species brought upon itself when it tried to master its own fate and to eliminate accident. It bent its knee to History; and History is a cruel god. Today, the commandments that fall from his lips are uttered by clever chaplains hiding in his empty interior. The eyes of the god are so constructed that they see wherever a man may go; there is no shelter from them. Lovers in bed perform their amorous rites under his mocking glance; a child plays in the sand, not knowing that his future life has been weighed and written into the general account; only the aged, who have but a few days left before they die, can justly feel that they have to a large extent escaped his rule.

The philosophy of History emanating from Moscow is not just an abstract theory, it is a material force that uses guns, tanks, planes, and all the machines of war and oppression. All the crushing might of an armed state is hurled against any man who refuses to accept the New Faith. At the same time, Stalinism attacks him from within, saying his opposition is caused by his "class consciousness," just as psychoanalysts accuse their foes of wanting to preserve their complexes.

Still, it is not hard to imagine the day when millions of obedient followers of the New Faith may suddenly turn against it. That day would come the moment the Center lost its material might, not only because fear of military force would vanish, but because success is an integral part of this philosophy's argument. If it lost, it would prove itself wrong by its own definition; it would stand revealed as a false faith, defeated by its own god, reality. The citizens of the Imperium of the East long for nothing so much as liberation from the terror their own thought creates.

In the Central Committee buildings, strategists move the little flags on the battle map of the war for men's minds. They can pinpoint ever greater successes; the red color, which in 1944 and 1945 was limited to a handful of believers coming from the East, spreads farther every day. But even sages are men, and even they fall prey to anxiety and dread. They compare themselves to the early Christians; they liken the march of the New Faith over the planet to the march of Christianity throughout the decaying Roman Empire. But they envy the Apostles their gift of reaching deep into the human heart. *"They knew how to make propaganda! How can we compare ourselves with them?"* mourned a certain Party dignitary hearing the Gospel read over the radio. The new (anti-) religion performs miracles. It shows the doubters new buildings and new tanks. But what would happen if these miracles suddenly stopped? Knives and pistols would appear in the hands that applaud today. The pyramid of thought would topple. For a long time, on the ground where once it stood there would be nothing save blood and chaos.

CHAPTER IX

The Lesson of the Baltics

"IF you keep thinking about the Baltics and the camps, do you know what will happen to you?" my friend asked me in Warsaw. He had recently acquired an admiration for the dialectical wisdom of the Center. "You will use up the rest of your time to live and you will present yourself before Zeus; and the god, pointing his finger (here my friend gestured accusingly), will cry: 'Idiot! You ruined your life by worrying about trifles!'"

It is true that I cannot stop thinking about the Baltics. Yet I can say something in my defense. Certainly, worry over the fate of nations trampled down by History—that elephant—leads nowhere, and is a proof of sentimentality. This much I grant. The rage one feels on reading sixteenth-century memoirs whose authors, mostly priests, recount the atrocities committed in America by Spanish Conquistadors is senseless. It cannot resurrect the Caribbean population slaughtered by Ponce de Leon, nor shelter the Inca refugees pursued through the mountains by knights fighting with faith and a sword. Those who have been defeated are forgotten forever; and anyone who would look too closely into the record of past crimes or, even worse, try to imagine them in detail, must either turn gray with horror—or become completely indifferent.

Historians know that a long time ago the area known as East Prussia was inhabited by the Prussian nation which, thanks to German-speaking followers of Jesus, met the same fate as the people of the Caribbean. But historians do not speak of mothers' despair or children's distress; and perhaps it is better so. The civilization that calls itself Christian was built on the blood of the innocent. To be nobly indignant at those who are trying today to create another civilization by similar means is to take a somewhat pharisaic attitude. The records of crime will remain for many years, hidden in some place that is remote and secure; then, a scholar of the future, reaching through dust and cobwebs for the old files, will consider the murders committed as insignificant misdeeds compared with the task accomplished. More probably, however, no such files will exist; for, keeping step with progress, the emperors of today have drawn conclusions from this simple truth: whatever does not exist on paper, does not exist at all.

Let us assume that this is what will happen. Nevertheless our attitude toward the present differs from our attitude toward the past, be that right or wrong. A *living* human being, even if he be thousands of miles away, is not so easily ejected from one's memory. If he is being tortured, his voice is heard at the very least by those people who have (uncomfortable as it may be for them) a vivid imagination. And even if he is already dead, he is still part of the present; for the man who killed him or who gave the order that he be killed is sitting down somewhere, at some precise point on the face of the earth, with his family; bread and tea are on the table, and his children rejoice over a gift he has brought them. To demand that a man regard the present as he would the past without, as my friend said, worrying about trifles, that he gaze at the ripening fruits of tomorrow through the telescope of History—that is asking too much. There must be, after all, some standard one dare not destroy lest the fruits of tomorrow prove to be rotten. If I think thus it is because for the last two thousand years or more there have been not only brigands, conquistadors, and hangmen, but also people for whom evil was evil and had to be called evil. Mass slaughter, the terror of revolution, the craze for gold, the misery of the working classes: who knows what dimensions these flaws might reach if every man believed he must keep silent and accept? In rebelling, I believe I protect the fruits of tomorrow better than my friend who keeps silent. I assume the risk and I pay. If I were not willing to do so, I would now be writing an ode in praise of the Generalissimo. When one has some training in poetic technique, it is not particularly difficult to compose fine-sounding, rhythmical praise of *The Glorious Hero*.

The Baltic states—Estonia, Lithuania, and Latvia—lie, as we know, on the edge of the great mainland of the continent. A gulf separates them from Finland; the Baltic Sea, from Sweden. Their inhabitants are not Slavic. The language of the Estonians is related to Finnish. The Lithuanian and Latvian tongues, which resemble each other, still constitute a linguistic riddle; no one knows the original home of these tribes who found their way to the lower reaches of the Niemen and Dvina rivers. We know only that the exterminated Prussians spoke a similar language. Of the three Baltic nations, only the Lithuanians succeeded in the past in creating and maintaining for a certain time a large state whose borders extended to the Dnieper.

These three sparsely settled countries underwent an intensive colonization, chiefly German and Polish, which marked the advance of Christianity. The result was that two different languages entered into use there: the masters, that is the landholders, spoke German (in Estonia and Latvia) and Polish (in Lithuania) in part because the newcomers brought with them their own language and customs, and in part because the local nobility adopted them. The common people, however, spoke their native tongue and preserved their cultural heritage from a legendary past. After the First World War, these three countries ceased to be provinces of the Russian Tsardom and became independent. Radical agrarian reforms curbed the influence of the great landowners. The native tongues became the official languages, while literature and education restored popular traditions.

In 1939, the population of these three states numbered about six million, that is, a little more than the population of Chile, a little less than that of Sweden. They were agricultural countries whose economies were maintained by a well-organized exportation of bacon, eggs, butter, grain, and fowl to Western Europe. In this, as well as in other respects, they resembled Denmark. Whoever knows the patterns of farming life can easily picture the mode of existence of these Baltic regions. A widespread system of cooperatives helped the farmer sell his products. His standard of living, judging by his appearance, his house and his diet, was higher than that of the Slavonic countries, with the possible exception of Czechoslovakia. Most Estonians and Latvians were Protestant; most Lithuanians, Catholic. All three nations were characterized by obstinate patriotism, or even chauvinism—which is understandable in terms of their hard past. Militarily, all three were defenseless.

The fate of these states was decided in the talks between Molotov and Ribbentrop. In the fall of 1939, Molotov demanded military bases; the Baltic governments hurried to grant them. (The press of all three countries consecrated much space, at the time, to articles proclaiming lasting, unshakeable friendship for the kind and powerful neighbor to the East.) In June 1940, on the pretext that Soviet soldiers stationed in these bases had not been assured proper security, the Red Army crossed the borders of Lithuania, Latvia, and Estonia, the NKVD moved into power, and all former state machinery ceased to exist.

My account of the Baltic states is not derived from books or manuscripts. The first sunlight I saw, my first smell of the earth, my first tree, were the sunlight, smell, and tree of these regions; for I was born there, of Polish-speaking parents, beside a river that bore a Lithuanian name. I am familiar with the events of the past years not from the dry notes of historians; they are as vivid for me as the faces and eyes of people one knows well.

The invasion of the Spanish must have been an appalling experience for the Aztecs. The customs of the conquerors were incomprehensible; their religious ceremonies, strange; the paths of their thought, impossible to follow. The invasion of the Red Army was no less of a shock for the Estonians, Latvians, and Lithuanians. Of course, the older people remembered the days of the Tsars; yet this was completely different, and much worse. In the years that had elapsed since the fall of Tsarism, Russia had not evolved closer toward Europe but further away, toward principles of social organization Europe had never before known. The thinking and reactions of these conquerors were just as alien to the conquered as the arcanum of Catholic theology and the Castilian concept of honor had been to the Aztecs.

New general elections were ordered immediately. But these elections had nothing in common with the elections held before then. There was a single list of candidates,

presented by the new authorities. Why, then, were the
cities and countryside covered with propaganda leaflets
and handbills; why did megaphones shout day and night;
why the trucks decorated with huge portraits of the candidates; why the garlands, the meetings, and the platforms?
Why the propaganda if one had no choice? No one could
understand. Yet on election day everyone flocked to the
polls. They had to vote; for when one turned in one's
ballot, one's passport was stamped. The absence of this
stamp meant that the owner of the passport was an enemy
of the people who had revealed his ill will by refusing to
vote. Some people, naïvely, handed in torn or crossed-out
ballots; but they were declared valid and affirmative. The
final tallies were impressive. The first act of the parlia-
ments thus elected was to make a formal request for incorporation into the Soviet Union. That favor was granted.

One of the new delegates to the Lithuanian parliament
was a friend from my early youth. Together we had traveled many kilometers down various European rivers in a
canoe, escaped drowning in rapids, wandered over mountain trails, seen the sun rise over the valleys of the Black
Forest and the castles of the Rhineland. A few years before the Second World War he became a Stalinist. He was
from Warsaw, and his presence in Lithuania at the outbreak of the war was more or less accidental. Nevertheless, he was proposed as a candidate (there were so few
Communists in these countries that every one was put to
use); and since candidacy was tantamount to election, he
became a delegate. It must have been quite an experience
of power for him; he could vote the incorporation of a
country he had nothing to do with into another country
which he knew only from its propaganda literature and
official statistics. At the time, that was something new; but
other innovations were to come. All over Eastern Europe,

foreigners (changing their names, if necessary) vote, represent, and rule.

Thus the inhabitants of the Baltic states became Soviet citizens. In the eyes of the new authorities this mass of people, who were so well off that they put the rest of the Union to shame, represented a scandalous relic of the past. They had to be educated. Prisons filled and, shortly, certain categories of citizens began to be deported to work camps, mines, and collective farms at the other end of Russia, chiefly in the polar regions. In 1941 the entire area was invaded by the German army. The Nazis, in turn, started to kill off that category of the population which their ideology classified as undesirable, namely the Jews, irrespective of age, sex, or class. To that task they applied their usual precision. At the same time they exported to the Reich a large number of forcibly enlisted workers.

In 1944 the Baltic states were recaptured by the Red Army and the Center set out to assimilate this area into the Union. The most urgent task was the destruction of the existing and wealthy farming economy. Collectivization met with considerable obstacles, however. The usual method, that of "intensifying the class struggle in the village," which speculates upon the antagonism between rich and poor farmers, had feeble results. Training in partisan units, together with the large number of arms left from war-time operations, encouraged opposition. Peasants fled to the woods and formed bands. In reprisal, disciplinary expeditions surrounded villages and killed those who had remained at home. This merely increased the opposition; for whole villages, including women and children, often preferred to join the partisans rather than expose themselves to the danger of being taken hostage.

The hostile attitude of these people forced those in power to resort to radical measures. Big man-hunts were instituted. Thousands of cattle-cars loaded with people moved towards uninhabited areas of Euro-Asia. The years in which Western Europe began to enjoy a precarious peace were far from peaceful for the Baltic countries. Villages whose inhabitants were dead, deported, or in hiding stood plundered and empty. The wind whistled through the apertures of broken windows and smashed doors. "Hitlers come and go, but nations remain," the Generalissimo declared in the moment when victory over Germany was certain. As far as smaller national groups are concerned, this statement should be amended to read: "Nations come and go, but the countries remain." In the words of an official of the Center, spoken in 1946: "There will be a Lithuania; but there will be no Lithuanians."

I do not know how many thousands of men and women these states lost before their economies were "reconstructed," i.e. before 1950. Perhaps no one knows the exact statistics. The number of foreign settlers ordered to the places left by the departed natives might serve as an index. Moreover, the process is not yet finished. Collective farmers have been imported into the rural areas; administrative cadres and their families, into the cities. In the streets one hears Russian spoken more frequently than Estonian, Latvian, or Lithuanian. The great majority of the Party leaders and higher government officials have Russian names.

The aim of all these moves is to inter-mix the population of the Union. Only by dissolving individual nationalities in the "Russian sea" can one attain the goal of a single culture and a single universal language. The territory that once linked the Baltic states with Germany has been settled by Russians. The city of Koenigsberg, within whose walls Kant was born and spent his entire life, has been re-named Kaliningrad and there is no longer any trace of the mild, orderly world the philosopher knew. On the islands lying off the coast of what was once Estonia, no Estonian fishermen push their boats toward the sea. The pot in which the Baltic peoples are being boiled down has its lid tightly clamped on. Obviously schools and universities, as well as books, all use native tongues. After all, the aim is not to destroy individual nationalities; the aim is to destroy the class enemy. When the young people learn in Lithuanian, Latvian, or Estonian how to be true patriots of the Union, and how to appreciate all that emanates from the Center, then the Russian language will triumph over all competition. At that point, a new level of understanding will be attained.*

What cause is there for anger? The little world that was the Baltic states is known to us from Breughel's country scenes: hands clutching jugs, cheeks red with laughter, heavy, bear-like kindness. There lived peasant virtues: industry, thrift, diligence; and peasant sins: greed, stinginess, constant worry about the future. The proletariat scarcely existed; industry was poorly developed; the agrarian reform had divided the large estates among the peasants. But why should this continue? Kulaks were an unforgivable anachronism. They had to be wiped out, and

---

* "I approached Stalin's portrait, took it off the wall, placed it on the table and, resting my head on my hands, I gazed and meditated. What should I do? The Leader's face, as always so serene, his eyes so clear-sighted, they penetrate into the distance. It seems that his penetrating look pierces my little room and goes out to embrace the entire globe. I do not know how I would appear to anyone looking at me at this moment. But with my every fibre, every nerve, every drop of blood I feel that, at this moment, nothing exists in this entire world but this dear and beloved face. What should I do?

"The Soviet government handles the enemies of the people with a firm hand. . . .

"These are thy words, comrade Stalin. I believe them sacredly. Now I know how to act."

From *Pergale* (Victory) magazine, organ of the Soviet Writers of the Lithuanian SSR, No. 4, April 1950, p. 52, cf. *The Lithuanian Bulletin*, New York, Nos. 7–12, July–December, 1950

the standard of living had to be lowered to match that of
the rest of the Union. As for the drastic methods employed
—after all, in the end everyone must die. Let us assume
that a large percentage of the population was killed off
by a plague, instead of by disciplinary expeditions. From
the moment we acknowledge historical necessity to be
something in the nature of a plague, we shall stop shed-
ding tears over the fate of its victims. A plague or an earth-
quake do not usually provoke indignation. One admits
they are catastrophes, folds the morning paper, and continues eating breakfast. One can revolt only against *someone*. Here, there is no one. The people who have brought
the plague are convinced they are merely fulfilling their
historical duty.

Yet the letter I one day held in my hand was painful. It
came from a family deported to Siberia from one of the
Baltic states in March 1949, and was addressed to relatives
in Poland. The family consisted of a mother and two
daughters. Their letter was a terse account of their work
on a kolkhoz. The last letters of every line were slightly
stressed, and reading vertically one made out the words
"Eternal Slave." If such a letter happened to fall into my
hands, then how many other, similarly disguised expressions of despair must have found their way to people who
could not make any use of them. And, calculating the
possibilities, how many such letters remained unwritten;
how many of those who might have written them died of
hunger and overwork, repeating those hopeless words,
"Eternal Slave"?

Perhaps at this very moment the mother and two daughters, if they are still alive, are carrying water in buckets
from a well. Perhaps the mother is worrying about the
insufficient bread ration which is their only salary. And
perhaps, too, she is worrying about the future of her

daughters. A citizen of New York transplanted to a native village in the Congo would feel more or less as does an inhabitant of the Baltic countries transported beyond the Ural mountains—such are the differences in standards of cleanliness, hygiene, and the most external evidences of civilization. The mother will die; the daughters will have to remain there for the rest of their lives, for one never returns from such exile. They will have to marry. But they will keep locked within themselves something which is incomprehensible to their environment, something they will never be able to transmit to their Russian-speaking children.

Possibly neither the mother nor the daughters were possessed of any particularly fine qualities. The mother went to church on Sundays with a thick prayer book, but at home she was a stingy shrew. The daughters had nothing on their minds but frippery and the Saturday dances on the grass that were so loved in their native province. They read no serious books; the names of Plato and Hegel, Marx and Darwin meant nothing to them. These three women were deported because they were kulaks; their farm had nearly thirty hectares of land. The benefit mankind got out of their quiet life in the country was, aside from a certain number of kilograms of butter and cheese, very little.

The question arises as to whether or not one is allowed to destroy three such creatures in the name of higher ends. The Stalinist will answer that it is allowed; Christians and pseudo-Christians will answer that it is not. Neither the former nor the latter are entirely consistent. Ninety per cent of the arguments used by Stalinists in their propaganda are based on man's injury to man. The appeal to moral indignation is always present in their slogans. Christians, on the other hand, maintain that it is wrong to harm others because every man has inherent value; but having voiced such a noble opinion, many of them would not move a finger to help another person. It is not merely the fate of the Baltic states that leaves them indifferent. They are equally unconcerned about forms of destruction other than slaughter and compulsory deportation. For example, they regard the spiritual death of people condemned to work hard all day and to swallow the poison of films and television at night as completely normal.

Pablo Neruda, the great poet of Latin America, comes from Chile. I translated a number of his poems into Polish. Pablo Neruda has been a Communist for some ten years. When he describes the misery of his people, I believe him and I respect his great heart. When writing, he thinks about his brothers and not about himself, and so to him the power of the word is given. But when he paints the joyous, radiant life of people in the Soviet Union, I stop believing him. I am inclined to believe him as long as he speaks about what he knows; I stop believing him when he starts to speak about what I know myself.

There is a great difference, indeed, between the believers of the East and those of the West. The Western Communist needs a vision of a golden age which is *already* being realized on earth. The Stalinist of the East does everything in his power to instill this vision in the minds of others, but he never forgets that it is merely a useful lie. His reasoning is correct. Every revolution has known a period of terror directed against the enemies of the new order. No one today weeps for the French aristocrats whose heads fell on the guillotine. Yet former revolutions are insignificant events compared with the revolution going on in our day. They aimed at the overthrow of a small class which stood in the way of artificially restrained, creative forces. The revolution of today cannot content itself with a moment of terror, necessary to the consolidation of the new power; the class struggle must continue until the economic bases for opposition have been destroyed. The class enemy consists of the millions of small producers, that is, of the peasants and artisans, as well as small businessmen. Their steady resistance, and the obstinacy with which they seize every opportunity to revive the old economic order, demand decisive punitive measures.

It must be added that the Revolution triumphed in a backward country; and ever since 1917 regression, in the form of internal decomposition or external intervention, has been a constant threat. It is, therefore, understandable that the moment of terror, proper to former revolutions, has been prolonged over decades in the greatest revolution the world has ever seen. And wherever terror and misery reign, no one can be happy. The golden age, therefore, belongs to the future. The Center has proclaimed that it has already reached the stage of socialism and is now headed toward the realization of communism. The present moment is dark but, seen from a distance, for example from the year 2953, it will appear as short as the Reign of Terror in the French Revolution seems to us today; and the number of victims (two or three hundred million, more or less) will seem scarcely more important than a few thousand beheaded French aristocrats.

Let us imagine a meeting between two fervent disciples of the Center—I base my account on personal observation of many such encounters. One is from the East. He has served perhaps three years behind the walls of prisons or slave labor camps *there*. He was not broken; he did not lose his faith. Wherever trees are being chopped down, splinters must fall. The fact that he, and many of his fellow-inmates were innocent, proves nothing: it is better to condemn twenty innocent people than to release a single evil-doer. To endure this trial successfully is a source of moral strength for him, and of esteem from his comrades in the Party. Having learned the workings of the machinery behind the scene, he knows the Country of Socialism to be a vale of tears and of gnashing of teeth. Nevertheless, the belief in historical necessity and the vision of the fruits of tomorrow persuade him that the harsh reality of the present—even extended over many years—is unimportant.

The other is a Communist from the West. His attention is directed above all toward the injustices of the system in which he lives. He is filled with a noble indignation against what is going on *here* and with a longing for what is going on *there,* in the land from which his companion has come. His companion looks at him benevolently, and his words fulfill all expectation. There may at times be a gleam of humor in his eyes; but that is only human, a mere weakness. His humor is lightly spiced with envy; the moral indignation and enthusiasm of the other are for him unattainable *luxuries* in the sphere of moral comfort. If the other *knew,* if he had undergone the same trials, what would his faith be like? Experience has proved that those from the West cannot hold up nervously under the strain of a protracted stay in the Center. The dose is too strong for them. They may be extremely useful as missionaries among the pagans, or when their countries are invaded by the "liberating" army. When it is too late, when they no longer have a choice, their inner doubts will do no harm.

I have spoken of Neruda. The problem of the Baltics is much more important for every contemporary poet than are questions of style, metrics, and metaphor. Today the only poetry worthy of the name is eschatological, that is, poetry which rejects the present inhuman world in the name of a great change. The reader of today is in search of hope, and he does not care for poetry that accepts the order of things as permanent. If someone is loaded with that little-known internal energy which bears the name of poetry, he will not be able to escape this universal expectation and he will search—falling, rising, again falling and searching again—for he knows that such is his duty. Revolutionary poetry is often artistically better than the poetry of cameral artists, for subject matter that is close to the longings of mankind emancipates the written word from the shackles of passing literary fads.

But revolutionary poetry becomes weak when it begins to extol the longed-for future as already realized, or in the process of realization, in a given part of the earth. To approve convincingly is difficult not because "positive" values are incompatible with the nature of literature, but because approbation, in order to be effective, must be based on truth. The split between words and reality takes its revenge, even though the author be of good faith. Sentimentality, that is, an exploitation of feelings for their own sake, and not for the sake of what occasions them, cannot lead to good writing. Reality puts literature to the test sooner or later. The ingenious methods by which Stalinists isolate themselves from reality are amazing. I know a poet who found himself in a city occupied by the Red Army after the Molotov–Ribbentrop pact. He was terrified by the mass arrests in which every day some friend or acquaintance disappeared. In panic, he sat down to work, and from his pen flowed gentle poems about the blessings of peace and the beauties of socialist society. I remember a verse in which he praised the "happy, prosperous collective farms" of the Soviet Ukraine. A few months later, when the German army began its invasion, these "happy, prosperous" collective farmers greeted the Nazis as liberators, and only the thoughtless cruelties of the conquerors convinced them they had made a mistake. This is no argument against the system—a few decades is too short a formative period. It is, however, an argument against the poet's verse.

The double ethical standard applied to what happens within the Imperium and without its borders makes honest art impossible. Dialectical reasoning may be well balanced, but art is not born of dialectical reasoning. Art is rooted in much deeper, primitive strata laid down in the individual by past generations. This fact may not be entirely convenient to the new rulers, to the philosophers who would like to see a purely dialectical literature, nourished by an understanding of historical processes. Yet what they prize as literature is nothing but its counterfeit. Repressed feelings poison every work, giving it a tinsel varnish which warns everybody: this is a synthetic product. Then, the most beautiful words are as dead as artificial wreaths.

Let us suppose we admit that terror is quite a useful measure and that the Baltic peoples must be destroyed, to a proper degree, as an anti-revolutionary group. Immediately, a difficulty arises: can one pose an equation sign between terror that is momentary and improvised on the one hand and, on the other, organized terror that extends over a long period? Who can tell whether someone given the perspective of a thousand years will regard the guillotine as identical with the murder or deportation of whole nations over months, years, decades? One month of terror and ten years of it are not the same. The element of time necessarily alters the quality of acts. A long period of terror demands an established apparatus and becomes a permanent institution. Deportees may try to escape. Their relatives can scarcely approve of their disappearance, and it is indicated that they be put on the next list. The families of these relatives are an uncertain element which can be kept in line only under threat. Only fear can inspire diligence in dissatisfied peasants tied to collectives.

Fear is well known as a cement of societies. In a liberal-capitalist economy fear of lack of money, fear of losing one's job, fear of slipping down one rung on the social ladder all spurred the individual to greater effort. But what exists in the Imperium is *naked* fear. In a capitalist city with a population of one hundred thousand people, some ten thousand, let us say, may have been haunted by fear of unemployment. Such fear appeared to them to be a personal situation, tragic in view of the indifference and callousness of their environment. But if all one hundred thousand people live in daily fear, they give off a collective aura that hangs over the city like a heavy cloud. Gold alienates man from himself; naked fear, which has replaced capital, alienates him even more efficiently.

To transcend this fear new means must be devised: one must breed a new man, one for whom work will be a joy and a pride, instead of the curse of Adam. A gigantic literature is directed toward this end. Books, films, and radio all have as their themes this transformation, and the instilling of hatred against the enemy who would want to prevent it. To the extent that man, terrified as he is, learns to fulfill his obligations to society of his own will and with joy, the dosage of fear is to be reduced. And eventually, a free man will be born.

Whether he can be born while such methods are applied is a question of faith. If everything in the world is ruled by rational laws, if freedom is nothing but the understand-

ing of that universal rational necessity, if man can achieve
that full consciousness to which what is necessary and
what should be willed are one and the same thing, then
a new, free society is possible in the future. In this sense,
the Communist who spent three years in a slave labor
camp was free, for he recognized his sentence and that of
his fellow-prisoners to be rational and necessary. In this
same sense, the writers of the people's democracies are
right when they say that a free man has *already* been born,
and that he is the man of the Soviet Union. But if god-like
consciousness (what could choice mean to a god who sees
all clearly?) is not accessible to man, then a certain number of people will always make what the ruling philosophers consider to be the wrong choice. That being so, to
ease the tension of fear would mean to allow the possibility of revolt. Naked fear is unlikely ever to be inclined
to abdicate. A young man in Moscow, born and raised in
the new system, is on the wrong path when he makes his
choice and (as, unfortunately, happens more and more
often) reads Dostoevski, who posed this problem in most
pessimistic terms.

At the moment we are concerned with the Baltics. They
are not being handled with thoughtless cruelty; their lot
is exactly the same as that of many nations living within
the borders of the Union. There is no reason for their
being treated differently. If their case is so striking, it is
only because they were incorporated so suddenly, were
so totally unprepared for their new circumstances. Moreover, they stood on a definitely higher level of civilization than other Soviet citizens. Not being Slavs, they have
difficulty in learning Russian. Their case confronts us with
the thorny question of nationalities.

When victory is won and socialism is realized on the
entire face of the planet, nations will—runs the prediction

—gradually cease to exist; a single universal language will appear which, according to the Generalissimo, will be neither Russian, nor German, nor English but a synthesis of many tongues. One can assume that before that happens a considerable portion of the world will learn Russian, which later will form the basis of the new universal language. (It is asserted that French is the language of feudalism; English, the language of capitalism; and Russian, the language of socialism.) The existence of nations cannot be justified rationally; at the present stage, however, one must deal with it as a fact. The encouragement of national cultures is indicated to the degree that it prepares the transition to the next phase. Whatever brings a given nation closer culturally to the Russians deserves protection; anything that fortifies the system also merits care. In the realm of science, one can even stimulate competition between nations, so long as Russian superiority is acknowledged. (In one people's democracy, a group of scholars were delicately persuaded not to publish the results of their scientific research because they were a little too good and so might seem to contest, indecently, Russian superiority in the same field.) One must always keep in mind the eventual goal, which is the melting down of all nations into a single mass. To this end, nationalism must be exterminated. Nationalism rests on the conviction that national culture is the expression of "national content in national form"; whereas, everybody knows that the content of national cultures has had until now a class character.

The opposite of nationalism is the formula of a "culture that is national in form, and socialist in content." And since the Russian nation made the Revolution and established the patterns of socialist culture, drawing them from its own past, nationalism can be defined simply as anti-

Russianism. If they suffer from that horrible disease, small national groups (like the Crimean Tatars, for example) can be liquidated in their entirety. Larger anti-Russian national groups must be dealt with gradually. Pride can be taken in the outstanding success in the Ukraine. More and more young Ukrainian writers move to Moscow and write in Russian. The poets and critics who dreamt of a *separate* Ukrainian literature have left this world; departed, also, are the actors whose pride in their national theater made them go a bit too far in competing with the Russians. So the self-congratulatory reasoning goes. One can be fairly satisfied with affairs in the Baltic states. As for the people's democracies, the pattern imposed there, modified in the light of past experience, is proving the wisdom of long-range planning.

The task is difficult because individual nations are burdened with their own past; for instance, the Baltic peoples tend to regard the culture of their kulaks as their own. They compare it with the culture of Russia. As if comparison were possible! Russia is a great nation; the Revolution was born in its womb. Only an impious fool could compare its past, pregnant with what was to be the greatest upheaval in history, with the past of the small nations it has liberated. Russia is the savior of the world.

No atrocities are being committed. One murders only those who must be murdered, tortures only those who must be made to confess, deports only those who must be deported. If deportees die off quickly, that is the fault of the climate, hard work, or insufficient rations, and nothing can be done about those inconveniences at the present stage. One cannot expect a country charged with so great a mission to take care of its prisoners as well as England cares for its soldiers. Perhaps if they were treated better these prisoners would die less quickly, but then their labor would cease to be cheap. In any case, before food can reach prisoners in camps, often situated five days' travel by boat from the nearest town, camp administrators will steal most of it. Everything will change when the standard of living improves. Then, the prisoners, too, will be better off.

The promoters of this kind of argument demonstrate by it their admirable far-sightedness. The nations of Central and Eastern Europe were nationalistic to the point of madness. They were ready to massacre each other over a scrap of land. Today they see how senseless this was, though probably that would not prevent them from leaping at each other's throat if the Center's control were lifted. Under the rule of the Center they "agree" to mutual compromises. The Poles relinquished their eastern territories; the East Germans accepted the Oder-Neisse line; the Czechs and Hungarians have renounced all claims to the Carpathian Ukraine. Expulsions put an end to minority issues. All the republics follow the same economic and cultural pattern worked out by the Center. The one factor that now separates the individual republics is that of language. The great plan is working.

The only trouble is the patient. He shrieks and struggles to get away. In *Madame Bovary*, Flaubert describes an operation on a club-foot performed by Doctor Bovary. This provincial doctor, together with his friend, the pharmacist Homais, decided to cure a servant in the village inn who was lame. After a great deal of difficulty, they persuaded him to surrender himself to their endeavors. Doctor Bovary, with the aid of medical handbooks, devised a wooden box weighing eight pounds, equipped inside with iron hooks, screws, and leather slings. The operation was a marvelous success, and the leg was strapped into the box. "Honor! Threefold honor!" cried the town paper. "Was it not said that the blind would see and the halt would walk! But what fanaticism once promised to the elect, modern science can accomplish for all men!" But alas, five days later something started to go wrong with the patient. He shrieked with pain. When the box was opened, the leg proved to be swollen and covered with sores. The two friends decided that the leg had not been strapped in well. So they tightened the screws. Yet the patient went from bad to worse. A doctor called in from a neighboring village diagnosed gangrene and amputated the leg. Obviously, Flaubert got a lot of malicious pleasure out of deriding Monsieur Homais's worship of progress. This does not mean that the same operation performed by good doctors would fail. Yet the doubt is always there: is the doctor we are dealing with really a good one?

"To tell the truth, all this is boring," an official of one of the people's democracies said to me. "I have already seen it happen in Russia. The stages are measured out in advance, and they succeed each other with mathematical precision. The only interest lies in watching the reactions of the human material."

Human material seems to have one major defect: it does not like to be considered merely as human material. It finds it hard to endure the feeling that it must resign itself to passive acceptance of changes introduced from above.

The parliamentary system may in many instances be a fiction designed to secure power to ever the same social groups. Still the possibility of casting a protest vote has a certain tonic value. Taking part in a manifestation against some minister of state, a strike, the reading of the opposition press, all furnish moments of emotional release which are probably good for the health of mankind. National pride many be an absurd feeling, yet a rooster's pride as he struts about in his own yard amid the hens is biologically useful.

The Center is, of course, not unaware of man's psychological needs; hence the parades, banners, posters, portraits, election-time propaganda, and demonstrations of hatred against the enemies of the state. National pride is flattered by the display of national flags as well as by daily announcements of the latest economic achievements, of the buildings, highways, and railroads constructed and the production quotas fulfilled. In general these means seem effective; yet the lack of some intangible element leads the human material to a feeling of *fiction*. Nothing is *spontaneous*. Within the limits of his profession a man can acquire some reason for pride. Beyond these limits, everything is predetermined. Overnight a single decree from on high can remove an entire government, change the borders of a country or order people to hate those who were called friends yesterday. Official safety valves are probably insufficient channels for feelings of national pride if most Estonians, Lithuanians, Latvians, Poles, Czechs, Hungarians, or Rumanians would willingly cut the throat of any available Russian were they not restrained by fear. Even Party cadres, one suspects, would not renounce such a pleasant prospect. One can only complain of the backwardness of these nations and hope that socialist upbringing will enlighten them. But it would be a mistake to deny these unpleasant facts and even worse ones, namely, that such hatred exists even in nations which have undergone a longer period of careful education.

The incorporation of the Baltic states into the Soviet Union may seem an unimportant incident to a Mexican or a Chilean, but not to the millions of people living in the people's democracies. For years they have been pondering over this rather extraordinary act on the part of a great

power, an act analogous only to some of the misdeeds of
colonial politics. If the Great Union as a "federation" is
capable of assimilating an unlimited number of "republics," then other countries will one day be swallowed up
in their turn. If what happened in the Baltics is a *pre-
figuration* of what will happen to them they can look forward to mass deportations and the settlement of colonists
from the Euro-Asian continent in their towns and villages.
The people of countries that Party propaganda likes to
call independent think of that future moment as the
Judgment Day. The lot of the Baltics has become a serious
psychological factor. In keeping the daily ledger of his
words and deeds, every citizen evaluates them not only
in terms of their present worth but in terms of that future
day of reckoning.

The friend who warned me against incurring the wrath
of Zeus is a philosopher. He lives amid his books knowing that no matter how much the human material may
tremble, there will be no lack of beautiful editions of
Lucretius printed in Moscow. As the new society expands,
more and more classics will be re-edited. A wise man,
scorning the poor literature of today, will always find
much delectation in the history of philosophy, in the
ancient authors, and in the complicated but exciting
studies of dialectical materialism. Truly, a philosopher
cannot be happier than when he is living in a country
ruled by men compared with whom the kings and prime
ministers of by-gone eras were no more than improvisers.
His days are devoted to intellectual effort. And when he
meets with his fellow-philosophers he knows that they
too are drawing wisdom from the well of dialectics.

The meetings of such people have nothing in common
with the sterile and irresponsible divagations of the intelli-

gentsia; they are the meetings of scientists engaged in erecting a social structure. My friend does not believe in "philosophizing." He believes that man is a social animal whose thought is the reflection of the movement of matter. Seekers after truth are no more than puppets trying to deny that their ideas are merely the reflection of historical processes. They are reactionaries serving the enemy of the proletariat; for it is the proletariat which, out of inescapable necessity, formulated the one true method of dialectical materialism. The Soviet Union will triumph as surely as trees will bud in the spring. The man who understands necessity is happy and free, for all freedom other than that based on an understanding of necessity is an illusion. My friend believes that those who suffer in the new society have only themselves to blame. Those who are deported or arrested are fools unworthy of our pity. They are so encumbered with the past that they are incapable of understanding the laws of progress. If they did understand, no evil would befall them and their lives would be active and serene.

My friend liked me because of my hatred of a dull and befogged mentality incapable of seizing a sharp impression of phenomena in full motion. He guessed rightly that I had always longed to see man bright, hard, and pure. Looking at man as he is, I turned my eyes away from him in shame, and I turned my eyes away from myself because I was like him. All my poetry had been a *rejection,* a derision of myself and others because men delight in what is unworthy of delight, love what is unworthy of love, suffer over what is unworthy of suffering. Did I not belong, on this score alone, to those creators of the new world who have a vision of a new man endowed with superhuman purity? Certainly I was a "good pagan," for my fury was the fury of the Bolsheviks. Everywhere outside the countries of the new man I would be bound to feel homeless.

I really had certain assets that could have assured my future happiness. In a Warsaw, rebuilding its ruins, I would have been working in harmony with the laws of history. I would have translated Shakespeare—what joy it is to breach a language barrier and find sentences as concise as the original. I would have undertaken Marxist studies on sixteenth-century England. Maybe I would have become a university professor. From time to time I would have published a poem stating my loyalty to the Revolution and its founders. Moving in the circles of the philosophers and occupying myself with dialectics, I would have treated the efforts of writers, painters, and musicians very lightly, knowing their art is, and must be, bad. I would have listened to Bach, and read Swift or Flaubert.

Yet I deceived my friend. What led me to do this I myself find it hard to define. If I could express it I would be a wise man, a teacher of philosophers. I believe that my motives lie deep in my past, in an incident I shall recount.

In my wanderings at the beginning of the Second World War, I happened to find myself, for a very short while, in the Soviet Union. I was waiting for a train at a station in one of the large cities of the Ukraine. It was a gigantic station. Its walls were hung with portraits and banners of inexpressible ugliness. A dense crowd dressed in sheepskin coats, uniforms, fur caps, and woolen kerchiefs filled every available space and tracked thick mud over the tiled floor. The marble stairs were covered with sleeping beggars, their bare legs sticking out of their tatters despite the fact that it was freezing. Over them loudspeakers shouted propaganda slogans. As I was passing through the station I suddenly stopped and looked. A peasant family—husband and wife and two children—had settled down by the wall. They were sitting on baskets and bundles. The wife was feeding the younger child; the husband, who had a dark, wrinkled face and a black, drooping mustache was pouring tea out of a kettle into a cup for the older boy. They were whispering to each other in Polish. I gazed at them until I felt moved to the point of tears. What had stopped my steps so suddenly and touched me so profoundly was their *difference*. This was a human group, an island in a crowd that lacked something proper to humble, ordinary human life. The gesture of a hand pouring tea, the careful, delicate handing of the cup to the child, the worried words I guessed from the movement of their lips, their isolation, their privacy in the midst of the crowd—that is what moved me. For a moment, then, I understood something that quickly slipped from my grasp.

Polish peasants were certainly far from the summits of civilization. It is possible that the family I saw was illiterate. My friend would have called them graceless, smelly imbeciles who had to be taught to think. Still, precious seeds of humanity were preserved in them, or in the Baltic people, or in the Czechs because they had not yet been subjected to the scientific treatment of Monsieur Homais. It may well be that the fondness with which Baltic women tended their little gardens, the superstition of Polish women gathering herbs to make charms, the custom of setting an empty plate for a traveler on Christmas Eve betoken inherent good that can be developed. In the circles in which my friend lives, to call man a mystery is to insult him. They have set out to carve a new man much as a sculptor carves his statue out of a block of stone, by chipping away what is unwanted. I think they are wrong, that their knowledge in all its perfection is insufficient, and their power over life and death is usurped.

Being on the side of that stammering and mumbling

with which human beings try to express themselves in their lonely helplessness, could I have walked on the thick carpet of my apartment, in a neighborhood reserved for privileged people, and savored Shakespeare? Instead of the hand through which warm blood flows from the heart to the fingers holding my pen, they would have given me an excellent artificial hand—the dialectic. Knowing there is a light in man, I could never have dared seek it; for light is not, I believe, the same as political consciousness, and it can exist in fools, monks, boys who dislike social duties, and kulaks. Knowing there is crime in man, I could never have pointed it out; for I would have had to believe, as does my friend, that crime is a product of history and not of human beings. There are past crimes: hundreds of thousands of Poles deported in the year 1940–41, those who were shot, or those who were drowned in the Arctic Ocean. But one must learn to forgive. I am concerned with the crimes that are being, and will continue to be, committed. Crimes in the name of the new and radiant man; crimes committed to the sound of orchestras and choruses, to the blare of loudspeakers and the recitation of optimistic poems.

Now I am homeless—a just punishment. But perhaps I was born so that the "Eternal Slaves" might speak through my lips. Why should I spare myself? Should I renounce what is probably the sole duty of a poet only in order to make sure that my verse would be printed in an anthology edited by the State Publishing House? My friend accepts naked terror, whatever name he may choose to give it. We have parted ways. Whether the side on which I now find myself is the future victor or the future victim is not the issue here. But I know that if my friend tastes the sweet fruits of victory, this planet will be improved according to plan for centuries—but woe to him who lives to see this happen. All over the world people are now sleeping in their beds, or perhaps they are engaging in some idiotic pastime; and one might easily believe that each in his own way is doing his best to deserve destruction. But that destruction will bring no freedom. Should the power my friend worships turn out not to be historical necessity, the earth will enter a period of terrible wars and bloody revolutions. But the quest will never end, and hope will always remain.

Let Pablo Neruda fight for his people. He is wrong, however, when he believes that all the protesting voices of Central and Eastern Europe are the voices of stubborn nationalisms or the yelps of wronged reaction. Eyes that have seen should not be shut; hands that have touched should not forget when they take up a pen. Let him allow a few writers from Central and Eastern Europe to discuss problems other than those that haunt him.

When, as my friend suggested, I stand before Zeus (whether I die naturally, or under sentence of History) I will repeat all this that I have written as my defense. Many people spend their entire lives collecting stamps or old coins, or growing tulips. I am sure that Zeus will be merciful toward people who have given themselves entirely to these hobbies, even though they are only amusing and pointless diversions. I shall say to him: "It is not my fault that you made me a poet, and that you gave me the gift of seeing simultaneously what was happening in Omaha and Prague, in the Baltic states and on the shores of the Arctic Ocean. I felt that if I did not use that gift my poetry would be tasteless to me and fame detestable. Forgive me." And perhaps Zeus, who does not call stamp-collectors and tulip-growers silly, will forgive.

About the Author

CZESLAW MILOSZ was born in 1911 in Lithuania, educated in Wilno and Paris, and began publishing while still in his early twenties. When Poland was invaded in 1939, Mr. Milosz became active in the Polish underground in Warsaw, working as a writer and editor for resistance publications. In 1946 he joined the postwar Polish diplomatic corps. He was stationed at the Polish embassy in Washington until 1950, when he was transferred to the Polish embassy in Paris as first secretary for cultural affairs. In February 1951 Mr. Milosz broke with the Polish government and went into exile, first in France, then in the United States. He was Professor of Slavic Languages and Literatures at the University of California at Berkeley, where he lived with his wife and two sons. His books include several volumes of poetry, several collections of essays, two works of fiction and an autobiography. In 1976 Mr. Milosz received a Guggenheim Fellowship for poetry and poetry translations, in 1978 the Neustadt International Prize for Literature, and in 1980 the Nobel Prize for Literature. He died in 2004.

VINTAGE INTERNATIONAL

VINTAGE INTERNATIONAL

VINTAGE INTERNATIONAL

Available at your bookstore or call toll-free to order: 1-800-733-3000.
Credit cards only.